IMMIGRATION AND THE REMAKING
OF BLACK AMERICA

IMMIGRATION AND THE REMAKING OF BLACK AMERICA

Tod G. Hamilton

Russell Sage Foundation NEW YORK

THE RUSSELL SAGE FOUNDATION

The Russell Sage Foundation, one of the oldest of America's general purpose foundations, was established in 1907 by Mrs. Margaret Olivia Sage for "the improvement of social and living conditions in the United States." The foundation seeks to fulfill this mandate by fostering the development and dissemination of knowledge about the country's political, social, and economic problems. While the foundation endeavors to assure the accuracy and objectivity of each book it publishes, the conclusions and interpretations in Russell Sage Foundation publications are those of the authors and not of the foundation, its trustees, or its staff. Publication by Russell Sage, therefore, does not imply foundation endorsement.

LIBRARY OF CONGRESS CATALOGING-IN-PUBLICATION DATA

Names: Hamilton, Tod G., author.
Title: Immigration and the remaking of Black America / Tod G. Hamilton.
Description: New York : Russell Sage Foundation, [2019] | Includes bibliographical references and index.
Identifiers: LCCN 2018045571 (print) | LCCN 2018057071 (ebook) | ISBN 9781610448857 (ebook) | ISBN 9780871544070 (pbk. : alk. paper)
Subjects: LCSH: African Americans—Economic conditions. | Africans—United States—Economic conditions. | West Indians—United States—Economic conditions. | Blacks—United States—Economic conditions. | African Americans—Social conditions. | Africans—United States—Social conditions. | West Indians—United States—Social conditions. | Blacks—United States—Social conditions. | Immigrants—United States.
Classification: LCC E185.8 (ebook) | LCC E185.8 .H244 2019 (print) | DDC 305.896/073—dc23
LC record available at https://lccn.loc.gov/2018045571

Cover art © 2018 Sam Gilliam / Artists Rights Society (ARS), New York.
Photo credit: The Art Institute of Chicago / Art Resource, NY
d00158139   ART539342
Gilliam, Sam (1933–) © Copyright. *Fire,* 1972. Color lithograph on white Japanese paper, 610 x 480 mm. Gift of Mr. Carl Horn, 1976.650.
The Art Institute of Chicago

Text design by Matthew T. Avery.

RUSSELL SAGE FOUNDATION
112 East 64th Street,
New York, New York 10065
10 9 8 7 6 5 4 3 2 1

To Mom and Tyneshia

CONTENTS

LIST OF ILLUSTRATIONS

Figures

Tables

ABOUT THE AUTHOR

TOD G. HAMILTON is assistant professor of sociology and a faculty associate of the Office of Population Research at Princeton University.

FOREWORD

For nearly a decade, Tod Hamilton has creatively applied rigorous statistical and demographic methods to high-quality national and international data to compare black immigrants and natives with respect to their socioeconomic status and health. His conclusions and the research behind them are clearly and persuasively laid out in *Immigration and the Remaking of Black America*. The book offers a comprehensive methodological and theoretical framework for understanding the integration of black immigrants into the United States. In so doing, it sheds important light on the ongoing importance of race in the American stratification system.

Since 1960, the number of black immigrants living in the United States has grown from around 125,000 to some 4.1 million persons. Foreign-born blacks now comprise about 10 percent of the U.S. black population, and their children make up 16 percent of black births in the United States. Beginning in the 1980s, studies revealed that black immigrants outperformed black natives on most indicators of social and economic achievement. These achievement gaps led some observers to attribute the lagging achievement of native African Americans in the post–civil rights era to a weakness of cultural norms that encourage work, effort, diligence, planning, and sacrifice. These values were assumed to prevail in the majority-black societies from which most immigrants emigrated. Obviously, the thinking went, if black immigrants did better than black natives, the difference could not be attributed to racial prejudice and discrimination. Since both groups shared similar racialized characteristics (for example, darker skin shade and hair texture), the explanation must be a cultural one.

Unsurprisingly such cultural claims were vigorously contested, contributing to a divisive debate about the importance of context versus culture, structure versus agency, in accounting for racial stratification within the United States. Until recently, opposing viewpoints were typically argued in the absence of sound research. Drawing on and expanding upon prior research, Hamilton offers instead a comprehensive theoretical and methodological framework for the analysis and understanding of black immigrants and their performance in the U.S. political economy. His approach begins with the observation that immigration is inevitably a selective process, a fundamental truth that, surprisingly, is all too often elided in scholarly and policy debates. The debates often degenerate into invidious comparisons between black immigrants and African American natives that lead to victim-blaming conclusions about the "cultural" causes of black disadvantage in the United States.

The people who depart the nation of their birth and relocate to a foreign country necessarily constitute a very select subset of the origin population. They are decidedly not a representative cross-section of a country's inhabitants. To model and accurately understand what happens to an immigrant group within the social and economic structure of a receiving country, one first needs to understand the process by which the immigrants were selected (or selected themselves) to leave their country of birth. Voluntary migrants virtually by definition are selected on the basis of unobservable characteristics such as ambition, risk-taking, endurance, and willingness to work, as well as on the basis of observable characteristics such as age, gender, health, and education. The selection of involuntary migrants depends on the reason for their coerced departure. People fleeing an environmental disaster that affects an entire population will be more representative than those escaping political or religious persecution, since the nature of the selectivity then depends on the nature of the persecution.

However migrants might have been selected to depart, the direction and degree of their selection must be assessed relative to the social and economic composition of the origin society. Among voluntary migrants, a modest level of education in the country of destination might indicate a high level of education in the country of origin. As a result, simple comparisons of the effect of education on earnings between immigrants and natives may overstate the influence of education among immigrants, since twelve years of education is likely to signal a much higher level of attainment in the home country than in the United States.

In addition, any analysis of the effect of immigrant selectivity requires serious attention to what the native-origin comparison group should be. If immigrants are selected on the basis of ambition, risk tolerance, and willingness to sacrifice, then representative samples of the foreign-born will reveal less about their "culture" than about the degree and nature of the selective process that brought them into the country of destination. Moreover, the degree and nature of immigrant selectivity is ultimately filtered through some receiving nation's immigrant admissions system.

Across nations, admission systems establish the criteria by which some immigrants are permitted to enter as legal residents with full rights, others are admitted as legal temporary workers with limited rights, and others are turned away, never to be observed in the country at all—or perhaps observed only as unauthorized migrants with very constrained rights and possibilities. Depending on how they emerge from any particular admission system, immigrants enter the receiving nation's social and economic structures, which in turn penalize or reward the selected characteristics in diverse ways.

In his book, Tod Hamilton develops a comprehensive model that explicitly recognizes processes of immigrant selectivity, attempts to measure and control them, and only then seeks to interpret intergroup differentials to understand any achievement gaps that remain between black immigrants and natives. He offers the first real attempt to elaborate an empirically and theoretically guided framework for the analysis of immigrants within a receiving society, and he makes good use of his framework to derive empirically defensible conclusions about how race and nativity operate within America's system of social stratification.

In addition to recognizing the core importance of selectivity in determining outcomes for black immigrants in the United States, Hamilton also takes into account the effects of arrival cohort, period of observation, and origin-country characteristics. He then draws upon these considerations to identify an appropriate reference group for immigrant-native comparisons. The resulting model achieves three specific aims: it provides a framework for understanding disparities between African Americans and black immigrants; it pieces together a detailed portrait of inequalities among blacks; and it shows how the growing number of black immigrants affects black-white disparities.

In the book, before applying his analytic framework, Hamilton sets the stage by offering a detailed descriptive analysis of the growth and diversification of black immigration since the 1960s. He then reviews prior research on social and economic disparities between immigrant- and native-origin blacks; pointing out the limitations of this work, he identifies three factors that may help to resolve the seemingly contradictory findings: the very different contexts within which pre- and post-1965 black immigration occurred, the changing selectivity of black immigration over time, and the wide variation in origin-country circumstances.

Given the inevitable selectivity of human migration, he argues that the overall African American population is not the proper reference group against which to compare the performance of black immigrants. Instead, he focuses on black internal migrants (those who move within the United States), who are similarly selected on the basis of observable and unobservable traits that promote movement. He shows that, like immigrants, native-born black movers display better labor market outcomes than nonmovers. Indeed, outcomes for black movers are quite similar to those observed for black immigrants, suggesting that it is *migrant selectivity* and not immigrant culture that accounts for immigrant-native performance differentials among blacks in the United States. However, these differentials were not present during the first four decades of the twentieth century and only emerged in the late twentieth and early twenty-first centuries. He concludes that reductions in racial discrimination enabled by civil rights policies were a necessary condition for the emergence of the immigrant-native differentials we observe today.

Hamilton's comparison of employment trajectories across different arrival cohorts finds that over time black immigrant employment rates have converged with those of black movers and whites. His analyses likewise reveal no differences in homeownership between immigrant and native blacks in the early twentieth century, but differential rates by nativity among blacks living in the United States today. Although upon arrival rates of homeownership for immigrant blacks are *lower* than those of native blacks, over time they rise and eventually come to exceed those of native blacks. At the same time, however, they never reach or exceed the rate of white homeownership, indicating the likely persistence of racial discrimination in housing markets.

With respect to health, black immigrants display a better profile upon arrival than either black movers or nonmovers. The health of both native black movers and native black nonmovers is always worse than that of whites, but the health of most black immigrant groups is similar to or better than that of white Americans, indicating strong positive selection on the basis of health. Immigrant health tends to deteriorate, however, as time spent in the United States increases.

With respect to rates of marriage, native blacks are less likely to marry than whites irrespective of their mobility status. In contrast, black immigrants have much higher marriage rates compared to black natives; the marriage profile of African immigrants is similar to that observed for whites.

Rates of intermarriage between native blacks and whites remain quite low compared with Hispanics and Asians, and black immigrants who were unmarried at the time of arrival have even lower intermarriage rates with whites than black natives. Instead, black immigrants tend to marry conationals, suggesting mate selection on the basis of common culture and languages. Nonetheless, black immigrants are more likely to marry native black Americans than native white Americans, indicating that race continues to be a salient barrier to black-white marriage in the United States. Among black natives, movers are more likely to marry whites than nonmovers are, consistent with the view that black movers are positively selected on a range of observable and unobservable characteristics.

In the rigor of its analytic model and the clarity of its conclusions, *Immigration and the Remaking of Black America* constitutes a tour-de-force climax to Hamilton's long record of first-rate sociological and demographic research on black immigrants and natives in the United States. The book not only documents how black immigration is reshaping black America today, but also reveals the continuing power of race as an influence on the social, economic, and health status of all those who trace their origins to Africa, regardless of where they were born. In the end, Hamilton marshals convincing evidence against the argument that the relative success of black immigrants compared to black natives somehow reflects the favorable influence of Caribbean or African culture and the weakness of African American culture, underscoring instead the continuing salience of race as a structural barrier to advancement in U.S. society.

Douglas S. Massey, Henry G. Bryant Professor of Sociology and Public Affairs, Princeton University

PREFACE AND ACKNOWLEDGMENTS

The research underlying this book represents my attempt to provide a more comprehensive portrait of the diversity within the black population of the United States and to recenter the importance of structural factors, rather than agentic concerns, in explaining the outcomes of black Americans. From studies of migrants from the Caribbean to the United States during the early twentieth century to research on African immigration of the 2000s, scholars have reported that groups of black immigrants tend to achieve better social and economic outcomes than black Americans. These findings have led some scholars and policymakers to dismiss the importance of racism and discrimination in shaping the outcomes of black Americans; they argue that because black immigrants and black Americans share similar racialized features, factors other than racism must explain the poor social and economic outcomes of black Americans. As a result, the cultural practices of black Americans have been pathologized for several decades.

My analysis in this book of social and economic disparities between black Americans and black immigrants from 1910 to 2014 challenges this view. The project brings new evidence to bear on the importance of selective migration in shaping the outcomes of both black immigrants and black Americans. I also analyze new data and show that the racial context of pre–civil rights America fundamentally shaped the outcomes of black Americans and put black immigrants and black Americans on different trajectories.

The book also highlights the growing demographic importance of black immigration to the United States and reveals the contours of the vast diversity within America's black population in the twenty-first century. By illustrating the many ways in which the U.S. black population is far from monolithic, the book cautions the research community about the consequences of failing to disaggregate the black population when measuring social and economic disparities. Given America's long and, at times, state-sanctioned history of racial discrimination against blacks, a large body of American social science research has focused on measuring and tracking changes in social and economic disparities between blacks and whites. The goal of these studies is generally to examine whether the country is making progress toward improving the social conditions of black Americans. Although the significant increase in the number of black immigrants has changed the meaning of black-white disparities, researchers tend to aggregate all blacks, regardless of nativity, when measuring changes in a range of social outcomes, from health and marriage to voting and labor market outcomes. This failure to account for black immigration can lead to incorrect estimates of both the social progress made by black Americans and changes in the intensity of racism and discrimination experienced by blacks in the United States. As the black immigrant population grows and becomes more diverse, empirical analyses must account for the effects of immigration on changes in the social outcomes of blacks in the United States. Assuming the homogeneity of the black population of the United States, as many social scientists still do, is an error. To assume homogeneity within the black immigrant population is another error. This book hopes to correct some of these errors.

Throughout the completion of this book, I amassed many debts. Intellectually, I am indebted to William Darity, who taught me to seek out the structural factors that underpin the social conditions of oppressed groups. I am also indebted to the many scholars who have advanced the study of race and immigration and upon whose work I have relied.

I thank Patricia Fernández-Kelly, Robert Wuthnow, Angel Harris, and Alejandro Portes for their initial encouragement to write this book. I would also like to thank Alejandro Portes and Douglas Massey for the many conversations we had and the advice they gave about this project. I have also benefited from working with several amazing graduate students at Princeton, including Janeria Easley, Angela Dixon, and Megan Blanchard. Linsey Edwards, Mary Lou Delaney, and Hye Jee Kim provided valuable research assistance on various parts of the project. I thank the Office of Population Research at Princeton University for providing financial and administrative support for the project. Many of the graphs and analyses in the book would not have been possible without the assistance of Dawn Koffman, a statistical consultant in the Office of Population Research. Of course, I am solely responsible for any errors or omissions.

I benefited from the feedback I received when I presented parts of this research at Duke University, Penn State University, the University of Pennsylvania, Ohio State University, the University of Michigan, the University of North Carolina at Chapel Hill, the University of Wisconsin at Madison, the University of Maryland at College Park, and Harvard University. I am particularly grateful for the comments I received from Robert Hummer, David Williams, Nancy Krieger, Ichiro Kawachi, Mark Hayward, Johnny Butler, and Mosi Ifutunji.

I made progress on the book at the Institute for Advanced Study in Princeton during the 2015–2016 academic year. I thank Didier Fassin for helpful comments on the project during my time at the institute, as well as my colleagues during the year for providing a stimulating intellectual environment in which to work on the project. I also acknowledge Princeton's Kahneman-Treisman Center for Behavioral Science and Public Policy for providing valuable support and office space that enabled me to complete this project during the fall of 2017.

Chapters 4 and 6 contain aspects of my research that have been previously published in academic journals, including *Social Science and Medicine*, the *Journal of Health and Social Behavior*, the *Review of Black Political Economy*, and *Demography*. I thank the editors and referees for their comments on these articles. Over the years, Amos Peters has provided an attentive ear and been an excellent academic sparring partner. Our discussions have helped sharpen many of my ideas. The insights on issues related to racial reporting among immigrants from the Dominican Republic in chapter 8 derives from collaborative research with Carmela Alcantara. The research in chapter 6 derives from collaborative research with Robert Hummer, Tia Palermo, and Tiffany Green. I have also benefited from my friendship and collaborations with Tiffany Green. She has provided steadfast encouragement over the years and critical feedback on issues related to immigration and health. Lefleur Stephens served as my writing partner at various points while completing this project. I thank her for providing the motivation to work through many days of writer's block.

I thank my editor at the Russell Sage Foundation, Suzanne Nichols, for seeing the merit in this work and for providing enthusiastic support for the project. While I completed the manuscript, Suzanne provided valuable guidance, encouragement, and ultimately friendship. I also thank Suzanne for enforcing deadlines, despite life's unexpected challenges. Her commitment to the project helped ensure the completion of the book. The book was also enhanced by the excellent comments and feedback from the anonymous reviewers who reviewed the book for the Russell Sage Foundation. In addition, the project benefited from superb editing at various points by Karen DeVivo, Jennifer Eggerling-Boeck, and Tamara Nopper.

I am thankful to Ann-Marie Deanna Peters, Keisha Brown, Melvin Brown, Renell Ballard, Lionel Jenkins, Rodney Priestley, and Dr. Robin Wilson-Smith for helping with a range of unexpected challenges while working on this project.

I thank my parents for giving me the courage to face life and its challenges. Their early lessons continue to sustain me. I am grateful to my mother for nurturing an early love of learning. My wife, Tyneshia, has been my greatest supporter. I acknowledge that being married to a researcher is not always fun. Despite the many challenges along the way, she never lost faith in my ability to complete the book. She was patient through the long nights of work and encouraging during my moments of doubt. For this and her immense love, I am most thankful. She means the world to me. This is our accomplishment.

Lastly, I am grateful to my children, Lena and Ethan, for their unwavering enthusiasm about the mere fact that I was writing a book. I thank them for their encouragement and unconditional love. They help me find perspective.

PART I

SETTING THE STAGE: THE SOCIAL AND DEMOGRAPHIC LANDSCAPE

CHAPTER ONE

INTRODUCTION

"Building Afromerica" was the July 11, 2015, headline of *The Economist* magazine. The article described a popular Washington, D.C., gathering spot where "Eritrean cab-drivers, students and pensioners chat politics and chow down on lamb stews served on spongy 'injera' bread. . . . Eritrean flags hang from the ceiling and the walls are lined with trinkets from the country." The article explained that Eritreans and several other African groups are migrating to the United States in growing numbers, noting that there are significant populations of Eritreans and Ethiopians in Washington, D.C.; Egyptians and Ghanaians in New York; Nigerians in Houston; and Somalis in Minneapolis. The story highlighted a trend that may be unfamiliar to many non-academics and perhaps some academics: immigrants from sub-Saharan Africa are becoming an increasingly large proportion of the black population in the United States. The article noted that these immigrants "stand out from American-born blacks" and concluded that, "over time, their growing numbers may change what it means to be 'African-American' and challenge the country's fraught race relations."

The migration of individuals who identify as black has been changing the contours of the U.S. black population since the mid-1960s, when changes in U.S. immigration policies made it easier for individuals from the Caribbean and sub-Saharan Africa to migrate to the United States. The black population of the United States became increasingly diverse through the end of the twentieth century, primarily owing to immigration from Jamaica, Trinidad and Tobago, Guyana, and other countries in the English-speaking Caribbean. In the first decade of the twenty-first century, diversity within the U.S. black population began to change yet again, this time owing to a growth in immigration from African countries. Since 2000, black immigrants from Africa have accounted for more than 50 percent of the growth in black immigrants to the United States.

By 2014, approximately 4 million black immigrants were living in the United States. At that time, 10 percent of the immigrant population identified as black, and 9.2 percent of the population who identified as black were immigrants. Black immigrants are one of the most diverse immigrant subgroups in terms of country of origin, arriving from home countries in the Caribbean, Africa, South America, and Europe. Despite this native-country diversity, most social scientific research on the experiences of black immigrants in the United States has focused on people from the English-speaking Caribbean. Few studies have comparatively investigated the experiences of the entire black immigrant population.

The Importance of Examining the Social and Economic Outcomes of Black Immigrants

Examining the social and economic outcomes of black immigrants is important for three reasons.

THE DECLINE IN IMMIGRATION FROM LATIN AMERICA

Much of the social science literature on contemporary immigrants residing in the United States focuses on immigrants from Latin America, particularly Mexico. Although Latin Americans were once the fastest-growing immigrant group in the United States, immigration from these countries has declined. By 2016, net migration between the United States and Mexico, the birth country of most contemporary U.S. immigrants, was negative, meaning that more Mexicans left the United States that year than arrived. Although the absolute number of African immigrants residing in the United States is small in comparison to other contemporary immigrant subgroups, African immigrants are now one of the fastest-growing immigrant populations. Indeed, Africans had the fastest growth rate (41 percent) of all major immigrant subgroups arriving in the United States between 2000 and 2013.[1]

Understanding the social impact of absorbing a population generated by decades of immigration from Latin America remains, of course, an important area of social inquiry, but in the coming decades black immigrants in general and African immigrants in particular will play a major role in immigration debates.

A SHIFTING COLOR LINE

A second reason to explore the social and economic outcomes of black immigrants is that their experiences are vital to understanding the new contours of the U.S. black population and the possible changes in the patterns of stratification among black people in the coming decades. Sociologists tend to agree that intermarriage rates are a good measure of an immigrant group's assimilation, with higher rates between immigrants (and their descendants) and members of the host society (particularly white Americans) demonstrating declining prejudice and fading division between members of the two groups, and thus representing the final stages of the immigrant group's incorporation into the host society.[2] Scholars have noted that, like European immigrants who came to the United States during the late nineteenth and early twentieth centuries, individuals of Asian and Latin American ancestry are marrying whites at a higher rate than blacks are marrying whites. This pattern suggests that the "boundaries of whiteness" will allow for the gradual incorporation of Asian and Latin American immigrant groups, and thus it reflects the "inconstant and changing nature of racial categories for all groups, except perhaps blacks."[3] These and similar findings have led scholars to conclude that high intermarriage rates between non-Hispanic white Americans and immigrants from Latin America and Asia will reduce the salience of the "black-white" divide that has historically characterized race relations and patterns of stratification in the United States, creating a new color line—a "black-nonblack" divide that reflects "the continued and unique separation of blacks not only from whites but also from other nonwhite ethnoracial groups."[4]

As this new color line is being drawn, however, black immigration is dramatically reconfiguring what it means to be black in America. Because of increased immigration from the Caribbean and Africa, as well as the relatively high birth rates among these groups, the percentage of black people who descend from American slaves has declined, albeit modestly, over the last three decades. Moreover, close to 20 percent of U.S.-born blacks under the age of eighteen have at least one foreign-born parent.[5] These trends necessitate an academic consideration of whether the social and economic outcomes of black immigrants will mirror those of black Americans, thus blurring distinctions between the two groups in later generations, or whether black immigrants and their descendants will alter the trajectory of black social and economic outcomes.

THE DETERMINANTS OF RACIAL DISPARITIES IN LIFE OUTCOMES

The third reason to analyze variation among black immigrants is that such research can provide insights into the primary causes of black-white disparities in social and economic outcomes in the United States. Although the traditional black-white binary may be fading as the focal racial divide in the United States, significant black-white disparities remain. Black Americans trail their white counterparts on almost every measure of social and economic well-being.[6] Because black immigrants and black Americans are phenotypically similar, some scholars have argued that they are subject to similar degrees of racial discrimination.[7] Consequently, if black immigrants outperform black Americans in the labor market, for example, factors other than racism must explain the disparities between black and white Americans.

Indeed, every U.S. census conducted since 1970 shows that, before adjusting for social and demographic characteristics, black immigrants from the English-speaking Caribbean earned more, were more likely to be employed, and had greater labor market participation rates than black Americans. These disparities have led some scholars to conclude that cultural deficiencies in attitudes toward work, rather than racism and discrimination, have impeded the progress of black Americans.[8]

A July 8, 1985, article in *Time* magazine entitled "Off to a Running Start" summarized the debate about the causes of disparities as follows:

The striking contrast between the disappointing economic achievements of American blacks and the progress made by immigrants is commonly attributed to racism. But the discrepancy is also evident when native-born blacks are compared with black immigrants from the West Indies and Africa. Because color is not a factor, such comparisons have fueled a sometimes acrimonious debate about the varying effects of race, class and culture on economic success in the U.S.

The belief that cultural differences are responsible for disparities between black Americans and black immigrants has emerged in both popular media and the scholarly literature. In *Ethnic America,* the economist Thomas Sowell explained nativity differences in labor market outcomes between black Americans and black immigrants as follows: "With many generations of discouragement of initiative and with little incentive to work anymore than necessary to escape punishment, slaves developed foot-dragging, work-evading patterns that were to remain as a cultural legacy long after slavery itself disappeared."[9] Similarly, the author of a 1986 *Wall Street Journal* article concluded:

> People in favor of affirmative action assume that the low rate of upward mobility of black Americans is largely due to racial discrimination. West Indians are black,[10] and they presumably must be targets of bigotry as much as black Americans. Yet, the percentages of blacks from the Caribbean who are successful in business and the professions surpass those of many white ethnic groups, and the group's jobless rate is lower than the national average. Its stunning success contradicts the claim that the dismal situation of black Americans is largely due to racial discrimination, thus calling into question the whole rationale for preferential treatment.[11]

This belief in black immigrants' cultural superiority has persisted in recent decades. In a 2006 *New York Times* op-ed, for example, the historical and cultural sociologist Orlando Patterson concluded that the developments of the 1990s "made it impossible to ignore the effects of culture," noting that "the Clinton administration achieved exactly what policy analysts had long said would pull black men out of their torpor: the economy grew at a rapid pace, providing millions of new jobs at all levels. Yet the jobless black youths simply did not turn up to take them. Instead, the opportunity was seized in large part by immigrants—including many blacks—mainly from Latin America and the Caribbean." Patterson continued, focusing on the role of wages:

> One oft-repeated excuse for the failure of black Americans to take these jobs—that they did not offer a living wage—turned out to be

irrelevant. The sociologist Roger Waldinger of the University of California at Los Angeles, for example, has shown that in New York such jobs offered an opportunity to the chronically unemployed to join the market and to acquire basic work skills that they later transferred to better jobs, but that the takers were predominantly immigrants.[12]

Given the persistent disparities between black and white Americans and the long-standing view that the accomplishments of black immigrants are evidence that the poor outcomes of black Americans stem from cultural dysfunctionality rather than racism and discrimination, it is vital to understand the mechanisms that produce disparities between black Americans and immigrants.

The Aims of the Book

This book has three primary aims. First, I seek to develop an improved framework for identifying and interpreting nativity-based disparities within the black population of the United States. Second, using a wide range of outcomes, I provide a detailed portrayal of inequality *among* blacks in the United States. Third, I examine how immigration-driven changes in the black population have influenced black-white disparities.

AIM 1: IMPROVING THE FRAMEWORK FOR UNDERSTANDING DISPARITIES AMONG BLACKS

The first aim of this book is to provide a more nuanced framework for understanding disparities between black Americans and black immigrants. Since the early 1900s, proponents of cultural explanations for disparities between black Americans and black immigrants have suggested that black Americans, particularly black men, simply do not want to work and immigrants, including black immigrants, simply do.[13] There are three primary reasons why the myth of black American cultural inferiority has persisted: the enduring influence of inaccurate anecdotal evidence; insufficient attention to how both selective migration and disparate pre- and post-1965 racial contexts shape the social and economic trajectories of black immigrants and black Americans; and a failure to fully account for differences in the relative benefits of employment in the United States.

The Shortcomings of Anecdotal Evidence

The myth of black American cultural inferiority originated in unrepresentative studies of blacks conducted during the early 1900s.[14] One reason the myth has endured is that scholars, the media, and politicians have been quick to accept such anecdotal evidence as an accurate representation of the entire black population and have not checked the validity of early conclusions via thorough empirical analyses.[15] Throughout this book, I address this limitation by rigorously analyzing disparities among blacks to uncover the mechanisms that facilitate the social integration of certain groups of black immigrants while hindering the integration of other groups. Specifically, I document disparities in education, labor market outcomes, homeownership, marriage, health, and intermarriage between black Americans and fourteen black immigrant subgroups from countries in the Caribbean and sub-Saharan Africa.

I examine economic disparities by analyzing data from the full U.S. census (100 percent) of New York City, home to most black immigrants in the early twentieth century, from 1910 to 1940. I then conduct a comprehensive analysis of disparities among blacks between 1980 and 2014, a period characterized by both rapid growth and increasing diversity of the black immigrant population. The goal of this analytical exercise is to identify the domains of social life in which black immigrants experience advantages over black Americans and uncover potential mechanisms explaining any disparities between the two groups. Across the chapters, I document several underappreciated disparities between black Americans and black immigrants, particularly in the domains of homeownership and marriage, and reveal that many of the immigrant advantages described in prior studies, particularly labor market advantages, were severely overstated.

Underappreciated Explanatory Mechanisms

A second reason for the persistence of the myth of black American cultural inferiority is that prior research has not fully explored important mechanisms producing nativity-based disparities among blacks. I highlight two understudied mechanisms: historical context and selective migration. My analysis of disparities among blacks in the early twentieth century shows that despite the volumes of research exalting the significant advantages of black immigrants during this period, few disparities actually existed between the two populations.[16] The results indicate that skin shade rather than nativity was the most important characteristic determining the outcomes of both black Americans and black immigrants at the time. Indeed, during the early twentieth century, the sheer magnitude of discrimination against all blacks allowed for very little variation to develop within the black population by either social class or nativity.[17] The analysis in the following chapters reveals that any meaningful advantages achieved by black immigrants over black Americans emerged in the post–civil rights era.

Although immigration scholars frequently acknowledge that the Immigration and Nationality Act of 1965 was largely responsible for allowing many black immigrants, particularly those from the Caribbean, to come to the United States, they often neglect the wider context: this policy change occurred during a period in which a broad array of newly implemented inclusionary policies facilitated greater social and economic variation within minority populations, particularly the black and Hispanic populations.[18] Just the year before the passing of this act, after decades of protests and legal battles, the U.S. Congress had passed the Civil Rights Act of 1964. This legislative victory, combined with the Voting Rights Act (1965) and the Fair Housing Act (1968), represented the key legal victories of the civil rights era.[19] These legislative victories decreased the acceptability of explicit forms of discrimination and eventually led to the creation of affirmative action programs, particularly in the government sector and higher education, which created pathways of upward mobility for some minority groups.[20] Taken together, these changes helped some blacks, both native-born and immigrant, make socioeconomic gains in the post–civil rights era.

The post–civil rights era policy changes, however, did not eliminate racism or discrimination. Blacks in the United States continued to experience extensive structural-level and individual-level barriers that created and maintained a high degree of residential segregation, mass incarceration, subpar education systems, and deficiencies in the health of black Americans. The best evidence suggests that contemporary discrimination and racism hinder the social outcomes of both black Americans and black immigrants, with some indications that black Americans experience higher degrees of discrimination than some black immigrants.[21] Throughout the book, I develop a somewhat more complex argument, showing that certain groups of black immigrants may have better outcomes than black Americans because they migrated to the United States at a time of expanding opportunities for all minorities and for women in general.

I am not arguing, however, that all black immigrants experienced the same post-1965 context or that black immigrants do not experience discrimination. Indeed, black immigrants from Haiti as well as those from majority-Muslim countries face unique forms of discrimination and racism. I argue instead that despite these variable experiences among black immigrants, not sharing the pre-1965 history that almost all black Americans experienced made it possible for some groups of black immigrants to achieve greater social and economic status than black Americans.

Selective migration is the second mechanism that helps explain disparities between black Americans and black immigrants. Black immigrants, like all other immigrants, are self-selected and thus differ systematically from other individuals in their birth countries. Studies have shown that regardless of national origin, immigrants are more educated and have better health profiles than those who remain in their countries of origin.[22] Thus, when they arrive in the United States, black immigrants already have certain advantages, at the aggregate level, over black Americans (and sometimes over white Americans). For example, in 2014, 63 percent of black Nigerian immigrants residing in the United States had at least a bachelor's degree, compared to an estimated 20 percent of black Americans and 36 percent of non-Hispanic white Americans.[23] In Nigeria, however, only 7 percent of the population had earned a bachelor's degree.[24] In addition to positive selection on observed characteristics (such as education), many immigrants are also selected on unobserved characteristics. Individuals with the necessary resources (for example, wealth), motivation, and ambition are most likely to take on the risk associated with moving to a new country.[25] Given the extent of the differences between immigrants and non-immigrants, comparisons between black immigrants and black Americans that do not account for selectivity in migration are meaningless.

To highlight the importance of selective migration, I compare the educational attainment of black immigrants to their compatriots in their origin countries, revealing that immigrants who migrate to the United States are often highly selected on education. Because migration is also selected on unobserved factors such as wealth, motivation, and risk tolerance, I also compare the outcomes of black immigrants to those of black American movers, a group that may be similarly selected on these unobserved characteristics. Across most outcomes, the profiles of black immigrants are more similar to those of black American movers than to those of black American nonmovers, suggesting that differences between black immigrants and black Americans stem, at least in part, from processes associated with selective migration.

Differences in the Relative Benefits of U.S. Employment

A third reason the myth of black American inferiority has persisted is researchers' failure to fully account for differences in the appeal of U.S. labor market opportunities for immigrants from less-developed countries (black or white). Because many jobs in the United States allow immigrants to fulfill a greater number of objectives than employment opportunities in most Caribbean and African countries, immigrants, particularly less-educated immigrants, may have a more favorable view of U.S. labor market opportunities than U.S.-born individuals, and this could lead to higher labor force participation and employment rates.

There are large wage disparities between many black immigrant-sending countries and the United States. For example, in 2015 the gross per person national income (GNI) was $53,245 in the United States but only $1,523 in Ethiopia. Thus, a full-time minimum-wage worker in Washington, D.C. (home to many of the Ethiopian immigrants living in the United States) would make more than fourteen times the annual earnings of the average person residing in Ethiopia.[26] Such wage differentials are a powerful motivating factor for people from all major black immigrant-sending countries.

Moreover, immigrants use their wages not only to support themselves but also to help family members build capital at home. Remittances account for a significant share of GDP in many countries in both the Caribbean and Africa. Because the cost of living is drastically lower in the home countries of most black immigrants than in the United States, even the worst-paying jobs in the United States offer appealing opportunities to fulfill financial objectives. In contrast, U.S.-born individuals, both black and white, have financial objectives and family networks grounded primarily in the United States and thus find many of the jobs filled by immigrant workers less attractive. Consequently, because the wage threshold for taking a job is lower for immigrants, particularly less-educated black immigrants, some immigrant groups may have higher labor market participation and employment rates than black Americans.

In summary, the combination of these three factors—migration to the United States during a period of expanding opportunities for minorities in general (historical context), selectivity among the immigrant population on both observed and unobserved skills and resources, and differing perceptions of the benefits of U.S. employment—set the stage for certain groups of black immigrants to achieve some social and economic advantages over black Americans.

AIM 2: CONSTRUCTING INFORMATIVE COMPARISONS: THE TOPOLOGY OF THE BLACK POPULATION

The second aim of the book is to paint a detailed portrait of inequality among blacks across a range of outcomes. The uncertainty about which factors are responsible for differences in social outcomes among blacks in the United States stems from a lack of research clearly documenting the demographic diversity of the country's black population. Few studies have attempted to rigorously detail the empirical facts needed to frame a substantive debate. Before the scholarly community can develop sound theories to explain disparities among blacks, scholars must first understand the nuances of the data. It is my hope that this book sheds light on these nuances and thus provides a lens through which scholars and policymakers can systematically understand racial disparities in the twenty-first century.

Immigrants

One of the shortcomings of the extant literature on black immigrants is that most research either treats the black immigrant population as monolithic or focuses on broad regional groups, such as immigrants from the Caribbean or Africa. This prior work overlooks the considerable subregional heterogeneity among black immigrants: In 2014, at least one black immigrant from nearly every country of the world resided in the United States.[27] I address this shortcoming in the literature by documenting the extensive birth-country variation in social outcomes among black immigrants. Although it is neither feasible nor informative to include every country of origin, I designed the country-level analysis outlined in this book to capture the meaningful variation in social outcomes among black immigrants residing in the United States. Because much of the literature on the importance of culture, selective migration, and discrimination in explaining disparities between black immigrants and black Americans pertains almost exclusively to first-generation black immigrants, this book focuses exclusively on the outcomes of this group.

Black immigrants from Latin America and the Caribbean come from a diverse array of countries. In the book, I analyze the outcomes of immigrants from the Dominican Republic, Haiti, Jamaica, Trinidad and Tobago, and Guyana. Collectively, these countries accounted for more than 75 percent of black immigrants from the Caribbean living in the United States in 2014, and just three of these countries—Jamaica, Haiti, and Trinidad and Tobago—accounted for nearly 64 percent of immigrants from the Caribbean region.

To incorporate the majority of immigrants from Africa and address the broad variation in underlying motivations for migration from this region, I examine the social outcomes of immigrants from nine of the primary source countries of African immigrants: Nigeria, Ethiopia, Ghana, Kenya, Liberia, Somalia, Cameroon, Sierra Leone, and Sudan. Collectively, these countries accounted for 70 percent of immigrants from sub-Saharan Africa in 2014.[28]

In addition to allowing for a better understanding of birth-country variation among black immigrants, the analysis captures a high degree of linguistic variation. English is the official language of Jamaica, Trinidad and Tobago, Guyana, Nigeria, Ghana, Kenya, and Liberia; Spanish is the official language of the Dominican Republic; French is the official language of Haiti and Cameroon; the official language of Sudan and Somalia is Arabic; and the official language of Ethiopia is Amharic. These countries also represent religious diversity: most black immigrants hail from Christian nations, but Sudan, Somalia, and Sierra Leone are primarily Muslim nations and tend to send large numbers of refugees to the United States. Although not every immigrant from

Sudan, Somalia, and Sierra Leone is Muslim or a refugee, including these countries in the analysis offers insight into the likely impact of inhabiting these two social statuses.

Black Americans

For several decades, researchers have sought to identify the source of labor market differences between black Americans and black immigrants by focusing primarily on three factors: cultural differences in work orientation, selective migration, and discrimination.[29] The convention in the literature is to compare the outcomes of black immigrants to those of representative samples of black Americans.[30] As documented in prior studies, however, black immigrants are not random samples of residents from their birth countries. Thus, using representative samples of U.S.-born blacks as the referent in labor market studies is likely to generate incorrect estimates of the importance of different mechanisms—culture, discrimination, or selective migration—in producing labor market disparities between the two groups.

In response to this problem, the economist Kristin Butcher has suggested that U.S.-born blacks who have also made a migration decision—domestic interstate migrants (black American movers)—are a more appropriate comparison group for evaluating nativity differences in labor market outcomes among the black population.[31] That is, if a correlation exists between favorable labor market outcomes and voluntary migration (whether international or domestic), then the outcomes of black immigrants should more closely resemble those of black American movers (interstate migrants) than those of black American nonmovers. Although it is unreasonable to expect the same degree of selectivity among black immigrants and black American movers, any meaningful change in estimates of social disparities resulting from the use of black American movers rather than all black Americans as the referent would highlight the importance of selective migration. Moreover, disparities between black American movers and black immigrants represent an upper bound on the importance of culture and discrimination in explaining disparities between black immigrants and black American movers. I apply this strategy to investigate the relative influence of selective migration in explaining differences in labor market outcomes, health, marriage, education, intermarriage, and homeownership. Black American movers are defined as individuals whose state of current residence is different from their state of birth.[32] Black American nonmovers are defined as individuals who reside in their state of birth.

AIM 3: EXAMINING THE INFLUENCE OF THE GROWTH IN BLACK IMMIGRATION ON BLACK-WHITE DISPARITIES

Given America's long and, at times, state-sanctioned history of racial discrimination against blacks, a large body of American social science research has focused on measuring and tracking changes in social and economic disparities between blacks and whites. The goal of these studies is generally to examine whether the country is making progress toward improving the social conditions of black Americans. Although the significant increase in the number of black immigrants has changed the meaning of black-white disparities, researchers tend to aggregate all blacks, regardless of nativity, when measuring changes in social outcomes, from health and marriage to voting and labor market outcomes. This failure to account for black immigration can lead to incorrect estimates of both the social progress made by black Americans and changes in the intensity of the racism and discrimination experienced by blacks in the United States. As the black immigrant population grows and becomes more diverse, empirical analyses must account for the effects of immigration on changes in the social outcomes of blacks in the United States.

Thus, the third aim of the project is to examine how the changing composition of the black population, spurred by immigration, has shaped black-white disparities. For example, the marriage gap between non-Hispanic white women and all black women began to widen during the 1960s. Few studies have examined how immigration has impacted the magnitude of the marriage gap between non-Hispanic white women and all black women. If black immigrant women have a higher marriage rate than black American women and researchers do not disaggregate the black population when calculating marriage disparities, immigration could conceal the extent of marriage decline among black Americans. Further, marriage is just one of the social outcomes that may have been affected by the increase in black immigration, and prior studies have examined very few of these outcomes. To fill this gap in literature, I examine the influence of the influx of black immigrants on a broad range of socioeconomic disparities between blacks and whites in the United States.

An Outline of the Chapters

The book is organized into three parts. Part I includes the introduction (chapter 1) as well as a demographic portrait of black America in the twenty-first century (chapter 2). In particular, chapter 2 outlines the demographic trends that motivate the project, including the growth of the black immigrant population since 1960, the changing birth-country distribution of the population, and differences in patterns of geographic settlement among black immigrants as well as how these patterns differ from those of black Americans. The chapter also highlights differences in the settlement patterns of black Caribbean immigrants and black African immigrants and discusses the impact of these differences on the social integration of these two groups of migrants.

Part II comprises chapters 3 to 5, which examine economic disparities among blacks in the United States. Chapter 3 provides the guiding theoretical framework for part II and motivates the analysis in the remaining chapters of the book. The chapter begins by summarizing the long-standing social and economic disparities between black and white Americans and discussing how, as early as the 1900s, scholarly interest in black immigrants was motivated not by an interest in understanding the social integration of that group, but rather by the goal of understanding variation among blacks and using this information to assess the influence of racism and discrimination in producing the poor standing of black Americans. Chapter 3 then summarizes nearly four decades of research, seeking to identify and assess explanations (for example, culture, disparate forms of discrimination, and selective migration) for labor market disparities between black immigrants (particularly immigrants from the English-speaking Caribbean, the group with the longest history of migration to the United States) and black Americans. The chapter highlights key limitations of prior work and develops a more comprehensive framework for understanding differences between native and immigrant blacks in the United States and among black immigrants.

I highlight three factors that help explain black immigrants' economic success: differential pre- and post-1965 racial contexts, selective migration, and conditions in immigrants' origin countries that shape how they perceive labor market opportunities in the United States.

Chapter 4 provides empirical support for the argument advanced in chapter 3. Although the chapter generates many nuanced results, four key findings emerge. First, black American movers tend to have better outcomes than black American nonmovers across most outcomes and in most years, highlighting the strong correlation between moving and labor market outcomes for black Americans. Second, the outcomes of black immigrants are more like the outcomes of black American movers than the outcomes of black American nonmovers, suggesting that the favorable outcomes of immigrants stem from selective migration rather than cultural differences. Third, for nearly every outcome studied, black immigrants had similar or worse outcomes than black American movers in the first four decades of the twentieth century, suggesting that any nativity-based variation in observed or unobserved characteristics associated with labor market success was not significant enough to produce a meaningful difference between the groups. This finding suggests that the legislative and institutional changes that reduced overt discrimination in the United States were a necessary condition for the emergence of disparities among blacks in the twenty-first century. Fourth, the most consistent black immigrant advantages occur in labor force participation. Almost every black immigrant arrival cohort from every country in the analysis eventually converged with or overtook the labor force participation rates of both black American movers and white Americans. If the favorable labor force participation rates of black immigrants are used to claim that black Americans suffer from a cultural deficit, white Americans must suffer from a similar cultural deficit. I argue, however, that rather than deriving from culture, the favorable labor force participation rates of black immigrants stem from the disparate benefits of low-skilled employment for immigrant and native populations.

Chapter 5 expands the focus on economic success, shifting from labor market outcomes to homeownership (a form of wealth). In 2010, the median wealth of white families was eight times that of black families.[33] Regardless of race, home equity makes up the bulk of the wealth portfolios for all but the wealthiest American families.[34] Thus, racial differences in homeownership account for a large portion of the overall racial wealth gap. While many studies have documented racial dispar-ities in homeownership, few have accounted for the impact of wealth disparities on black demographic diversity, particularly changes in the foreign-born share of the country's overall black population.[35]

Mirroring the labor market findings, I document negligible dispar-ities in homeownership during the early twentieth century. Among contemporary blacks, I find that shortly after arriving in the United States, all country subgroups of black immigrants exhibited lower rates of homeownership than black American movers and nonmovers. Yet as their tenure in the United States increased, most of these subgroups achieved higher homeownership rates than black Americans. During the period of study, homeownership rates increased for most black immigrant groups but remained flat for black Americans. All groups of blacks have lower homeownership rates than white Americans.

Part III completes the portrait of social and economic well-being among blacks in the United States by examining disparities in health (chapter 6) as well as marriage and intermarriage (chapter 7). Each chapter contains a discussion of the origins of racial disparities in focal outcomes; because of data limitations, however, the analysis focuses on the contemporary period. Chapter 6 shows that upon arrival in the United States, every black immigrant subgroup has a more favor-able health profile than black American movers and nonmovers. Black immigrants from Africa tend not only to have better health but to maintain this advantage the longer they live in the United States. In comparison, the health advantage of black immigrants from the Carib-bean erodes over time. Mirroring the patterns for other outcomes, black American movers have more favorable health profiles than black American nonmovers. While black Americans tend to report worse health than white Americans, most black immigrant subgroups report health outcomes that are similar to or more favorable than those of white Americans.

Chapter 7 provides an analysis of disparities in marriage and intermarriage, perhaps the oldest sociological measure of assimila-tion, among the black population and between blacks and whites in the United States. Despite evidence from the General Social Survey (GSS) suggesting that the percentage of Americans opposed to marry-ing a black spouse has declined, the intermarriage rate among blacks, particularly the rate of marriages with white Americans, has remained relatively low, even as the rate of intermarriage with whites increased for both Hispanics and Asians.[36] Chapter 7 examines whether this general pattern of intermarriage holds across America's diverse black population and also analyzes the degree of intramarriage among black subgroups. This analysis explores whether subgroups of black immigrants are creating social boundaries between themselves and black Americans or whether native- and foreign-born blacks are uniting via marriage. I find that, relative to black Americans, black immigrants who were unmarried at the time of immigration have lower rates of intermarriage with non-Hispanic whites. Although most black immigrants marry conationals, they tend to marry black Americans more than whites. Among all black people, regardless of nativity, black American movers are more likely than nonmovers to marry white Americans. I discuss the implications of these findings for understanding the racial color line in the twenty-first century.[37]

Chapter 8, the concluding chapter, summarizes the book's key findings and discusses the meaningful ways in which black immigrants are contributing to a more diverse black population in the United States. In addition, I explore the implications of the findings for explanations of social disparities among black people and between blacks and whites. Specifically, I discuss how the changing birth-country distribution of black America has affected the way policymakers and academics understand the trajectory of racial inequality in the United States.

CHAPTER TWO

A DEMOGRAPHIC PORTRAIT OF BLACK AMERICA

This chapter provides an overview of the historical developments related to black immigration to the United States and presents a current demographic profile of the black population. I begin by exploring the primary demographic phenomenon motivating the project: the rapid growth of the black immigrant population residing in the United States since the 1960s. I examine several aspects of the historical and recent streams of black immigration, including the policy changes that led to the post-1965 increase in black immigration, diversity among black immigrants with regard to country of origin and reason for migrating, and the geographic settlement patterns of black immigrants in the United States.

The Mechanisms Driving Black Immigration

The overwhelming majority of blacks residing in the United States descend from American slaves, but their share of the overall black population has gradually decreased ever since the flow of black immigrants, primarily from the Caribbean to the United States, began in earnest in the 1910s and 1920s. According to the sociologist Suzanne Model, two factors are largely responsible for the initiation of black immigration to the United States during this period: the banana trade between Caribbean and Central American countries and the United States in the wake of the Spanish-American War, and the completion of the Panama Canal.[1] Sugar had been the dominant crop grown in the Caribbean during the nineteenth century, but the banana industry began to flourish there during the early and mid-twentieth century. The economist Ransford Palmer noted: "While banana growing gave new life to the small farmer because the crop could be grown on terrain unsuitable for sugar cane, it also brought the banana boat, which signaled the development of a tourist industry. The banana boats also brought passengers and marked the beginning of regular steamship travel between the Caribbean and the Atlantic ports of the United States, especially New York."[2] Indeed, the development of passenger travel by ship created the infrastructure needed to facilitate travel to New York, which over time created a mechanism for bringing visitors to the Caribbean and Caribbean migrant workers to the United States.[3]

The second major development was the building of the Panama Canal. In search of better living conditions and wages, over 100,000 black immigrant men from the Caribbean, particularly from Jamaica and Barbados, migrated to the Panama Canal zone to help build the canal.[4] After the project was completed in 1914, many of these individuals, now accustomed to earning higher wages than would be possible in the Caribbean, continued their northward journey to the United States in search of higher pay and better living conditions.[5]

Model used data from the U.S. Immigration Commission on the annual number of blacks migrating from the Caribbean to link the flow of black Caribbean migrants to the United States with the completion of the Panama Canal and the creation of trading routes between the two regions.[6] In 1900, only a few hundred black immigrants came to the United States. By 1910, this number had increased to just under 4,000, and it grew to over 10,000 by 1924.

Black immigration to the United States slowed dramatically after 1924, the year the Johnson-Reed Act was implemented. This immigration act contained provisions designed to curtail the flow of immigrants from both southern and eastern Europe and severely restricted immigration from northern Africa, Arab states, and Asia. Because black immigrants from the English-speaking Caribbean, the primary source of black immigrants to the United States during this period, came under the quota for Great Britain, the Johnson-Reed Act had no direct impact on immigration from this region. Indeed, most of the quota for Great Britain between 1924 and 1929—which was approximately 34,007 individuals—went unfilled.[7] Despite this fact, the flow of black immigrants declined to 1900s levels and remained low throughout the 1930s and 1940s. In 1924, 10,000 black immigrants from the

Caribbean arrived in the United States. This number fell to 308 in 1925 and averaged 617 persons a year from 1924 to 1932.[8]

Several factors are likely to have contributed to the reduction in black immigration to the United States. Although residents of the English-speaking Caribbean were not directly impacted by the Johnson-Reed Act, symbolically the policy change reflected the anti-immigrant sentiment of the period, which probably inhibited individuals from moving to the United States. Additionally, those wishing to move to the United States had to obtain a visa from local consulate offices. Research has suggested that many consulate offices engaged in subversive and discriminatory behavior throughout the Caribbean and Latin America, often denying individuals who were eligible to obtain visas.[9] The historian Roger Daniels notes that "The statutory requirement of a visa, which had to be obtained at an American consulate, was felt to be most important by restrictionists. It was, in their terminology, a way of controlling immigration at the source and it gave considerable discretion authority to individual consular officials."[10]

In addition to potential discriminatory behavior by various consulate offices, the onset of the Great Depression, which lasted from 1929 to 1939, also discouraged many Caribbean residents from making a move to the United States. Indeed, owing partly to poor employment conditions during the Great Depression, between 1932 and 1937 net migration between the United States and the West Indies was negative.[11] According to U.S. census data, 98,620 black immigrants resided in the United States in the 1930s; this number dropped to 83,941 in the 1940s.[12] Black immigration would remain low for the next two decades.

The 1960s brought a significant shift in patterns of black immigration (see figure 2.1). Fueled in part by poor economic conditions in the post–World War II era, many blacks in the Caribbean, like their predecessors who migrated to the Panama Canal zone during the first two decades of the twentieth century, began searching for better living conditions outside of the Caribbean. While labor market conditions served as a powerful motivator for blacks from the Caribbean, changes in immigration policies in both Great Britain and the United States were the most notable factors that ultimately allowed blacks from the Caribbean to act on their desire to migrate.[13]

Because many countries in the English-speaking Caribbean are former British colonies, even after they gained independence they remained members of the British Commonwealth. All Commonwealth

Figure 2.1 *Growth of the Black Immigrant Population by Region of Birth,*
1960–2014

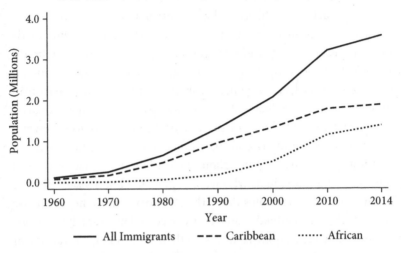

Source: U.S. census and 2014 American Community Survey (ACS).

citizens were recognized as British subjects. The Nationality Act, passed by Great Britain in 1948, essentially created an open-door immigration policy between Great Britain and member states of the British Commonwealth, including residents of the island nations in the English-speaking Caribbean.[14] Thus, Great Britain was an easy option for individuals seeking to improve their living conditions by moving to a more-developed country. A side effect of this policy was that demand for immigration from this region to the United States was low.

Britain's immigration policies changed, however, in 1962. Motivated in part by nativist tensions over jobs and housing and the view by many in Britain that black migrants could not assimilate into British society, in 1962 Great Britain passed the Commonwealth Immigrants Act.[15] The new policy instituted admissions restrictions that significantly reduced the flow of new migrant workers to Great Britain, particularly the flow of blacks from the English-speaking Caribbean.

Just as migration to Great Britain was becoming more difficult for these immigrants, the United States began to relax its immigration policies.[16] In 1965, Lyndon Johnson signed the Immigration and Nationality Act, also known as the Hart-Celler Act. Perhaps the act's most significant change to U.S. immigration policy was the removal of quota provisions, a hallmark of previous policies that disproportionately benefited immigrants from northern Europe. Under the previous system, the annual number of immigrants allowed from a specific country was based on the percentage of foreign-born persons from that country living in the United States at the time of the 1890 census. Because few black immigrants from either the Caribbean or Africa resided in the United States in 1890, the quota system allowed very few people from these regions to migrate to the United States each year.[17] The Hart-Cellar Act replaced these provisions with a hemisphere-based quota system. Countries in the Western Hemisphere could send a total of 120,000 migrants per year to the United States, and no country in the Eastern Hemisphere could send more than 20,000 immigrants per year.[18] In addition, nations in the Eastern Hemisphere—but not those in the Western Hemisphere—were subject to a preference system in which 20 percent of each country's allotted immigration visas were reserved for people with specific skills and 80 percent were reserved for family reunification.[19]

Although these policy changes were a dramatic shift from the restrictive provisions embedded in previous U.S. immigration policies and signaled to some degree an increased acceptance of racial and ethnic divisions, as Philip Kasinitz notes:

> No one, particularly not the bill's supporters, envisioned that Hart-Cellar would produce a dramatic change in the ethnic composition of new arrivals. On the eve of the bill's passage, Attorney General Robert Kennedy testified that the number of new immigrants was not expected to increase greatly, and other experts, while acknowledging that immigration from Jamaica and Trinidad would exceed the limit of one hundred, predicted that it would stabilize at approximately 5,000 to 7,000 per year for the Caribbean as a whole. . . . Not one witness or legislator disagreed with this estimate.[20]

Figure 2.1 shows, however, that these predictions were drastically incorrect. In 1960, approximately 118,000 black immigrants resided in the United States, nearly all of whom were born in the Caribbean. By 1970, that number had risen to 258,000—a 118 percent increase in just ten years. As Model explains, the exemption of Western Hemisphere countries from the skills and family preferences that were applied to Eastern Hemisphere countries had certain implications for the composition of the flow of black immigrants from that region: "If they [West Indians] were not parents, spouses, or children of American citizens, if they did not qualify for a preference, and if they were not refugees, Hart-Celler required that they obtain certification from the U.S. Department of Labor."[21]

Because it was relatively easy for immigrants from the West Indies to acquire labor certification for two specific occupations—nurses and domestic servants—much of the growth in the U.S. black population between 1960 and the mid-1970s was driven by Caribbean women who could secure visas for employment in these two professions.[22] Figure 2.1 shows that between 1970 and 1980, the dramatic increase that began in the prior decade continued: the number of black immigrants residing in the United States grew from 257,800 to 653,460, a 153 percent increase in a single decade.

During the 1980s, several additional changes to U.S. immigration policy significantly affected the number of blacks immigrating to the United States. The Refugee Act of 1980 changed U.S. refugee policy to conform with United Nations protocols by providing 500,000 visas per year to individuals applying to move to the United States as refugees.[23] The Refugee Act started streams of migration from Somalia, Ethiopia, and Eritrea and increased the flow of refugees from Haiti. Additional changes came a few years later, when the 1986 Immigration Reform and Control Act provided a path to legal residence status for roughly 35,000 sub-Saharan Africans and 100,000 migrants from the English-speaking Caribbean who were living as undocumented immigrants in the United States.[24] During the 1980s, the number of black immigrants residing in the United States increased from 653,460 to 1,308,678, partly because of these policy changes.

Much of the growth of the black immigrant population from the 1960s through the 1980s was driven by Caribbean immigration, but during the 1990s African immigration became increasingly important.[25] The eroding economies, poverty, corrupt governments, and political violence that have long affected many African nations also generated highly mobile populations within the African region.[26] To improve their living conditions, many black Africans have historically moved to countries with strong economies within Africa, particularly South Africa, or, like Caribbean immigrants, to former colonial powers such as Belgium, France, Portugal, and the United Kingdom.[27]

U.S. policy changes implemented in the 1990s, primarily the 1990 Immigration Act, provided a new and relatively welcoming venue for Africans seeking to improve their living conditions. The 1990 act had two provisions that spurred immigration from Africa. First, by raising the number of immigrants admitted on the basis of skills, it increased the flow of migrants from both the Caribbean and sub-Saharan Africa.[28] Second, the act created a diversity visa system designed to increase the number of immigrants from countries that were underrepresented in the current immigrant population of the United States. Although originally designed to expand the number of immigrants from European countries, the lottery had an unintended but significant impact on immigration from sub-Saharan Africa.[29] Between 1998 and 2007, 27 percent of diversity visas were granted to immigrants from this region, and by 2013 the proportion had grown to approximately 39 percent.[30] As a result of the changes implemented as part of the 1990 Immigration Act, as of 2014 black immigrants from sub-Saharan Africa were one of the fastest-growing immigrant populations in the United States. In fact, some scholars have shown that the number of African immigrants who have come to the United States since 1990 as voluntary migrants now exceeds the number of black Africans brought to the United States during the slave trade.[31]

Figure 2.2 demonstrates these trends by showing the number of lawful permanent residents arriving in the United States from sub-Saharan Africa and the Caribbean between 1960 and 2009.[32] Although the number of new permanent residents arriving from the Caribbean has always exceeded the number coming from sub-Saharan Africa, the growth rates of the two populations, shown by the slopes of the respective curves, have changed dramatically over time. Between 1960 and 1980, the Caribbean growth rate was significantly greater; during the 1980s, the two rates began to converge; and by the 1990s, the number of permanent residents from Africa was growing much faster than the number of new residents from the Caribbean, a trend that continues to the present day.

Figure 2.3 further illustrates the influences of shifts in immigration policy over the past fifty years by showing the total number of black immigrants arriving in the United States as well as the distribution of these immigrants by home region for each five-year arrival cohort from 1970 to 2014 (based on data from the 2014 American Community

Figure 2.2 *Lawful Permanent Residents Arriving from Africa and the Caribbean, 1960–2009*

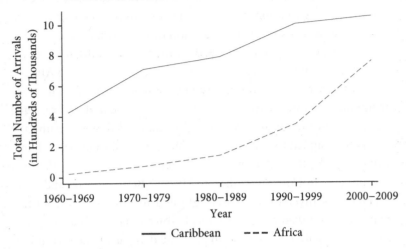

Source: U.S. Department of Homeland Security 2014.
Note: Persons obtaining lawful permanent resident status by region of last residence.

Figure 2.3 *Immigrant Population in 2014 by Birth Region and Arrival Cohort*

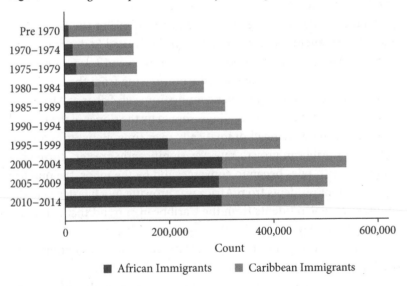

Source: 2014 ACS.

Figure 2.4 *Top Ten Countries of Origin for All Black Immigrants in 2014*

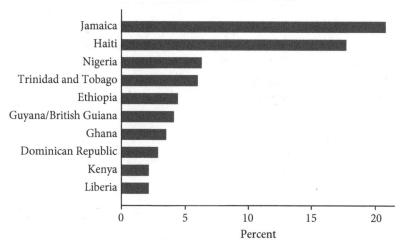

Source: 2014 ACS.

Survey). In the 1970s, most black immigrants were from the Caribbean. In comparison, large-scale immigration from Africa is more recent, with the vast majority of black African immigrants arriving after 1990. In addition to this shift in home region distribution, the overall number of black immigrants coming to the United States has increased considerably. Between 1980 and 1989, 601,545 black immigrants came to the United States. By contrast, between 2000 and 2010, 1,147,167 black immigrants arrived in the country, and the majority (645,953) of these immigrants hailed from Africa.

Variation by Country of Origin

Understanding the increase in the number of black immigrants and the shifts in immigrants' home regions over the past fifty years is important, but these trends do not tell the entire story. Another critical aspect of black immigration is the immense variation by country of origin among these immigrants. Figure 2.3, which shows that black immigrants tend to arrive from two primary regions of the world (the Caribbean and Africa), provides only a partial picture of the extensive diversity of the black immigrant population in the United States. Figure 2.4 lists the ten most common national origins of black immigrants living in the United States as of 2014.

Figure 2.5 *Top Ten Countries of Origin for Black Caribbean Immigrants in 2014*

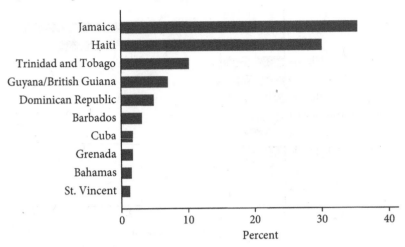

Source: 2014 ACS.

Given the long and sustained period of black migration from the Caribbean, it is not surprising that Jamaica, Haiti, and Trinidad and Tobago are three of the four top sending countries. More notable is the fact that fully half of the top ten origin countries—Nigeria, Ethiopia, Ghana, Kenya, and Liberia—are in sub-Saharan Africa. Given that relatively few African immigrants arrived before 1990, the presence of so many African countries on a list of the top ten sending countries highlights the rapid growth of these migration flows during the 1990s and 2000s.

Figures 2.5 and 2.6 add further detail by showing the top ten sending countries for Caribbean immigrants and the top ten sending countries for African immigrants, respectively, in 2014. Notably, the top five home countries of Caribbean immigrants—Jamaica, Haiti, Trinidad and Tobago, Guyana, and the Dominican Republic—account for almost 90 percent of all black immigrants from this region in 2014. Barbados, Cuba, Grenada, the Bahamas, and St. Vincent contributed much smaller flows of black immigrants.

The sub-Saharan African countries sending the largest number of black immigrants to the United States are Nigeria, Ethiopia, and Ghana (see figure 2.6). One important difference between migration from the

Figure 2.6 *Top Ten Countries of Origin for Black African Immigrants in 2014*

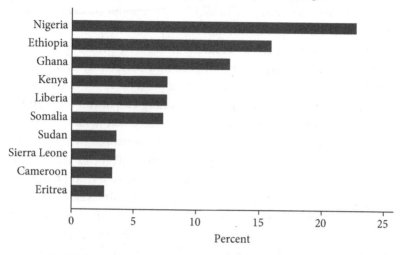

Source: 2014 ACS.

Caribbean and migration from Africa is the degree of birth-country variation within the two populations. Nearly 75 percent of immigrants from the Caribbean hail from just four countries. In contrast, the five largest immigrant streams from Africa—those from Nigeria, Ethiopia, Ghana, Kenya, and Liberia—account for approximately 50 percent of the African immigrant population. Thus, the growth in immigration from Africa has significantly increased the overall birth-country diversity within the U.S. black immigrant population.

Variation by Visa Category

Another way in which black immigrants in the United States are quite diverse is in their wide variety of reasons for migrating. Although it is difficult, at least quantitatively, to fully capture immigrants' underlying motivation for migration, the type of visa they hold provides some insight into how U.S. immigration policy affects the types of immigrants who come to the United States. That is, although many immigrants with non-employment-based visas may fully intend to work in the United States and were primarily motivated by the potential economic benefits of immigrating, some immigrants with, for example, family-sponsored visas may have non-economic goals. This factor could lead to greater diversity in social and economic outcomes among immigrants who migrate with different types of visas.

The U.S. Department of Homeland Security provides information on five visa categories: refugees and asylees, diversity visas, employment-based preferences, immediate relatives of U.S. citizens, and family-sponsored preferences.[33] Among Caribbean immigrants who arrived between 2000 and 2013, 35 percent had family-sponsored preference visas and 53 percent had visas sponsored by immediate relatives who were U.S. citizens.[34] All other categories were much smaller: 3 percent arrived via employment-based visas, 5 percent were refugees or asylees, and none had diversity visas (because immigrants from the Caribbean do not qualify for this type of visa). The large share of Caribbean immigrants who arrive on family-sponsored visas and visas sponsored by immediate relatives underscores the strength of chain migration among individuals from the region—where more established migrants sponsor newcomers.

Among sub-Saharan African immigrants, the most common visa categories were diversity visas, visas sponsored by relatives who were U.S. citizens, and refugees and asylees. Between 2000 and 2013, 19 percent of these immigrants received diversity visas, 39 percent were sponsored by relatives in the United States, and 28 percent migrated as refugees or asylees. The level of family-sponsored preference visas was much lower for African immigrants than for Caribbean immigrants: only 6 percent of immigrants from sub-Saharan Africa arrived via family-sponsored preference visas.[35]

In addition to this regional variation, visa type varies significantly by country of origin for both immigrants from the Caribbean and those from Africa. For example, table 2.1 shows the distribution of visas awarded to immigrants from the primary sending countries of black immigrants in 2014. While the majority of immigrants from the Caribbean had visas sponsored by family members or immediate relatives of U.S. citizens, Haitians were the only Caribbean subgroup with a significant proportion of immigrants (8.8 percent) arriving under the refugee/asylee admissions category. For all other Caribbean countries, fewer than 1 percent of immigrants were refugees or asylees.

Among immigrants from sub-Saharan Africa, refugees and asylees made up a very large share of the immigration flows from Somalia

Table 2.1 *Persons Obtaining Lawful Permanent Resident Status by Broad Class of Admission and by Region and Country of Birth, 2014*

Country of Birth	Total	Family-Sponsored Preferences	Employment-Based Preferences	Immediate Relatives of U.S. Citizens	Diversity	Refugees and Asylees	Other
Caribbean							
Dominican Republic	44,577	25,025	293	19,000	6	111	142
Jamaica	19,026	6,379	629	11,917	4	44	53
Haiti	15,274	6,998	110	6,617	—	1,344	205
Guyana	6,267	4,179	87	1,958	12	9	22
Trinidad and Tobago	3,988	913	244	2,677	68	7	79
Belize	789	224	42	497	D	D	18
Africa							
Nigeria	12,828	1,882	884	7,147	2,740	126	49
Ethiopia	12,300	1,310	182	4,271	2,494	4,020	23
Ghana	7,115	926	280	4,266	1,556	65	22
Kenya	5,884	459	363	2,711	1,298	1,019	34
Somalia	5,190	176	D	1,645	79	3,276	D
Cameroon	3,943	358	103	1,212	1,381	876	13
Liberia	3,874	408	14	1,265	1,638	543	6
Sudan	2,442	129	D	529	592	1,161	D
Sierra Leone	1,740	158	48	724	686	119	5

Source: U.S. Department of Homeland Security 2014.
Note: D = data withheld to limit disclosure.

(63.1 percent), Sudan (47.5 percent), and Ethiopia (32.7 percent), but a very small share of flows from Nigeria and Ghana (less than 1 percent for each country). With the exception of immigrants from Somalia, only 2 percent of whom arrived under the diversity visa category, diversity visas were responsible for more than 20 percent of new arrivals from the other focal African countries. For example, among immigrants from Liberia, 42 percent of new lawful residents in 2014 arrived under the diversity visa category. Like immigrants from the Caribbean, a large share of individuals from each of the African countries examined arrived on family-sponsored preference visas or visas reserved for immediate relatives of U.S. citizens.

Black Immigration in Context

To discern how the rapid growth in black immigration in recent decades has affected broader patterns of immigration and racial dynamics within the United States, it is essential to understand not only the nuances of the increase in black immigrants but also the context in which this growth occurred. One way of contextualizing this trend is to compare the number of black immigrants from all sending countries to the number of immigrants from the primary source country of contemporary immigrants to the United States: Mexico. Figure 2.7 shows the number of black immigrants from all source countries living in the United States between 1960 and 2014 as well as the number of immigrants from Mexico living in the United States during the same period. When viewed in this context, the number of black immigrants in the United States seems rather small. For example, in 2014 the black immigrant population was approximately 3.4 million, while the Mexican immigrant population was more than three times larger, at roughly 12 million.

Given the relatively small number of black immigrants, it may initially seem that the growth of the black immigrant population does not warrant substantial scholarly attention. However, when the focus shifts from how black immigrants are changing the makeup of the entire population to how these new arrivals are changing the composition of the black population in the United States, the significance of this immigration trend is more obvious. Figure 2.8 shows that in 1960, less than 1 percent of the black population was foreign-born. By 1990, that share had increased to just under 5 percent, and by 2014, 9.2 percent of

Figure 2.7 *Growth of the Mexican-Origin and Black Immigrant Populations, 1960–2014*

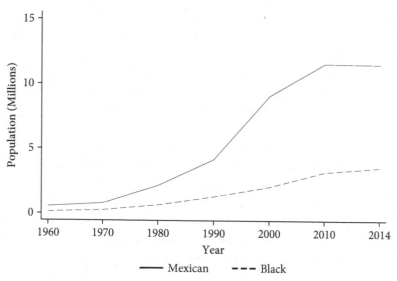

Source: U.S. census and 2014 ACS.

Figure 2.8 *Black Immigrants as a Proportion of All Blacks Living in the United States, 1960–2014*

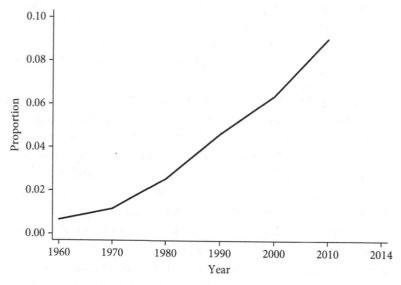

Source: U.S. census and 2014 ACS.

the U.S. black population was foreign-born. During the 2000s, black immigrants accounted for more than 20 percent of the growth in the black population in the United States.

This demographic trend is even more consequential because the growth of the black immigrant population is concentrated in two areas of the country: the Northeast and the South. In 2014, fully 83 percent of black immigrants resided in these two regions. Indeed, nearly 35 percent of blacks in the northeastern United States were foreign-born in 2014. Residence within this region varies greatly, with some states having much larger populations of black immigrants than others.

Table 2.2 shows the top ten states of residence for all black immigrants, as well as for the Caribbean and African subgroups, in 2014. The two regional lists have several states in common, but there are some clear differences in the settlement patterns of Caribbean and African immigrants. For example, Minnesota, Virginia, and Ohio are common destinations for immigrants from Africa, while Florida and Pennsylvania are popular only among immigrants from the Caribbean. Some of this variation is driven by visa type: owing in part to refugee resettlement assistance from the U.S. government, many black African immigrants reside in states that are not typical destinations for contemporary immigrants, regardless of race.

Table 2.3 shows the top ten states of residence for all native-born blacks in 2014, as well as the top states for subgroups based on domestic migration status (those who have moved across state lines and those who have not). Although the order differs to some degree, seven states—New York, Florida, Maryland, Texas, Georgia, California, and Virginia—appear on both the list for black immigrants and the list for black Americans. Three states—New Jersey, Massachusetts, and Pennsylvania—are unique to black immigrants, and two—North Carolina and Louisiana—are unique to black Americans. The data in tables 2.2 and 2.3 reflect the long periods of migration from the Caribbean to states in the Northeast, the historical settlement of black Americans in the South, and the movement of black Americans from southern states to midwestern states during the Great Migration. A comparison of tables 2.2 and 2.3 reveals a demographic fact often overlooked in studies that compare native-born and immigrant blacks: many black immigrants reside in places and work in labor markets where they have little contact with black Americans.

Table 2.2 State of Residence for Black Immigrants by Region of Birth, 2014

	All Black Immigrants			Caribbean Immigrants			African Immigrants	
Rank	State of Residence	Number	Rank	State of Residence	Number	Rank	State of Residence	Number
1	New York	831,517	1	New York	641,458	1	Texas	150,271
2	Florida	656,277	2	Florida	602,448	2	Maryland	138,379
3	Maryland	204,203	3	New Jersey	130,972	3	New York	131,784
4	Texas	203,578	4	Massachusetts	86,234	4	Minnesota	87,221
5	New Jersey	200,353	5	Georgia	72,388	5	California	81,201
6	Georgia	178,019	6	Pennsylvania	53,729	6	Virginia	80,420
7	Massachusetts	162,062	7	Connecticut	52,093	7	Georgia	75,937
8	California	145,769	8	Maryland	51,657	8	Massachusetts	67,554
9	Virginia	110,159	9	Texas	31,846	9	New Jersey	57,486
10	Pennsylvania	101,088	10	California	28,703	10	Ohio	48,250

Source: 2014 ACS.

Table 2.3 State of Residence of Black Americans by Migration Status, 2014

	All Black Natives			Black Movers			Black Nonmovers	
Rank	State of Residence	Number	Rank	State of Residence	Number	Rank	State of Residence	Number
1	Georgia	2,810,584	1	Georgia	900,796	1	Texas	2,084,353
2	Texas	2,795,207	2	Texas	776,824	2	Georgia	1,939,455
3	Florida	2,324,426	3	Florida	666,764	3	Florida	1,721,859
4	North Carolina	1,976,616	4	Maryland	659,270	4	New York	1,712,850
5	New York	1,918,686	5	California	606,831	5	North Carolina	1,712,850
6	California	1,886,692	6	North Carolina	535,828	6	California	1,359,792
7	Illinois	1,677,843	7	Virginia	436,430	7	Illinois	1,349,021
8	Maryland	1,485,019	8	New York	352,257	8	Louisiana	1,293,352
9	Louisiana	1,422,918	9	Illinois	350,723	9	Alabama	1,047,892
10	Virginia	1,383,263	10	Ohio	285,828	10	South Carolina	1,015,313

Source: 2014 ACS.

Figure 2.9 *Metropolitan Statistical Area Destinations for Caribbean Immigrants in the United States, 2010–2016*

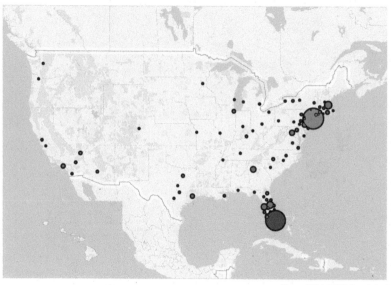

Share of Total MSA Population
0.1%   20.7%

Source: Migration Policy Institute tabulation of data from the U.S. Census Bureau's pooled 2010–2016 ACS. Originally published on the Migration Policy Institute's Migration Data Hub as "U.S. Immigrant Population by Metropolitan Statistical Area (MSA), 2012–2016," www.migrationpolicy.org/programs/data-hub/charts/us-immigrant-population-metropolitan-area.

Figures 2.9 and 2.10 further illustrate the degree of spatial diversity among immigrants from the Caribbean and sub-Saharan Africa.[36] As shown in figure 2.9, most immigrants from the Caribbean reside in Florida and metropolitan areas in the Northeast, with small populations spread throughout the rest of the country. In contrast, African immigrants are more geographically dispersed, with significant populations in California, Texas, and several midwestern states, as shown in figure 2.10.

Conclusion

This chapter has highlighted the long and complex history of migration from Africa and the Caribbean to the United States and the impact of U.S. immigration policy on immigration flows from these regions.

Figure 2.10 *Metropolitan Statistical Area Destinations for African Immigrants in the United States, 2010–2016*

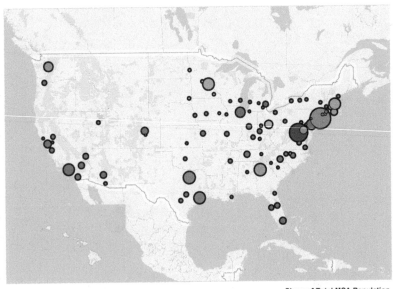

Share of Total MSA Population
0.2% ▓▓▓▓▓▓▓▓▓ 3.2%

Source: Migration Policy Institute tabulation of data from the U.S. Census Bureau's pooled 2010–2016 ACS. Originally published on the Migration Policy Institute's Migration Data Hub as "U.S. Immigrant Population by Metropolitan Statistical Area (MSA), 2012–2016," www.migrationpolicy.org/programs/data-hub/charts/us-immigrant-population-metropolitan-area.

Most black immigrants hail from either the Caribbean or Africa, but there is considerable diversity among immigrants from these two regions in country of origin, type of visa, time of arrival, and state of residence—factors that could lead to meaningful variation in socioeconomic outcomes among black immigrants. This variation provides the background for analyzing several demographic and social developments discussed in subsequent chapters.

First, this chapter has documented three significant waves of black immigration to the United States. The first occurred during the first three decades of the twentieth century. The vast majority of these immigrants hailed from the English-speaking Caribbean and tended to settle in New York City. Few immigrants migrated to the United States between 1940 and 1965.[37] The second occurred between 1965 and 1990. While significant flows came from Africa, again, the majority hailed from the Caribbean. The third wave began in the 1990s and continues to the present. African immigration accounted for the majority of the growth of the black immigrant population during this period.

In comparison to the first wave of voluntary black immigration, the second and third waves faced a drastically different social and political context. During the early 1900s, even in more progressive states in the Northeast where black immigrants tended to reside, both black Americans and black immigrants were profoundly affected by intense state-sanctioned racism. As I show in chapter 4, despite popular myths regarding the economic success of black Caribbean immigrants in New York during the 1920s and 1930s, regardless of social class or skills, black Americans and black Caribbean immigrants were mostly confined to jobs in the lower rungs of the occupational distribution.

In chapter 3, I argue that the social and political changes brought about by the civil rights movement of the 1950s and 1960s greatly impacted the experiences of the second and third waves of black immigrants. In the post–civil rights era, educational and occupational opportunities that were once reserved for white American men became available to women and minorities. Black immigrants, many of whom were positively selected on good education and work experience, were able to translate the skills acquired in their home countries into employment opportunities in the United States.

Second, this chapter has also shown that the factors that helped produce the social standing of black immigrants who arrived between 1960 and 1990 may not apply to post-1990 immigrants. In the 1980s, for example, the overwhelming share of black immigrants residing in the United States hailed from the Caribbean, particularly from countries such as Jamaica, Trinidad and Tobago, Guyana, and Haiti. Black immigrants during this period tended to live in close proximity to black American population centers, with those from the English-speaking Caribbean residing primarily in the Northeast and Haitians settling in South Florida. While black Caribbean immigrants largely continue to settle in these regions, the reasons behind these immigration flows have changed over time. Compared to those who arrived in the 2000s, a greater proportion of immigrants from the Caribbean arrived in the United States in the 1970s with visas reserved for individuals seeking employment. However, by 2014, only a small share of Caribbean immigrants were arriving on employment visas. Instead, most had family-sponsored visas. This change suggests that the underlying motivation for coming to the United States has shifted over time among Caribbean immigrants, and any such shift could lead to greater diversity in social and economic outcomes among more recent cohorts from the region. Because of changes in immigration regimes across arrival cohorts, throughout the book I highlight the changes over time in the social and economic outcomes of immigrants from the same region or country. The arrival cohort analysis also sheds light on changes in the social and political context faced by different waves of immigrants from the same region or country.

Caribbean immigrants dominated black migration during the 1970s and 1980s, and then Africans became the primary drivers of black immigration in the 1990s and 2000s. In the 1980s and 1990s, social, economic, and political conditions in many African countries worsened, motivating many residents of the region to seek better lives in more-developed countries. At the same time, changes to U.S. immigration policies during the 1980s and 1990s made it easier for refugees from Africa to come to the United States, and the new diversity visa program created a surge in migration from the continent.

This chapter has shown that African immigration increased the size and diversity of the black immigrant population of the United States as well as the spatial diversity of the overall black population. Certainly, many African immigrants reside in traditional black immigrant destinations in the Northeast. However, largely because of U.S. refugee resettlement programs, many black immigrants, particularly those from Somalia, Sudan, and Ethiopia, reside in states throughout the Midwest and Northwest. Not only is black immigration new to some of these destinations, but few black Americans reside in these parts of the country. Because much of the sociological literature on the social integration of black immigrants relies on data for Caribbean immigrants in the Northeast, the social integration of African immigrants, particularly in new black destinations, is new territory for researchers. Will new waves of black Africans have social and economic outcomes that resemble those of prior waves of immigrants, or will an entirely new pattern of social adaptation unfold for these groups? I provide answers to this question in later chapters.

Third, given America's long and sometimes state-sanctioned history of racial discrimination against blacks, a major focus of American social science research involves measuring and tracking changes in social and economic disparities between blacks and whites. The goal of these studies is generally to examine whether the country is making progress toward improving the social conditions of black Americans. This chapter has highlighted that black immigrants—a group that collectively accounted for more than 20 percent of the growth in the overall black population in the 2000s—have complicated and changed the meaning of black-white disparities in multiple domains.[38] The recent large influx of black immigrants could lead researchers to incorrectly estimate both the social progress made by black Americans and changes in the intensity of racism and discrimination experienced by blacks in the United States.

For example, cross-sectional studies that aggregate the entire black immigrant population or focus on regional subgroups conceal the remarkable birth-country variation within the aggregate population. This could produce inferences that apply only to the larger black immigrant subpopulations and thus generate misleading conclusions about the mechanisms producing the social standing of particular black immigrant subgroups. Moreover, studies examining trends in social outcomes for the aggregate black population in the United States capture at least two factors: changes in the conditions of the stock of blacks residing in the country at the start of the period and changes in the composition of the black population driven by immigrants. Throughout the book, across multiple measures of social well-being, I show the implications of ignoring subgroup heterogeneity within the black population and its impact on our understanding of the mechanisms driving racial disparities in social and economic outcomes.

PART II

UNDERSTANDING SOCIAL AND ECONOMIC DISPARITIES BETWEEN BLACK IMMIGRANTS AND BLACK AMERICANS: TOWARD A MORE COMPREHENSIVE FRAMEWORK

CHAPTER THREE

THEORETICAL CONSIDERATIONS

Much of the extant literature, as well as the social and political debates on black immigration, focus on economic disparities between black Americans and black immigrants. Part II of this book builds on this literature. In this chapter, I summarize the existing research on the causes of labor market disparities between black Americans and black immigrants and provide a comprehensive framework for understanding historical and contemporary disparities between the two groups. I support the arguments advanced in the chapter by providing original analyses of historical and contemporary labor market (chapter 4) and homeownership (chapter 5) disparities between black Americans and black immigrants.

Deep Disparities: Understanding the Debate

Every U.S. census of the population has shown that African Americans trail their white counterparts on nearly every measure of social and economic well-being. In terms of labor market outcomes, compared to white Americans, black Americans are less likely to be in the labor market and more likely to be unemployed and to have lower average earnings.[1] These disparities hold even after accounting for important determinants of labor market success, such as educational attainment, work experience, and marital status.

Large disparities in wealth, an important determinant of family well-being, social status, neighborhood quality, and school quality, also exist between black and white Americans.[2] The sociologist Thomas

Shapiro showed that wealth disparities between black and white Americans are larger than the labor market disparities between the two groups.[3] Using figures from 1999, Shapiro made a striking observation:

> White American households in every income quintile have significantly higher median wealth than similar-earning black households. In the lowest quintile, net worth for typical white households is $17,066, black households in the same quintile possess only $2,400. Among the highest-earning households, white median net worth is $133,607, while net worth for black households in the highest income register is $43,806.[4]

These statistics indicate that even when the labor market accomplishments of black and white families are similar, substantial wealth disparities exist. Further, black-white disparities in net worth have increased since the 1990s. In the late 1990s, the median net worth of white American households was $192,500, ten times as much as the median net worth of black households ($19,200). Although the median net worth of both black and white American households had decreased by 2013, the gap between the two groups actually increased in the years following the Great Recession, with the net worth of white Americans ($141,900) increasing to thirteen times that of black Americans ($11,000).[5]

THE CAUSES OF RACIAL DISPARITIES

The existence of disparities between black and white Americans is clear. Scholars continue, however, to debate exactly what causes these disparities, from two primary opposing positions. On one side are scholars who place considerable weight on structural conditions, such as the past and current forms of racism and discrimination faced by black Americans: residential segregation, poor-quality neighborhoods, and underperforming schools.[6] On the other side of the debate are scholars who argue that the position of black America is determined by cultural inferiority, including poor attitudes toward work, shiftlessness, poor diets, oppositionality, promiscuity, and the general lack of family values.[7]

During the first three decades of the twentieth century, scholarly attempts to understand the social conditions of black Americans merged with examinations of the history of black immigrants. In many ways, early scholarly interest in black immigration derived not from an attempt to understand the social integration of the group in the United States, but rather from efforts to understand the causes of disparities between black and white Americans.[8] That is, researchers used the social and economic outcomes of black immigrants as an analytic tool to disentangle the roles of culture and structural conditions (for example, racism and discrimination) in generating the poor economic standing of black Americans. Because black immigrants and black Americans shared similar racialized features (such as dark skin and coarse hair), researchers surmised that examinations of disparities between the two groups would hold race constant and thus identify the impact of culture.[9] Therefore, all else being equal, if black immigrants could obtain better social and economic outcomes than black Americans, the poor standing of the latter group must be due to culture rather than discrimination. For example, the economist Thomas Sowell noted:

> West Indians in the United States are significant not only because of their overrepresentation among prominent or successful blacks, but also because their very different backgrounds make them a test case of the explanatory importance of color, as such, in analyzing socioeconomic progress in the American economy and society, as compared to the importance of the cultural traditions of the American Negro. Their history also provides a test of beliefs about the particular aspects of slavery which constitute the most crippling continuing handicaps as far as socioeconomic advancement is concerned. Moreover, since West Indian immigrants to the United States—unlike the "free persons of color"— are seldom mulattoes, biological influences may also be gauged.[10]

Such analytic frameworks have guided decades of research on immigrant-native disparities among blacks in the United States and, by extension, analysis of disparities between black and white Americans.

In the early twentieth century, researchers using primarily non-representative studies of black immigrants residing in the United States found that black immigrants, who at the time hailed primarily from the English-speaking Caribbean and tended to reside in New York, had higher rates of entrepreneurship and were overrepresented in professional occupations (for example, doctors, dentists, and lawyers) relative to black Americans.[11] Moreover, during the first three decades of the twentieth century, when it was difficult for blacks to obtain loans from traditional financial institutions, blacks from the English-speaking

Caribbean, scholars suggested, established rotating credit associations to help coethnics purchase homes and obtain capital to start businesses.[12] Indeed, according to James Weldon Johnson, during the first three decades of the twentieth century, black immigrants were stereotyped as "characteristically sober-minded and [having] something of a genius for business, differing almost totally in these respects from the average rural Negro from the south."[13]

In the 1960s, after changes in U.S. immigration policy made it possible for larger waves of black West Indian immigrants to migrate to the United States, scholars once again compared black Americans to blacks from the Caribbean and touted their findings as evidence of black immigrants' cultural superiority. The second wave of such research mirrored the academic accounts of black immigrants who migrated to the United States between 1900 and 1930, noting that black immigrants who arrived in the 1960s and 1970s seemed to outperform black Americans on many measures of social and economic well-being.[14] Post-1965 black immigrants had greater earnings, were more likely to be employed, and held jobs with greater occupational prestige than black Americans. Again, these findings led many scholars and policymakers to argue that cultural deficiencies in attitudes toward work rather than discrimination explained the poor social position of black Americans.

Although the academic and policy discourse has become more polite and latent in recent years, many of today's scholars and policymakers continue to promote the thesis that black Americans' cultural deficiencies explain disparities between black and white Americans. For example, in his speech at the Democratic National Convention, then-Illinois state senator Barack Obama indirectly utilized a cultural narrative to explain the poor educational achievement of black Americans: "Go into any inner-city neighborhood, and folks will tell you that government alone can't teach our kids to learn; they know that parents have to teach, and children can't achieve unless we raise their expectations and turn off the television sets and eradicate the slander that says that [a] black youth with a book is acting white."[15] Obama was speaking specifically to the marked racial disparities in education, a primary determinant of labor market outcomes in the United States. However, his core statement, particularly his reference to "acting white," is rooted in the oppositional culture thesis advanced by the anthropologist John

Ogbu, which states that involuntary minorities (black Americans) underperform in education relative to voluntary minorities (black immigrants) because they have developed cultural tools (for example, resisting schooling) that hinder their academic success.[16]

In contrast to early research on labor market disparities between black immigrants and black Americans, in which cultural arguments were explicit, contemporary cultural arguments are often veiled in notions of cultural capital or ethnic resources. Moreover, despite both persistent black-white wage gaps and robust perceptions of racial discrimination among black Americans, some scholars argue that discrimination is no longer a barrier to upward mobility.[17] Recent studies report that between 1977 and 2000, a decreasing number of whites readily supported assertions that blacks are intellectually inferior to whites or stated opposition to residing in the same neighborhoods as blacks.[18] A 2011 study, for example, concluded: "In 1977 nearly 30 percent of whites believed that racial inequality in jobs, income, and housing existed because blacks have a lower capacity to learn, [while] less than 10 percent held this belief by 2000."[19] It seems logical for those who accept the notion that blacks no longer experience racial discrimination to attribute the persistent labor market inequalities between black Americans and white Americans to a cultural deficit.[20]

In the remainder of this chapter, I advance two goals. First, because most of the foundational work on nativity-based disparities among blacks focuses on labor market disparities, I review the theoretical work on the factors that produce differences in labor market outcomes among blacks in the United States. Second, I highlight the key limitations of prior work and develop a more comprehensive framework for understanding both differences between native and immigrant blacks in the United States and differences among black immigrants.

Labor Disparities between Black Americans and Black Immigrants: Traditional Explanations

For nearly three decades, scholars have attempted to understand the factors underlying labor market disparities between foreign-born and native-born blacks. Researchers have examined three main factors as possible reasons for these disparities: cultural differences, different experiences of discrimination, and selective migration.

CULTURAL DIFFERENCES

Distinct Historical Legacies of Slavery

Some researchers have argued that distinct historical legacies of slavery in the United States and the English-speaking Caribbean produced cultural differences, which in turn led to disparities between Caribbean immigrants and native-born blacks.[21] This literature has focused on three key historical differences. First, relative to slaves in the United States, slaves in the Caribbean were more likely to attempt to escape from slavery and be successful in their attempts, both because the environment and terrain on most Caribbean islands made it easier for fugitive slaves to find food and shelter and because blacks made up a majority of the population on many of the islands. Second, Caribbean slaves cultivated their own food and were permitted to sell surplus crops for profit, whereas American slaves received food rations from their owners. The Caribbean system of slavery provided more opportunities for slaves to engage in commerce and more incentives to increase work effort than the U.S. system. Third, relative to slaves in the United States, those in the Caribbean had greater opportunities to develop human capital because the relative size of the black population made it impossible to confine slaves to a narrow set of very low-skilled positions, as was common in the American South. Sowell argues that this distinctive history led Caribbean slaves to develop a cultural orientation that placed a relatively greater value on diligence, rational thinking, delayed gratification, and autonomous work.[22] He posits that current-day disparities in labor market outcomes between black Americans and blacks from the English-speaking Caribbean stem, at least in part, from these differences in culture and values.

Socialization in a Majority-Black Society

Scholars have also advanced a second cultural argument based on contemporary differences in the racial composition of the United States and the Caribbean. This line of research emphasizes the psychological benefits of socialization in a majority-black society. For example, the sociologist Milton Vickerman argues that because blacks are the numeric majority on many islands in the English-speaking Caribbean, whites cannot relegate the entire black population to low-skilled jobs that offer minimal responsibilities or opportunities for human capital development.[23] Consequently, Caribbean immigrants hail from countries where blacks occupy a greater range of jobs than in the United States, which in turn creates more black role models and serves to normalize success among blacks socialized in the region. These factors could lead to greater aspirations and labor market success for Caribbean immigrants.

In addition, Mary Waters argues that because they were raised in a majority-black society, Caribbean immigrants are less likely than black Americans to expect to have negative cross-race interpersonal relations with white Americans.[24] Further, when white Americans interact with black West Indians, their perceptions and emotions are not tainted by the intense history of strained race relations in the United States as they are in interactions with black Americans. In addition, black immigrants are aware that they will face racism in the United States and thus are prepared to fight for their rights. Waters concludes that this combination of high ambitions, more harmonious interpersonal relations with whites, and strong reactions in the face of perceived discrimination leads to better labor market outcomes for West Indians than for black Americans.[25]

DISPARATE PATTERNS OF DISCRIMINATION (WHITE FAVORITISM)

Scholars have also suggested that black immigrants and black Americans experience different degrees of racial discrimination, which could account for labor market differences between the two groups. Evidence of the influence of differential patterns of discrimination comes from three sources: black immigrants who report that white employers have a strong preference for black immigrants over black Americans, black Americans who perceive worse treatment from white employers than black immigrants do, and white managers who state a preference for black immigrants over black Americans.[26] Differences in discrimination toward American and immigrant blacks could stem from either productivity differences between the two groups or from an underlying source of bias.

In her study of a food services firm in New York, Waters was directly told by white employers that they preferred to hire West Indian immigrants over black Americans because black Americans were lazy, less flexible at work, and preferred welfare to working.[27] By contrast, they referred to their immigrant employees as highly motivated, loyal, and more concerned about working than finding instances of discrimination. When Nancy Foner asked Jamaican immigrants about racial tension in New York, most referenced tension between Jamaican immigrants (and other West Indians) and black Americans, rather than tension with white Americans.[28]

Researchers have suggested two other reasons why white employers favor Caribbean immigrants over native blacks: either because they occupy a higher position in the U.S. social hierarchy or because they were not colonial subjects of the United States. Foner argues that these frameworks explain why West Indians in New York fare better than West Indians in London.[29] In London, West Indians are migrating to their former colonial power, which, according to Ramán Grosfoguel, places them in a less favorable position in the country's discrimination hierarchy.[30] Conversely, no country in the West Indies was ever a U.S. colony, which puts immigrants from this region in a more favorable position in the discrimination hierarchy of the United States. Similarly, Imoagene finds that black immigrants from Nigeria, also a former colony of Great Britain, fare better in the United States than their counterparts do in Great Britain.[31] In contrast, black Americans, because of their connection to the racialized history of slavery in the United States, occupy the least favorable position in America's discrimination hierarchy.[32]

Discrimination based on skin shade could also produce variation in labor market outcomes between black Americans and immigrant blacks as well as among blacks in general. A substantial body of research suggests that lighter-skinned black Americans have better labor market outcomes than their darker-skinned counterparts.[33] Studies have found similar labor market penalties associated with skin shade among immigrants.[34] Given that, on average, black African and Haitian immigrants are darker than those from Latin America or the English-speaking

Caribbean, the labor market success of African and Haitian immigrants may be hindered by skin shade discrimination.[35]

SELECTIVE MIGRATION

Selectivity arguments focus on the motivation spurring the immigration decision. Many immigrants, including black immigrants, come to the United States to pursue educational advancement and to find better employment opportunities. Therefore, black immigrants might have better labor market success than some groups of black Americans because the decision to migrate is correlated with hard-to-measure characteristics such as ambition and motivation.[36] Upon arrival in the destination country, immigrants tend to have worse labor market outcomes than natives because it takes time to learn the nuances of the new labor market.[37] Over time, however, the labor market outcomes of immigrants improve and, depending on their initial labor market deficiencies and the degree to which immigrants are positively selected, could surpass those of native individuals.

The economist Barry Chiswick suggested that the earnings crossover—the point when immigrants overtake the earnings of native workers—is more likely to occur for immigrants who are motivated by economic opportunities than for immigrants who move to escape political tensions in their home countries.[38] Among black immigrants, most political refugees hail from Haiti and Africa, with very few from the English-speaking Caribbean. Chiswick's predictions imply that, relative to black immigrants from the English-speaking Caribbean, black immigrants from Haiti and Africa—particularly those from Somalia, Liberia, Sudan, and Ethiopia—are less likely to overtake the earnings of black Americans.

Building on the work of Chiswick, George Borjas argues that immigrants who move to improve their economic well-being are positively selected on skills when the degree of income inequality in the receiving country is greater than that of the sending country. That is, if the income distribution in the receiving country is more dispersed than in the sending country, then immigrants of a particular skill level should be able to occupy a relatively better position in the receiving country's income distribution than at home.[39]

Borjas also notes, however, that the degree of selectivity among immigrants increases as the costs associated with migration increase.[40] These costs, which can be both monetary and psychic, may vary based on the immigration infrastructure as well as the degree of cultural distance between the destination country and the origin country. Most black immigrants hail from countries with greater income inequality than that of the United States, but the cost of immigration varies considerably among black immigrants. For example, the costs of emigrating from Africa are typically much higher than from the Caribbean, suggesting that most African immigrants would be more positively selected on observed and unobserved skills. Other research has suggested, however, that skills obtained abroad—particularly skills acquired in less developed countries than the United States—do not transfer easily to the U.S. labor market. Thus, highly skilled immigrants who were educated in such countries—such as in Africa—could have less favorable labor market outcomes than they would have if their education was obtained in the United States.

Selectivity arguments also emphasize the differences between people who choose to immigrate and those who stay in their home countries. Black immigrants, like all other immigrants, are self-selected and thus differ systematically from other individuals in their native countries. Those who emigrate often have better health, higher education levels, higher levels of motivation, and more ambition than their peers who stay in the home country.[41] For example, in 2014, 63 percent of black Nigerian immigrants residing in the United States had at least a bachelor's degree, while only 7 percent of the Nigerian population had earned a bachelor's degree.[42] This self-selection process almost certainly affects the disparities between black immigrants and black Americans, making black immigrants relatively more advantaged.

EMPIRICAL EVIDENCE ON THE IMPORTANCE OF CULTURE, DISCRIMINATION, AND SELECTION

Several studies have attempted to determine the relative importance of the three factors described in this section—culture, discrimination, and selective migration—in explaining disparities between black Americans and black immigrants.[43] Model has provided the most comprehensive empirical test of the three frameworks to date.[44] In terms of culture, she uses variation in the organization of slave plantations in the United States and the Caribbean to test whether having a legacy of slavery that relied on the provision grounds system produced better labor market outcomes for the descendants of slaves. In many island nations, slaves were allotted land for growing subsistence food. Any food not consumed could be sold at market for a profit. She found that this mechanism did not consistently explain variation in labor market outcomes between black Americans and immigrants from the English-speaking Caribbean. Model also tested the relative importance of socialization in a majority-black country by examining whether black immigrants from Caribbean countries with mixed-race populations, such as Trinidad and Tobago and Guyana, displayed poorer labor market outcomes than immigrants from majority-black countries like Jamaica. She did not detect a consistent advantage for Caribbean immigrants from majority-black countries.

Model ran a second test of the majority-black society hypothesis by comparing the labor market outcomes of black immigrants from sub-Saharan Africa to those of native-born black Americans.[45] Although most African countries were colonized by whites, black Africans were never enslaved in the same manner as black Americans. Indeed, blacks have held most of the key economic and political positions in African countries for many decades. Model argued that if socialization in a majority-black society is the primary mechanism leading to the relative success of immigrants from the English-speaking Caribbean over black Americans, then immigrants from sub-Saharan Africa should also have stronger labor market outcomes. Further, like blacks from the English-speaking Caribbean, blacks from sub-Saharan Africa should not perceive skin color or race as a barrier to achievement and thus should be more ambitious and successful than black Americans.[46] Model found, however, that blacks from sub-Saharan Africa generally have worse labor market outcomes than black Americans.

In summary, the results from prior studies, particularly Model's, do not support the two primary cultural theories used to explain labor market differences between native and immigrant blacks: socialization in majority-black countries or differential legacies from the era of slavery. Prior studies have also examined the role of selective migration in producing disparities between black Americans and black immigrants from the English-speaking Caribbean. Butcher used data from the

1980 U.S. census to compare the earnings and employment probabilities of black immigrants with those of native black movers (interstate migrants) and native black nonmovers.[47] If culture is embedded in the group, her mover-nonmover comparison would allow her to hold culture constant and vary migration. She found that the outcomes of black immigrants are more like those of native black movers than nonmovers. Butcher concludes that selective migration, rather than culture, more consistently explains labor market differences between black immigrants and American blacks.

Further evidence of the selective nature of internal migration for black Americans comes from studies examining the labor market outcomes of blacks who moved during the Great Migration, which began in the United States around 1910 and lasted through the 1960s.[48] During this period, more than four million native blacks migrated from the South to cities in the Northeast, Midwest, and West.[49] Using data on more than five thousand men tracked from 1910 to 1930, the economists William Collins and Marianne Wanamaker found that black in-state migrants were positively selected and that economic gains from migration were large for black Americans who moved during the Great Migration.[50] The economist Leah Boustan also found evidence of positive selection among southern-born black Americans residing in northern cities between 1940 and 1970.[51] Suzanne Eichenlaub, Stewart Tolnay, and Trent Alexander, however, found a contrasting pattern. The authors used data from the 1910 to 1970 U.S. censuses to compare black migrants who left the South with their compatriots who remained in the South (both individuals who moved within the southern region and those who remained in their state of birth). They found that blacks who moved across regions often fared worse than both southern-born blacks who moved within the southern region and blacks who remained in their state of birth.[52]

In terms of how migration status affects non–labor market outcomes, in their study of mortality the economists Dan Black, Seth Sanders Evan Taylor, and Lowell Taylor find that survival rates declined among older African Americans as a result of moving north.[53] In sum, studies of the labor market outcomes of people who left the South during the Great Migration offer mixed conclusions. Whether leaving the South benefited those who moved out of the South in the Great Migration economically, and, if so, how much, remains a contested issue in the social sciences.[54]

In many ways, the mixed findings for black Americans who moved during the Great Migration align with the experiences of international migrations. Depending on the time period and group studied, some immigrants have better labor market outcomes than individuals who remained in their countries of origin.[55] Patterns of return migration among immigrants, however, suggest that individuals who stay in the United States might have better labor market outcomes than individuals who return to their home countries.[56] Moreover, although during their initial years in the United States immigrants' health and mortality profiles are better than those of the native-born population, immigrants experience significant declines in health the longer they live in the United States.[57] Thus, immigrants with a long tenure of U.S. residence might have worse mortality profiles than their nonmigrating compatriots in their country of origin.

Studies have also documented differing patterns of selective migration among immigrants from the same region or country based on when the immigrants arrived in the United States.[58] Model finds that earlier arrivals from the West Indies tended to have more favorable labor market outcomes than more recent immigrants.[59] In addition to confirming this result, my own prior work shows that only the most recent arrival cohorts from English-speaking African countries are projected to overtake the earnings of black American movers.[60] These findings imply that the underlying factors that affect labor market outcomes among Caribbean and African immigrants vary across time, and that only a subset of immigrants from the Caribbean overtake the outcomes of black American movers, which is strong evidence of differential patterns of selectivity among immigrants from the same region of the world who migrate at different time periods.

The empirical evidence on the role of differential experiences of discrimination is somewhat mixed. Mary Waters, F. W. Arnold, and Ramán Grosfoguel all find evidence that white employers prefer to hire Caribbean immigrants over native blacks, and Nancy Foner argues that native-born blacks experience more discrimination than any black immigrant subgroup.[61] Although qualitative studies suggest that black Americans and black immigrants experience different degrees of discrimination, when Model operationalized the mechanism argued to produce a labor market advantage for black West Indian immigrants, she produced statistical results that dispute the linkage between white favoritism (differential patterns of discrimination) and Caribbean advantage. She notes the following, however: "Ordinary white Americans may favor West Indians over African Americans. Discarding the hypothesis that white favoritism is a cause of West Indian economic advantage does not require abandoning the hypothesis that white favoritism is a real phenomenon."[62] In other words, it is entirely possible that white employers favor black immigrants over black Americans, but that this preference does not lead to an economic advantage for black immigrants.

Expanding the Discussion: Neglected Factors in Prior Comparisons of Black Immigrants and Black Americans

Although the findings summarized thus far are informative, the literature on labor market disparities between black immigrants and black Americans is limited in several significant ways. First, perhaps owing to an overemphasis among scholars on trying to understand what the experiences of black immigrants say about the extent of racism and discrimination faced by black Americans, prior research has often focused on factors pertaining specifically to those of African descent (for example, the historical legacy of slavery) while overlooking factors that influence the outcomes of labor migrants or the outcomes of immigrants more generally.[63]

Second, relatively few studies have addressed variation in outcomes within the black immigrant population—for example, by country of origin or time of arrival. Although immigrants from the Caribbean have historically made up the lion's share of flows of black immigrants to the United States, since the 1990s black immigration has been driven primarily by African migration.[64] Few theoretical perspectives have viewed black African immigrants as a distinct set of migrants.[65]

Third, most work on disparities between black immigrants and black Americans does not consider how the racial contexts of the pre- and post–civil rights eras have shaped the outcomes of the two groups in the United States.[66] Since becoming free people, black Americans' experiences have been influenced by exclusionary policies (such as Jim Crow policies) that have confined the population to socially and economically isolated neighborhoods, underfunded schools, and disproportionate rates of incarceration.[67] Moreover, black Americans have been systematically excluded from post–World War II social policies that lifted large segments of white Americans—particularly first- and second-generation German, Irish, and Italian immigrants—into the middle class.[68] Although reforms of the civil rights era attempted to remove barriers to upward mobility, the legacy of prior exclusionary policies continues to influence the life outcomes of black Americans.[69] Most contemporary black immigrants do not share black Americans' link to the legacy of Jim Crow, which, along with patterns of positive selective migration, might generate disparities between black Americans and black immigrations.

Lastly, much of the extant work on disparities among blacks implicitly assumes that a single factor—either culture, selection, or discrimination—is the primary driver of disparate outcomes across the groups. The three mechanisms, however, are not mutually exclusive. For example, it is entirely possible that both selective immigration and discrimination, past and present, affect the upward mobility of black immigrants.

FACTORS THAT AFFECT IMMIGRANTS MORE GENERALLY: THEORIES OF LABOR MIGRATION

Most prior studies of labor market disparities among blacks have focused almost exclusively on earnings, ignoring the labor market outcome over which individuals exert the most control: labor force participation.[70] Although some studies have considered multiple outcomes, including earnings, employment, and labor force participation, variation across these outcomes is typically assumed to have the same theoretical implications.[71] Disparities in labor force participation, however, differ from disparities in employment and earnings.[72] Structural conditions such as access to public transportation and the availability of affordable child care certainly affect labor force participation, but because there are fewer structural constraints on labor force participation, variation in this outcome sheds more light on an individual's disposition toward work than either earnings or employment.[73]

Proponents of the cultural explanation for disparities in labor market outcomes suggest that black Americans, particularly black men, simply do not want to work. Although previous studies have disputed the theorized mechanism thought to produce a cultural advantage for immigrants (for example, the legacy of slavery, the racial composition of the origin country, and greater self-efficacy), the core argument advanced by cultural theorists is that black Americans simply do not want to work whereas black immigrants do.[74] Because labor force participation measures the sheer willingness of adults to stay involved in the labor market by either holding a job or searching for work, it provides a direct measure of motivation, a key component of any framework that conceives culture as the primary determinant of work-related outcomes.

An individual's cultural disposition toward work, however, is not the only factor determining labor force participation. Indeed, international migration is often motivated by a combination of "push" factors at origin and "pull" factors at destination.[75] Political instability, crime, and poor labor market conditions are perhaps the most notable drivers of emigration. For example, the homicide rate in the United States was 3.9 per 100,000 individuals between 2010 and 2014. During the same period, the homicide rate in Nigeria was 10.1 per 100,000 individuals, more than two times that of the United States. For those in Jamaica, the difference was even more dramatic: 36.1 per 100,000 individuals were homicide victims each year, a rate more than nine times greater than that of the United States.[76]

Poverty also affects immigration. After accounting for in-kind transfers (such as those provided by nutrition assistance or housing and energy programs), few individuals residing in the United States live on less than $2 per day, a measure of extreme poverty used by the World Bank. Across the primary African sending countries, however, between 2005 and 2015 the percentage of individuals living on less than $2 a day ranged from 14.9 percent in Sudan to 68.6 percent in Liberia. Although labor market conditions vary from year to year across countries, 5.3 percent of the American workforce was unemployed in 2015, a rate lower than that of nearly every major black immigrant-sending country. In the same year, 13.7 percent of the Jamaican workforce and 13.6 percent of the Sudanese workforce were unemployed.

Even though substantial racial disparities have always existed in the United States, compared to the conditions many black immigrants face at home, moving to the United States and achieving the mean outcomes of black Americans offers greater opportunities for immigrants to fulfill financial objectives than employment opportunities in their home countries. For example, in 2015, the U.S. black unemployment rate of around 9.5 percent was lower than the unemployment rates in Jamaica, the Dominican Republic, Guyana, and Sudan. In sum, poverty, crime, and the lack of jobs in their home countries are powerful push factors causing many blacks to emigrate.

The substantial wage differential between origin and destination countries is a primary pull factor for many contemporary immigrants. The gross per person national income (GNI) in Jamaica was $8,350 in 2015, compared to $53,245 in the United States. This difference implies that the average full-time worker in New York, the state with the largest share of Jamaican immigrants, earning just the minimum wage of $13 per hour in 2015, would make more than three times the annual earnings of the average person residing in Jamaica in 2015. Such wage differentials are a powerful motivating factor for people from all the major black immigrant-sending countries, where per capita GNI ranges from $28,000 in Trinidad and Tobago to just $294 in Somalia.

Closely related to push-pull factors are neoclassical economic theories of labor migration. The microeconomic theory of individual decision-making suggests that a person decides to move if the benefits of moving outweigh the costs. Within this framework, the financial and economic burden of leaving home, migrating, and settling in the new country are conceptualized as "costs," and favorable economic circumstances such as higher wages and better employment conditions are "benefits."[77] Thus, people make the decision to move based on whether they can maximize returns on their individual human capital. If the benefits outweigh the costs, migrating is the rational decision.[78] Under this framework, if there are limited barriers to migration and a large wage differential between two countries, migration between the countries should continue.

Migration scholars, however, have highlighted several drawbacks to the neoclassical theory of migration. First, many nations have large wage differentials but lack significant migration flows.[79] Second, the framework does not explain the substantial patterns of return migration to countries when significant wage differentials remain.[80] Like Mexican migrants, each year thousands of black immigrants, particularly those from the English-speaking Caribbean, return home. According to the sociologists Douglas Massey, Jorge Durand, and Nolan Malone: "If the world really worked according to neoclassical principles, why would anyone migrate abroad temporarily to remit money back home in anticipation of an eventual return? A rational utility-maximizing actor logically should want to stay abroad permanently to enjoy forever the higher wages and consumption available in the United States."[81]

Such patterns exist because many immigrants, including black immigrants, do not intend to reside permanently in the United States. Many move to acquire capital or improve the economic conditions of family members. This is true even among those from sub-Saharan Africa, for whom the Atlantic Ocean creates a significant barrier to return migration. Every year black immigrants remit millions of dollars back to their origin countries, partly to support family but also to invest in homes and businesses. Indeed, in 2015 nearly 17 percent of Jamaica's and 9 percent of Guyana's gross domestic product (GDP) came from remittances. Similarly, nearly 25 percent of Haiti's GDP and 13 percent of Ghana's GDP came from remittances.

The new economics of migration (NEM) theory helps explain patterns of return migration.[82] The key difference between microeconomic theory and NEM theory is how the agent of migration is conceptualized. NEM theory suggests that the household unit, not the individual, is the agent of migration. The decision to move is not based solely on an individual optimizing his or her own gains; rather, moving is considered an opportunity to maximize income and minimize risk for an entire household unit.[83] In the absence of credit and lending markets or government-sponsored safety net programs, such as unemployment insurance and government-organized retirement programs, often the only resource that households have at their disposal is the labor of family members.[84] To improve the economic welfare of the entire household and mediate the risk of economic conditions in the country of origin, households often elect to send a family member to a more-developed country to work and send remittances back to the family in the home country.[85] Thus, unlike microeconomic theory, NEM theory considers the complex social and familial conditions of migrants to better explain monetary remittances and significant return migration. The household is seen as the unit with the strongest influence on migration decisions.[86]

Other more structural or macrolevel theories attempt to explain migration flows. World systems theory is a particularly influential perspective in this literature.[87] Unlike the neoclassical economic theories of individual decision-making, world systems theory considers the changing historical context in which migration occurs. Instead of assuming that individuals make their cost-benefit analysis in a vacuum, world systems theory recognizes that a changing global system influences whether an individual will decide to migrate. More specifically, the largely capitalistic economies of many dominant nations penetrate noncapitalist nations and create incentives for migration. The natural "disruptions and dislocations" of capitalism in peripheral nations encourage migration. Thus, migration is not solely a function of an individual analysis but the result of capitalist forces.[88]

For contemporary black immigration to the United States, world systems theory seems to describe at least part of the motivation for black migrants. Many Caribbean and African countries are former colonies of European nations, particularly the United Kingdom, France, Spain, and Portugal.[89] Many of these former colonies are hindered economically by the residual governments, institutions, political conflict generated from forced labor, extraction of material resources, and other forms of exploitation designed to fuel European capitalism. Consequently, migration from the Caribbean and Africa results partly from economic and social problems internal to capitalism and these nations' histories as former European colonies.[90]

In line with world systems theory are theories that explain the demand for immigrant labor in developed Western economies. Most notable is the theory of segmented labor markets, which suggests that the advanced economies of the world have an almost unlimited demand for unskilled labor. The result is a constant pull factor for immigrants from less-advanced countries.[91] For many immigrants, the move to the United States will bring them higher wages than they could ever achieve in their home countries. Moreover, many immigrants are motivated by a desire to fulfill a particular goal at home. In their discussion of the factors motivating the decisions of Mexican migrants, Massey, Durand, and Malone state:

> Migrants generally begin foreign labor as target earners: they are seeking to make money for a specific goal that will solve a problem or improve their status at home (such as building a new house, buying land, or acquiring consumption goods). Moreover, the disjuncture in living standards between developed and developing societies makes

low wages abroad appear generous by the standards of the sending country. Finally, even though a migrant may realize that a foreign job carries low status, he does not view himself as a part of that society but as embedded within the status system of his home community, where hard-currency remittances buy considerable social status.[92]

In sum, for a variety of reasons, many advanced economies produce a persistent number of jobs at the lower end of the occupational structure that are difficult to fill with native workers but are very attractive to low-skilled immigrant workers. Researchers attempting to understand labor market disparities between black Americans and black immigrants have often overlooked this factor. Moreover, because of black immigrants' status as "black," many researchers examine their labor market experiences without fully considering the contextual factors that shape the outcome of "immigrants." As this section highlights, a combination of factors in the country of origin and the destination country determine how black immigrants value labor market opportunities in the United States.

The substantial improvement in living conditions associated with moving, as well as the factors outlined in the theories of migration, may make the reservation wage of immigrants—the minimum wage required to induce individuals into the labor market—considerably lower among many subgroups of black immigrants, particularly less-educated immigrants. Indeed, even the worst-paying jobs in the United States offer greater opportunities for less-educated Caribbean and African immigrants to fulfill financial objectives than jobs available in their home countries. At the same time, because the financial motives and family networks of U.S.-born individuals were formed in the context of the United States, many Americans, black or white, would consider many of the jobs held by immigrants to be dead-end employment. Consequently, it is reasonable to expect that, depending on how U.S. jobs compare to those in their home country, less-educated black immigrants might have higher labor market participation rates than black Americans.

FACTORS THAT AFFECT IMMIGRANTS MORE GENERALLY: THE CONTEXT OF RECEPTION

Alejandro Portes and Rubén Rumbaut argue that the relative success of immigrant groups in the United States is determined by the different modes by which they become incorporated into the host society—whether as entrepreneurs or as wage or salary workers—and their context of reception, which is "defined by the policies of the receiving government, the character of the host labor market, and the features of immigrants' own ethnic communities."[93]

Federal Immigration Policy

The U.S. government affects the reception context that immigrants face by taking actions that either encourage immigration from a particular country (for example, the United States has long granted legal status to all Cubans upon arrival on U.S. soil) or constraining the flow of immigrants from a particular nation or region (such as attempts by President Donald Trump's administration to end the Deferred Action on Childhood Arrivals [DACA] policy, which provides temporary protected status for undocumented immigrants who arrived as children). Black immigrants are subject to a wide range of federal policies, based on their country of origin. Since 1965, the U.S. government has taken a relatively neutral stance toward most black immigration from the Caribbean. In 2017, most Caribbean immigrants arrived on family-sponsored preference visas or visas intended for immediate relatives of U.S. citizens. Many black immigrants from sub-Saharan Africa also migrate under these categories, but in 2014 large numbers of immigrants from Nigeria, Ethiopia, Ghana, Kenya, Cameroon, Liberia, Sudan, and Sierra Leone received diversity visas, which were designed to increase the diversity of U.S. immigrant flows.[94] In addition, many recent immigrants from Ethiopia, Kenya, Somalia, Cameroon, Liberia, and Sudan arrived as either refugees or asylum-seekers.[95] Many black immigrants who arrive as refugees benefit from resettlement programs, including assistance with health needs, employment, and home purchases as well as entrepreneurship support.

Four black immigrant-sending countries—Haiti, Somalia, Sudan, and Sierra Leone—have received less favorable treatment in U.S. immigration policy. Despite Haiti's history of political turmoil and civil unrest, the U.S. government has long restricted or denied petitions from Haitians seeking political asylum. In addition, in 2017 the Trump administration, citing concerns about potential terrorist attacks, attempted to institute a travel ban on immigrants from several Muslim-majority countries, including the African countries of Somalia and

Sudan. If these bans remain in place, they will dramatically limit immigration from Somalia and Sudan. Further, negative media attention and the new label on their countries as highly likely to send Muslim terrorists to the United States very well may hinder the social adaptation of immigrants from Sudan, Somalia, and other Muslim-majority countries.

The Host Labor Market

The character of the host labor market is another important component of immigrants' context of reception. Portes and Rumbaut argue that immigrants' labor market outcomes are influenced by both regional variation in labor market conditions and employers' beliefs about the types of work that different immigrant groups can perform.[96] As described earlier, prior qualitative research has found that employers, especially those who hire low-wage workers, prefer to hire black immigrants, particularly immigrants from the English-speaking Caribbean, over native-born blacks. However, other aspects of the host labor market have not been thoroughly considered in research comparing the labor market outcomes of black immigrants and black Americans.

Gender dynamics also shape the host labor market experiences of immigrant groups, including black immigrants. Although the wage gap between white American men and black American men is large and persistent, the differences between black American women and white American women are smaller and often statistically insignificant.[97] One reason for this smaller gap may be that, as some research has found, employers discriminate against black American women less than they do against black American men.[98] The extant research suggests that gender dynamics are also responsible for labor market disparities between black immigrants and black Americans. The same gender pattern that characterizes black Americans extends to black immigrants: black immigrant women perform better than black immigrant men in the U.S. labor market.[99]

Coethnic Communities

A third factor that shapes immigrants' reception context is the strength of the existing coethnic communities developed by previous waves of conationals. Portes and Rumbaut argue that waves of immigrants who are received by communities of economically vibrant and socially respected conationals are much more likely to achieve economic success than those received into coethnic communities that are economically weaker and have experienced high degrees of discrimination.[100]

A disproportionate share of early black migrants were women, and the legacy of these gendered migration streams can still be seen today in sustained occupational niches in health care professions, nanny services, and domestic work, especially among immigrants from the English-speaking Caribbean.[101] Thus, newly arriving black immigrant women from the Caribbean who settle in communities of conationals have a link to jobs in these niches, in which employers often rely on referrals for hiring.[102]

Because many immigrants from Somalia, Sudan, Ethiopia, and certain other African countries arrive as refugees and participate in refugee resettlement programs, they tend to reside in areas that are not home to communities of earlier black immigrants and thus have limited access to the benefits of ethnic niches. Portes and Rumbaut note that new immigrants who do not settle in an established community of conationals face a unique situation.[103] Highly skilled immigrants who experience a positive or neutral reception context are in an ideal position because they can succeed on the strength of their human capital. In contrast, those with few skills who face a negative context of reception are at a serious disadvantage because they must endure discrimination without the aid of a community to ease their adaptation to the host community.[104]

EXTENDING THE CONTEXT OF RECEPTION FRAMEWORK

Black American Population

I argue that focusing exclusively on how earlier waves of black immigrants aided the economic adaptation of more recent immigrants severely underestimates the strength of black immigrants' coethnic communities. In fact, the presence of a large native-born black community has helped the economic adaptation of every wave of black immigrants to the United States.

Phillip Kasinitz has noted that the "immigrants of the first three decades of the twentieth century, whatever their cultural propensities, were profoundly affected by the fact that they were part of a massive expansion in New York City's black population."[105] A large fraction of black professionals were doctors, dentists, and lawyers who were born in the Caribbean.[106] Many of these migrants received their credentials in the Caribbean, but others trained at historically black colleges and universities in the United States.[107] During this period, Kasinitz contends, few whites were willing to contract the services of black professionals, regardless of nationality. Similarly, blacks in general had trouble obtaining professional services from whites. Black Americans therefore were a natural clientele for West Indian professionals, who had trained outside the United States and would not have been able to work in their chosen professions in the United States without the patronage of black Americans.[108]

The presence of black Americans also influenced the intensity of the racism and discrimination experienced by black immigrants.[109] Since the early 1900s, black immigrants, particularly those from the English-speaking Caribbean, had resided in close proximity to black Americans. Consequently, as the black immigrant population grew, particularly in New York, they became an invisible minority within a larger minority population because Americans hardly noticed their presence. Thus, many black immigrants, as blacks, suffered high levels of discrimination, but as immigrants, unlike more visible immigrant minorities, they faced little hysteria or discrimination from natives.[110] This fact clearly aided the assimilation of black immigrants from the Caribbean and Africa into traditional destinations.

The outcomes of black Africans who reside outside traditional destinations are likely to differ from those of Caribbean immigrants. In addition to the absence of a black American population to buffer experiences of discrimination and ease the process of social adaptation, many black immigrants who reside outside traditional black immigrant destinations are from Muslim-majority countries. Because of their religious practices and customs, new arrivals from Ethiopia, Somalia, and Sudan are likely to face intense threefold discrimination: as Muslims, as blacks, and as immigrants.

Historical Context: The Pre–Civil Rights Era

Few studies on disparities between black immigrants and black Americans have examined the distinct experiences of these two groups in the U.S. context. Slavery officially ended in the United States in 1865. From 1880 to 1910, at both the federal and state levels, exclusionary policies were implemented throughout the United States to roll back many of the modest gains made by black Americans during Reconstruction (1863–1877). These policies included poll taxes and literacy tests that restricted the voting rights of black Americans in southern states and both explicit and implicit policies designed to hamper the housing decisions of blacks throughout the country.[111] Racism and discrimination were prevalent throughout the country, but living conditions in the South were considerably harsher than conditions in the northern states. For this reason, and because of the draw of industrial jobs in the Northeast, more than 1.6 million black Americans moved from the rural South to industrial cities in the Northeast and Midwest between 1916 and 1930.

Ever since slaves in the English-speaking Caribbean were freed in 1838, blacks have been on the move. Initially, many former slaves moved to other islands in the Caribbean.[112] In search of still better working and living conditions, many former slaves from this region, particularly those from Barbados and Jamaica, eventually headed southward to work on the Panama Canal project. Although these migrants were met with harsh working conditions and lower remuneration than promised by recruiters, working on the Panama Canal allowed them to earn considerably more than was possible in the Caribbean.[113] After the Panama Canal was completed, many former canal workers, accustomed to higher wages, journeyed farther north to the United States in their quest to earn a living wage.[114] These workers, along with individuals who came directly from the Caribbean, would eventually join the large black American population in New York City that had recently migrated from the U.S. South. Among the blacks living in New York State in the 1930s, 59.1 percent were black American migrants and 16.7 percent were from the Caribbean region.[115] Only 24.2 percent of New York's black population was born in New York State.[116]

During this period, all blacks living in the United States faced an extremely high degree of racial hostility. In New York, as in the rest of the United States, both blacks from the West Indies and northern- and southern-born black Americans, because of limited residential options, resided almost exclusively in the few areas open to them, including

Harlem and Brooklyn.[117] These neighborhoods were highly segregated and overcrowded. The sociologist Philip Kasinitz notes: "Whether by choice or not, the first cohort of West Indian immigrants lived in neighborhoods that were segregated by race and integrated by ethnicity and class."[118] Kasinitz described the effects of this pattern of residential segregation:

> Faced with physical proximity, the impossibility of remaining sojourners indefinitely and, increasingly, a second generation who were at least partially assimilated into their African-American surroundings, the first cohort of West Indian migrants eventually joined the mainstream of New York's black community. . . . Thus a feeling of commonality, based partially on an awareness of a common history and heritage, but also on an awareness of common problems faced in racist America, helped forge a shared black identity.[119]

The introduction of restrictive immigration policies in 1924, in combination with the Great Depression and World War II, caused black immigration to the United States to decline significantly during the 1930s and 1940s, a trend that continued until the 1960s. At the same time, until 1970, millions of southern-born blacks continued moving to cities in the Midwest and Northeast. The first generation of blacks from the Caribbean, who migrated to the United States before 1924, lived under Jim Crow policies along with black Americans. Segregated neighborhoods, schools, and hospitals and acts of physical violence effectively restricted the upward mobility of both groups.

Historical Context: The Post–Civil Rights Era

The black immigrants who are the focus of much of the extant literature on the social incorporation of black immigrants, those who arrived in the United States after 1965, experienced a profoundly different context than their predecessors. The Immigration and Nationality Act of 1965 signaled a less xenophobic stance toward immigrants from non-Western nations, and at the same time the civil rights movement was creating a less overtly discriminatory context for minorities in the United States.[120] Although improving economic conditions for black Americans was the primary motivation of the civil rights movement, generations of immigrants of many hues also benefited from the Civil Rights Act of 1964, which outlawed discrimination based on race, color, religion, sex, or national origin and ended racial segregation in schools, workplaces, and the public sphere. Moreover, the Voting Rights Act of 1965 prohibited discrimination in voter registration. Subsequently, voter registration increased throughout the American South, and minority political representation increased across the country. These changes helped raise the country's sensitivity to issues of racial injustice, and the government bureaucracy began to shift toward efforts to address racial inequalities. Moreover, the affirmative action policies of the post–civil rights era, including targeted recruitment and government mandates to contractors to integrate minorities and women, increased the representation of both minorities and women across many segments of the American workforce and educational system.[121]

Prior research has debated the relative magnitude of the interpersonal racial discrimination experienced by black immigrants and black Americans, but the best evidence suggests that both groups of blacks had worse labor market outcomes than white Americans, even after adjusting for labor market characteristics.[122] Further, both groups saw a significant and, perhaps most importantly, similar reduction in their earnings deficit relative to white Americans between 1970 and 1990, the period that witnessed the largest expansion in civil rights policies and affirmative action programs.[123] These parallel shifts suggest that the same mechanism drove improvement in labor market conditions for black Americans as for many black and Hispanic immigrants. The fact that structural changes produced similar outcomes for both black Americans and black immigrants is often neglected by scholars who advance cultural explanations for nativity disparities among blacks. Indeed, civil rights changes that made America a less overtly discriminatory country are perhaps the most influential contextual factors shaping the social integration of black immigrants.

UNDERSTANDING THE CONTEXT OF EDUCATION: SELECTIVITY AND SOCIAL CLASS

The last contextual factor that helps explain disparities between black Americans and black immigrants relates to hidden disparities in educational attainment, particularly among less-educated individuals. Since they became free persons in 1865, the educational outcomes of black

Americans, long shaped by their inability to obtain education during slavery, were affected after slavery by both the quality and quantity of good schools, particularly in the American South.[124] Despite these challenges, however, over time the education profiles of black Americans improved.[125] Robert Margo notes:

> On the eve of the Civil War the overwhelming majority of slaves were illiterate. During the late antebellum period it was generally illegal to teach slaves to read and write. Even if it had been legal, it is doubtful that slaves' literacy rates would have been very high. Only a small percentage of slaves were involved in making economic decisions in which literacy would have been an asset to the slave owner. A literate slave was presumed to be discontented chattel—or worse, a potential trouble-maker or runaway.[126]

Immediately after slavery ended in the United States, black Americans began to make significant improvements in literacy. In 1900, thirty-five years after the official end of slavery in the United States, 50 percent of black men between the ages of twenty and sixty-four residing in the U.S. South were illiterate, compared to only 11 percent of white Americans. By 1940, only 12 to 17 percent of black Americans were illiterate, compared to 4 to 5 percent of white Americans.[127] Literacy rates differed considerably, however, between black Americans residing in the South and those residing in northern states. Census estimates for the total U.S. population in 1910 reveal that only 5 percent of New York's black American population was illiterate, and that nearly all of the state's white population was literate.

In short, historically black Americans, in large part because of structural constraints, particularly under Jim Crow conditions in the U.S. South, have tended to complete fewer years of schooling than white Americans.[128] In the decades following emancipation, black-white gaps in literacy and educational attainment resulted from the legacy of slavery as well as de jure exclusionary policies in the American South and de facto policies in the American North that confined blacks to poorly funded and racially isolated schools. Moreover, despite the landmark *Plessy v. Ferguson* decision by the Supreme Court in 1896, which upheld the constitutionality of racial segregation laws for public facilities (including public schools) *only if* the segregated facilities were equal in quality, the vast majority of black Americans continued to attend underfunded schools in impoverished neighborhoods while whites attended vastly better schools.[129]

As employment and housing opportunities improved for some blacks in the post–civil rights era, more affluent members of the black community moved into better neighborhoods. This expansion of opportunities for some blacks, however, coincided with a transformation of the economies in areas with large black populations: in a new development for black Americans, geographic areas arose in which less-educated blacks were trapped in neighborhoods segregated, not along racial lines (as in the pre–civil rights era), but along class lines.[130] The out-migration of affluent blacks and the economic restructuring of black and minority communities created living environments that lacked the necessary resources to maintain vital neighborhood institutions and public services and whose residents thus lived in persistent poverty and underemployment.[131]

Consequently, despite the improvements made during the civil rights era, significant black-white disparities persist today in both schooling context and achievement. According to the 2014 American Community Survey (ACS), among adults between the ages of twenty-five and sixty-four, nearly twice as many blacks as whites dropped out of high school (9 percent and 5 percent, respectively), and only 20 percent of black adults held at least a bachelor's degree, compared to 36 percent of white Americans. As in the pre–civil rights era, relative to whites, blacks continue to reside in and attend schools in poor and racially homogenous communities. The average black student attends a school that is 49 percent black, and the average white student attends a school that is 75 percent white.[132] Moreover, 25 percent of students attend schools where 99 percent or more of the student body are students of color.[133] In 2014, 48 percent of black children attended schools in high-poverty neighborhoods, compared to only 8 percent of white students.[134]

This brief summary of the history and current state of black education in America illustrates how the legacy of slavery, de jure Jim Crow laws that mandated segregation in both housing and education, and de facto exclusionary policies during the post–civil rights era have shaped the context for understanding the educational and economic profiles of black Americans. Despite moving from near-complete illiteracy

just prior to emancipation to the probability of having a college education being 10 percentage points lower for black Americans compared
to white Americans, the black American population has never had an
equal opportunity to acquire high-quality education.

Immigration Context and the Education Profiles of Black Immigrants

Black immigrants do not share black Americans' legacy of being
restricted to poor-quality educational institutions. This difference, in
combination with the effects of selective migration, fundamentally
shapes how comparisons between black Americans and black immigrants should be interpreted. Although a significant number of black
immigrants, particularly from the Caribbean, immigrated to the United
States in the first three decades of the 1900s, the vast majority migrated
to the United States after 1965, a period of expanding opportunities for
minorities as a whole. Indeed, although both U.S.-born and immigrant
blacks still receive lower economic returns to education than white
Americans, black Americans faced even more extreme educational
inequality in prior periods, while most black immigrants immigrated
to the United States in arguably the most favorable period for blacks
to acquire and capitalize on education. The educational outcomes of
blacks residing in the Caribbean and Africa reflect those regions' own
histories of slavery (the Caribbean) and colonialization (Africa), but
with the selectivity of migration, these historical factors are not as
acutely reflected in the education profiles of some black immigrants
in the United States. In other words, many black immigrant subgroups
are more highly educated, on average, than their counterparts in their
countries of origin. Although there is considerable variation in social
class among black Americans, there is even more social class variation
among individuals in the primary black immigrant sending countries.[135]

Educational Selectivity and Social Class

Table 3.1 presents the ratio of mean years of education among black
immigrants in the United States to the mean years of education of individuals living in the origin country.[136] Using this ratio as a measure of
education selection—the degree to which the education profiles of immigrants differ from those of residents in their country of origin—black

Table 3.1 *Mean Education in the United States and Immigrants' Country of Origin*

Country	Mean Years of Education in the United States in 2014	Mean Years of Education in Origin Country in 2015	Ratio of Destination to Origin Country Education
White Americans	13.75		
Black Americans	13.00		
Black American movers	13.41		
Black American nonmovers	12.81		
Ethiopia	12.85	2.58	4.98
Sierra Leone	13.62	3.33	4.09
Sudan	13.01	3.52	3.69
Liberia	13.15	4.44	2.96
Nigeria	14.97	6.00	2.50
Haiti	12.27	5.18	2.37
Cameroon	14.44	6.11	2.36
Kenya	14.25	6.31	2.26
Ghana	13.62	6.94	1.96
Guyana	13.16	8.42	1.56
Dominican Republic	11.89	7.68	1.55
Jamaica	13.13	9.64	1.36
Trinidad and Tobago	13.31	10.88	1.22
Somalia	9.85	—	

Source: United Nations Development Program (UNDP) 2016 *Human Development Report* and the 2014 ACS.

immigrants from Ethiopia are the most highly selected group of black immigrants residing in the United States, with nearly five times as much education as their compatriots in Ethiopia. The next two most highly selected black immigrant groups hail from Sierra Leone and Sudan. Immigrants from Trinidad and Tobago, Jamaica, and the Dominican Republic are the least-selected groups of immigrants. Overall, African immigrants have more than twice the amount of schooling as their compatriots in their origin country. This high degree of selectivity highlights the fact that immigration is a costly process, requiring the ability to navigate the bureaucracy of less-developed countries and secure sufficient resources to make the physical move. People with more education are more likely to have the resources to accomplish both goals.

Another important factor embedded in education selectivity is social class.[137] Returning to the example of Ethiopian immigrants, the mean years of education among Ethiopians living at home was 2.58 in 2015. In the same year, black Ethiopian immigrants residing in the United States averaged 12.85 mean years of education. Although Ethiopian immigrants, on average, have less education than black American movers and white Americans, they have almost five times as many years of education as Ethiopians who have not immigrated. Thus, prior to migration, these individuals probably occupied the highest rungs of Ethiopian society. This degree of education selection implies that prior to migrating to the United States, Ethiopian immigrants had access to jobs that allowed them to develop skills reserved for the most-educated members of their home country's population. Yet in the United States, Ethiopian immigrants have an average education, which typically affords them access only to jobs below their actual skill level. Selectivity arguments often suggest that immigrants are selected on soft skills such as motivation and ambition.[138] The estimates in table 3.1 suggest, however, that black immigrants may also be selected on hard skills, knowledge networks, wealth, and other hard-to-measure resources associated with membership in the higher social classes. Therefore, comparisons between black immigrants and black Americans at a given education level, particularly the lower education levels, could hide important advantages for the immigrant population.

Selectivity on social class is closely tied to the lateral mobility hypothesis, which makes two primary predictions regarding the social mobility of immigrants. First, in America, immigrants will achieve socioeconomic status similar to what they held or would have held in their country of origin. Consequently, black immigrants of middle or higher socioeconomic status in their country of origin will achieve the same relative status in the United States. Second, because of social class differences, some black immigrants are likely to obtain higher socioeconomic status than native black Americans, who are disproportionately poor and of lower socioeconomic status.[139] Given that immigrants' numeric years of education do not accurately capture their social class position in their home countries, the lateral mobility hypothesis suggests that some immigrants with low education levels could surpass the outcomes of black Americans with similar years of schooling.

Conclusion

In this chapter, I explored four issues that are essential to framing empirical comparisons of black Americans and black immigrants. First, I outlined the three primary theoretical frameworks—cultural differences, different experiences of discrimination, and selective migration—that have guided the last several decades of work on labor market disparities among blacks in the United States. In addition, I reviewed the existing empirical evidence on the relative explanatory power of each of these theoretical frameworks. The research shows little support for the theory that culture, at least as formulated in the extant literature, plays a significant role in explaining disparities between black immigrants and black Americans. Much of the evidence, particularly the seminal work of Model, shows that selective migration is the primary driver of disparities between black Americans and black immigrants from the English-speaking Caribbean.[140] Studies that find that the outcomes of black immigrants are remarkably similar to those of black American movers provide the most compelling evidence that contemporary nativity disparities are the result of selective migration.

The similarity between black American movers and black immigrants has implications for how researchers theorize the role of culture, the mechanism historically thought to produce disparities between black Americans and black immigrants. Much of the early work on the role of culture is based on a rather simplistic understanding of the concept. For example, Thomas Sowell's framing of culture is based on historical differences in the organization of slavery, but he does not offer a mechanism by which culture transfers across generations; his framework simply assumes that once disparate work orientations appear, they become fixed and independent.[141] Given the enormous social, political, and economic changes that have occurred in both the Caribbean and the United States, a more flexible and nuanced notion of culture is required. Patricia Fernández-Kelly provides a useful summary of such a perspective:

> An alternative interpretation of ethnic and racial outcomes does not require that we cast a blind eye on personal decision-making or culture but it demands that we consider history and social context. Individuals make choices and they adhere to belief systems but decisions

and values do not materialize in a vacuum—they are shaped by specific relationships and power differentials; by the physical spaces in which people live; and by the character and quantity of the information they receive. In other words, culture cannot be seen as an *independent variable*, as Sowell and other market advocates do. A better way to define that term is as an ideational repertory from which individuals and groups select symbols and narratives to make sense of their experience and of the environments that surround them. Culture matters and markets exist but not in the ways that neo-liberal thinkers adduce.[142]

Fernández-Kelly's argument has clear implications: Scholars must view culture as an endogenous factor, a variable determined by other factors. Therefore, cultural explanations can never be the primary source of disparities between groups, a conclusion that challenges researchers to better understand the structural conditions that determine group outcomes, particularly those that impact the outcomes of all immigrants, regardless of race, as well as those that uniquely shape the economic outcomes of black Americans.

As a second step in framing current-day comparisons of black immigrants and black Americans, I have highlighted the importance of several structural factors that limit the upward mobility of black Americans. In particular, I analyzed the relevant historical contexts that influenced the social outcomes of black Americans and black immigrants—a relatively understudied factor. Some studies have found evidence that black Americans experience more discrimination than some black immigrants.[143] Other studies, however, find that differential patterns of discrimination do not explain disparities between the two groups.[144] Few scholars, however, have thoroughly examined the impact of differential exposures to a legacy of institutional racism.

During the pre–civil rights era, implicit and explicit Jim Crow policies impeded the progress of both black Americans and black immigrants. Migration from the Caribbean slowed in the 1930s, but millions of black Americans still journeyed from the South to midwestern and eastern cities, as they had done since the 1910s and would continue to do until the 1970s. Some migrants found pathways to upward mobility, but many more found themselves stuck in cities with declining opportunities and residing in highly segregated communities.[145]

Millions more would remain in the South, facing limited opportunities for upward mobility and threats of violence by whites determined to maintain the status quo. I argue that both the trauma inflicted on black Americans by Jim Crow and the selectivity among black immigrants (particularly by education, wealth, and social class) are understudied factors that produced disparities between black Americans and black immigrants.[146]

Although educational and economic opportunities expanded for blacks after 1965, the racism and subpar schooling most had received in earlier eras prevented all but a small minority of U.S.-born blacks from taking full advantage of these new opportunities.[147] These factors had a smaller effect on many post-1965 black immigrants from the Caribbean and Africa. Because many black immigrants, particularly those from sub-Saharan Africa, had more education than both black Americans and the average resident in their home countries, they were better able to capitalize on the expanding opportunities in the United States.

Third, I have argued that one of the key limitations of prior research on black immigrants is the tendency for studies to focus solely on the experiences of black immigrants from the Caribbean. Not all black immigrants share the same historical or contemporary reception context, and differences in these contexts can produce disparate outcomes within the black immigrant population. For example, while black immigrants from Jamaica, Trinidad and Tobago, Guyana, Nigeria, Ghana, Kenya, Cameroon, Liberia, and Ethiopia have received a neutral or favorable context of reception, which improves their likelihood of economic success, immigrants from Somalia, Sierra Leone, and Sudan, because they are more likely to be Muslim and to reside outside traditional black immigrant destinations, are likely to face a negative context of reception. Moreover, because of the harsh political rhetoric surrounding Haitian immigration and the negative stigma of being both black and Hispanic for immigrants from the Dominican Republic, blacks from these countries are also likely to experience a negative reception context, which reduces their likelihood of upward mobility.

Fourth, few studies have examined how the relative benefits of U.S. employment for black immigrants and black Americans might produce labor market disparities between the two groups. Many black immigrants hail from countries with weaker labor markets than that of the

United States. Moreover, prior research has suggested that many black immigrants' decision to move to the United States is not solely based on a desire to fulfill individual objectives but also represents an opportunity to assist family members in their home countries, a factor that is likely to explain the high remittance flows to many of the primary black immigrant sending countries. These factors, along with considerable differences in living standards between the United States and the many origin countries in the Caribbean and Africa where modest remittances can substantially improve individuals' living standards, suggest that many jobs, even those on the lower rungs of the occupational distribution, allow immigrants to fulfill a greater number of objectives than employment opportunities in their home countries. As a result, many immigrants, particularly less-educated immigrants, may have a more favorable view of U.S. labor market opportunities than do U.S.-born individuals (both black and white), and such a view could lead to higher labor force participation and employment rates. Because the financial objectives and family networks of the U.S.-born are embedded in the United States, many of the jobs held by black immigrants do not offer the same benefits for black or white Americans.

Finally, I have argued that much of the existing research on disparities between black immigrants and black Americans has ignored important aspects of the social class differences between the two populations. Researchers tend to adjust for education when making comparisons, but they often overlook the contextual importance of education. That is, comparisons between black Americans and black immigrants at a specific level of education conceal social class differences between the two groups. For example, immigrants, particularly those who are considered low-skilled or moderately skilled in the U.S. context, occupy a more favorable position in their host countries' education distributions, which means that, relative to black Americans with similar years of education, immigrants occupied a more favorable social class position in their origin countries. Consequently, less-educated immigrants had access to more opportunities to develop skills, wealth, and knowledge than native-born blacks with a similar level of education. This difference in context could produce significant disparities between immigrants and native-born blacks, particularly among those with lower levels of education.

The Path Forward

In each of the remaining chapters of the book, I begin with either a discussion or empirical analysis of historical data, with the goal of helping readers understand the origins of the social and economic standing of black Americans and providing a lens for interpreting disparities between black Americans and black immigrants. Each chapter also outlines changes over time in disparities between and among black Americans, white Americans, and black immigrants, with the goal of highlighting how black immigration is shaping the ways in which scholars and policymakers understand racial disparities in the twenty-first century.

In these subsequent chapters, I also provide empirical support for the arguments advanced in this chapter. While each chapter develops an argument specific to the focal outcome in that chapter, several methodological strategies are applied throughout the book. First, given the importance of selective migration in shaping the outcomes of immigrants, I systematically compare black American movers to black immigrants.

In this chapter, I have argued that black immigrants from Jamaica, Trinidad and Tobago, Guyana, Nigeria, Ghana, Kenya, Cameroon, Liberia, and Ethiopia have received a neutral or favorable context of reception, which improves their likelihood of favorable social integration. In contrast, immigrants from Somalia, Sierra Leone, Sudan, Haiti, and the Dominican Republic have experienced a negative reception context, which has a negative impact on their likelihood of upward mobility. Prior studies typically use labor market outcomes to test the context of reception framework, but a broad interpretation and a strong test of this framework suggest that immigrants who experience a favorable context of reception should experience not only better labor market outcomes but better outcomes across a range of social and economic outcomes. I test this proposition in the remainder of the book.

Lastly, I examine whether historical context provides an explanation for disparities between black Americans and black immigrants. In this chapter, I have argued that the civil rights movement is one of

the most significant contextual factors that shaped the post-1965 outcomes of black Americans. To test this hypothesis, in chapters 4 and 5,
I show that in the pre–civil rights era, when the degree of racism faced
by all blacks was greatest, disparities between black immigrants and
black Americans were modest. Significant disparities between the two
groups emerged only after legislative changes made the United States a
less overtly racist society.

CHAPTER FOUR

HISTORICAL AND CONTEMPORARY LABOR MARKET DISPARITIES

Black Americans trail their white counterparts in nearly every measure of social and economic well-being. Compared to white Americans, black Americans have lower earnings, are less likely to be employed, and have lower labor force participation rates.[1] Although some of these disparities result from differences in education, even when black Americans are compared to white Americans with similar education levels, disparities remain. In 2008, among individuals with at least a college degree, black men earned 74 percent of what white men earned, and among workers with less than a high school education, black men earned 61 percent of what white men earned.[2] Similar disparities exist in employment. At every education level, white American men have higher employment rates than black American men.[3] Given the importance of labor market success in shaping overall social well-being, understanding the magnitude of labor market disparities between black Americans and black immigrants as well as the mechanisms that produce these disparities will provide important insights into the social standing of all blacks as the black immigrant population grows and diversifies.

Early Twentieth-Century Disparities

In this chapter, I present a detailed analysis of educational attainment, labor force participation, employment, and earnings for white Americans, black Americans, and black immigrants. I start with an analysis of race- and nativity-based disparities between 1910 and 1940. A substantial body of qualitative work examines disparities among blacks during the first four decades of the 1900s.[4] During this period, most black immigrants hailed from the English-speaking Caribbean and almost all resided in New York City. Many southern-born blacks also migrated to New York City during the same period in search of better living conditions.[5] Indeed, during the earlier 1900s, the vast majority of blacks residing in New York were born in either the Caribbean or the American South.[6]

Early work on labor market differences between Caribbean-born blacks and both northern- and southern-born blacks exalts the Caribbean-born population for both their high rates of entrepreneurship and high rates of employment in skilled professions.[7] W. A. Domingo, a journalist and political activist, noted:

> It is safe to say that West Indian representation in the skilled trades is relatively large; this is also true of the professions, especially medicine and dentistry. Like the Jew, they are forever launching out in business, and such retail businesses as are in the hands of Negroes in Harlem are largely in the control of the foreign-born. While American Negroes predominate in forms of business like barber shops and pool rooms in which there is no competition from white men, West Indians turn their efforts almost invariably to fields like grocery stores, tailor shops, jewelry stores, and fruit vending in which they meet the fiercest kind of competition. In some of these fields they are the pioneers or the only surviving competitors of white business concerns.[8]

Much of this work attributes the success of Caribbean-born blacks to their favorable cultural values and practices—hard work, an ability to defer gratification, entrepreneurial skills, a love of learning—and attributes the lack of success among black Americans, both northern- and southern-born, to shiftlessness and a general acceptance of a subordinate role in society.[9] Comparing blacks from the South and those born in the Caribbean, James Weldon Johnson, the author of *Black Manhattan,* noted:

> Those from the British West Indies average high in intelligence and efficiency. There is practically no illiteracy among them, and many have a sound English common school education. They are characteristically sober-minded and have something of a genius of business, differing, almost totally, in these respects, from the average rural Negro of the South.[10]

My analysis of within-race disparities among blacks in the early twentieth century challenges the proclaimed existence of significant disparities among blacks during the period. I argued in chapter 3 that any advantages experienced by black immigrants over black Americans in the contemporary era are driven primarily by two factors: selective migration and the benefits of moving to the United States in the post–civil rights era, a period marked by an expansion of opportunities for all minority populations. Counter to accounts in prior studies based largely on unrepresentative samples of black people in the 1930s, I argue that the harshness of discrimination and racism experienced by all blacks in the early 1900s left little room for significant within-group disparities among blacks by nativity.[11]

Despite the considerable literature on differences among blacks in the early 1900s, only one published study has quantitatively examined the claims made regarding disparities between black Americans and black immigrants in this period. Model used data from the 1 percent samples of the 1910, 1920, 1930, and 1940 U.S. census to analyze these disparities in labor force participation, employment, occupational prestige, and earnings.[12] Her analysis produced only two statistically significant findings: one supporting an immigrant advantage and the other against an immigrant advantage. First, she found that West Indian men held more prestigious occupations than black American men in 1940. Second, she found that the probability of being in the labor force was 23 percent lower for West Indian women compared to black American women in 1940. All other comparisons of labor force participation, unemployment, occupational prestige, and earnings between the two groups were statistically insignificant across the study period.

Although Model's results support the argument I advanced in chapter 3, her findings must be interpreted with a degree of caution. As Model noted, in any given year, the 1 percent samples contain a very small number of foreign-born blacks—usually between one and two hundred. Although many of her finding are statistically insignificant, some of her estimates point in the direction of an advantage for the immigrant population. Given the small number of immigrants in the sample, some of the insignificant findings may be driven by insufficient sample sizes.

To better understand the disparities among blacks during this period, I build on Model's estimates in two significant ways. First, rather than relying on the 1 percent samples of the U.S. census, I utilize the complete (100 percent) census of individuals residing in the New York metropolitan area between 1910 and 1940. The complete count of Caribbean-born individuals between the ages of twenty-five and sixty-four contains 4,990 individuals in 1910, 14,544 in 1920, 32,287 in 1930, and 36,889 in 1940.[13] Given that the estimates are based on the entire census of New York City, any differences between the groups represent the actual population estimates.

Second, much of the literature on nativity-based disparities among blacks involves trying to understand the theoretical importance of culture, selective migration, and discrimination. To address this debate, I divide the black American population into two groups: those born in New York and those born in a state other than New York (primarily southern migrants). This methodological strategy allows me to place an upper bound on the importance of culture and discrimination in explaining disparities between black immigrants and native-born blacks. That is, if disparities between these two groups are partly driven by factors associated with selective migration, partitioning the black American population into movers and nonmovers essentially holds culture constant and varies migration status. Prior research shows that black Americans who moved to northern cities were positively selected compared to the general southern black American population.[14] Moreover, while some studies suggest that black American migrants were also positively selected on motivation and determination compared to northern-born blacks, other research suggests that compared to northern-born blacks, "migrants did not seem to suffer an earnings penalty associated with having been born and educated in the South, neither did they enjoy the earnings premium that in previous work has been interpreted as a sign of positive selection on the basis of personal attributes."[15] To set the stage for the discussion of labor market disparities, I first document differences in educational attainment for non-Hispanic whites, black Americans, and black immigrants in the United States during the early twentieth century.

EDUCATIONAL ATTAINMENT

Prior to 1940, the U.S. census contained only one measure of adults' educational attainment: literacy. Most individuals residing in New York prior to 1940, both white and black, were literate. For example, among men residing in New York City in 1930, nearly 100 percent of whites were literate, compared to 98 percent of black American movers and 99 percent of black American nonmovers. The 1940 census reveals further variation across these groups in educational attainment. Among men, white Americans averaged 10.22 mean years of schooling, approximately two years more than black American movers (8.12) and approximately one year more than black American nonmovers (9.13). Men from the Caribbean averaged 8.71 years of education—slightly more than black American movers and slightly less than black American nonmovers.

In terms of education selectivity, the degree to which education differed between migrants in New York and those residing in their birth country, both black American movers and black Caribbean immigrants were positively selected on education. In 1940, among adults between the ages of twenty-five and sixty-four, 83 to 88 percent of blacks residing in the American South were literate.[16] By comparison, almost the entire black population of New York was literate. In Jamaica, one of the primary source countries during this period, close to half of the population was illiterate during the early 1900s.[17] In comparison, close to 100 percent of Jamaicans residing in New York City were literate. George Roberts and Ira De Augustine Reid showed that holding a job in a skilled occupation was more common among immigrants from Jamaica residing in the United States than among home-country stayers.[18] From 1916 to 1925, 4 percent of Jamaicans in the United States were in professional occupations, compared to 2.6 percent of Jamaican stayers in 1921. Moreover, during this period the percentage of individuals holding jobs in low-skill occupations was smaller among Jamaican immigrants (50 percent) than among those living in Jamaica (76.2 percent).[19]

LABOR MARKET OUTCOMES

Tables 4.1 to 4.4 show the labor market outcomes of black American movers, black American nonmovers, Caribbean-born blacks, and white Americans in 1910, 1920, 1930, and 1940.[20] The tables show two estimates for each group, the first from a base model that adjusts only for age differences across the groups, and the second from an adjusted model that accounts for differences in age (survey years 1910, 1920, and 1930), marital status, literacy (survey years 1910, 1920, 1930) or education

Table 4.1 *Regressions of Labor Force Participation for Black American, White American, and Caribbean-Born Adults, Ages Twenty-Five to Sixty-Four, 1910–1940*

| | 1910 | | 1920 | | 1930 | | 1940 | |
	(1) Base	(2) Adjusted	(3) Base	(4) Adjusted	(5) Base	(6) Adjusted	(7) Base	(8) Adjusted
Men								
Country of birth (reference: black American movers)								
White Americans	-0.015***	-0.016***	-0.011***	-0.012***	-0.009***	-0.010***	0.031***	0.025***
Black American nonmovers	-0.007***	-0.006**	-0.011***	-0.011***	-0.009***	-0.008***	-0.003	-0.003
Caribbeans	0.001	0.000	-0.002	-0.004*	-0.000	-0.002	0.012***	0.011***
Observations	488,885	488,885	651,200	651,200	974,875	974,875	1,388,566	1,348,196
Women								
Country of birth (reference: black American movers)								
White Americans	-0.400***	-0.353***	-0.345***	-0.306***	-0.347***	-0.291***	-0.234***	-0.199***
Black American nonmovers	-0.121***	-0.098***	-0.089***	-0.060***	-0.113***	-0.075***	-0.083***	-0.053***
Caribbeans	-0.004	-0.017	-0.019*	-0.021***	-0.042***	-0.032***	-0.042***	-0.010**
Observations	534,337	534,337	719,725	719,725	1,051,395	1,051,395	1,512,584	1,476,733

Source: Full count of the U.S. Census of Population for the New York Metropolitan Area from 1910 to 1940.
*p < .05; **p < .01; ***p < .001

(survey year 1940), and experience (survey year 1940). Adjusted models for women also control for both number of own children and number of own children under the age of five in the household. I focus the discussion on the fully adjusted models.

Table 4.1 shows that among men, during the three earlier periods (1910, 1920, and 1930), the probability of being in the labor force was slightly lower (less than two percentage points) for both white Americans and black American nonmovers than for black American movers. However, from 1910 to 1930, there was no statistical or substantive difference between black American movers and Caribbean-born blacks. Indeed, the estimates are near zero in each year.

The data from 1940 show slightly more variation among men. Probably because the Great Depression was ending and labor demand was increasing at the beginning of the World War II period, the probability of being in the labor market was 2.5 percentage points greater for white American men than for similarly skilled black American movers. The disparity in labor force participation between black American movers and black Caribbean men increased very modestly in 1940, with Caribbean men being slightly more likely (one percentage point) to be in the labor market than black American movers.

Among women, a more straightforward picture emerges from the data. Between 1910 and 1940, compared to black American movers, white Americans and black Caribbean immigrants had significantly lower labor force participation rates. Perhaps owing to the gendered nature of work during the period (a large share of white American women worked exclusively in the home), the difference in labor force participation relative to black American movers was largest for white American women, followed by black American nonmovers, and then by Caribbean-born women. Indeed, by 1940, the probability of being in the labor force was 1 percentage point lower for Caribbean immigrants than for black American movers.

Table 4.2 examines disparities in employment across the groups. Focusing on the adjusted models in the period from 1910 to 1940, relative to black American movers, the probability of being employed was greater for white Americans (among both men and women) and was either similar or lower for black American nonmovers (among both men and women). With the exception of estimates for men in 1910 and 1930, when the probability of being employed was approximately one

Table 4.2 Regressions of Employment for Black American, White American, and Caribbean-Born Adults, Ages Twenty-Five to Sixty-Four, 1910–1940

	1910		1930		1940	
	(1) Base	(2) Adjusted	(3) Base	(4) Adjusted	(5) Base	(6) Adjusted
Men						
Country of birth (reference: black American movers)						
White Americans	0.029***	0.028***	0.047***	0.046***	0.033***	0.020***
Black American nonmovers	0.006	0.006	0.005	0.005	-0.015***	-0.015***
Caribbeans	0.012*	0.011*	0.010***	0.008**	-0.027***	-0.028***
Observations	346,437	346,437	942,812	942,812	1,298,160	1,264,320
Women						
Country of birth (reference: black American movers)						
White Americans	0.021***	0.016***	0.019***	0.016***	0.022***	0.016***
Black American nonmovers	-0.011*	-0.011*	-0.001	0.001	-0.033***	-0.033***
Caribbeans	-0.009	-0.009	-0.014***	-0.014***	-0.013***	-0.010**
Observations	114,600	114,600	324,663	324,663	541,324	528,517

Source: Full count of the U.S. Census of Population for the New York Metropolitan Area from 1910 to 1940.

Note: Information on employment for 1920 is not available.

*p < .05; **p < .01; ***p < .001

percentage point greater for Caribbean men compared to black American movers, in every other period the probability of black Caribbean immigrants being employed was either statistically similar to or lower than the probability for black American movers.

The next set of estimates for the early twentieth century uses occupational prestige scores (table 4.3) to assess disparities in the types of occupations held by individuals. The occupational prestige scale is an ordinal measure of the status associated with different occupations. For example, doctors would have a higher score than house servants, and house servants would have a higher score than agricultural workers. The estimates from models of occupation prestige offer several interesting insights. First, as expected for the period, compared to black American movers, white Americans, both men and women, had occupations with more prestige. In addition, for both men and women, black American nonmovers and Caribbean immigrants held jobs with slightly more prestige than the jobs held by black American movers. Black movers fared more poorly than black nonmovers on occupational prestige because most of them were educated in and had amassed their skill sets in the southern states. These findings also comport with prior research on the Great Migration.[21] Interestingly, however, the results indicate that black American nonmovers held jobs with more or similar prestige as the jobs held by Caribbean immigrants, suggesting that Caribbean immigrants had no consistent advantage in occupational prestige. Despite these differences, the magnitude of the coefficient estimates on disparities in occupational prestige suggests that few substantive differences existed among black American movers, black American nonmovers, and Caribbean blacks during the early twentieth century.

Unfortunately, data on earnings were not collected in the U.S. census until 1940. Table 4.4 provides estimates based on these data. Again, focusing on the adjusted models, white American men and women earned more than black American movers. Moreover, consistent with the occupational prestige models, both men and women among black American nonmovers earned more than black American movers. Again, this finding is probably related to the high proportion of black American movers in New York who were born and educated (or had limited access to education) in the U.S. South. Both Caribbean men and Caribbean women earned less than black American movers of the same sex.

Table 4.3 Regressions of Occupational Prestige for Black American, White American, and Caribbean-Born Adults, Ages Twenty-Five to Sixty-Four, 1910–1940

	1910		1920		1930		1940	
	(1) Base	(2) Adjusted	(3) Base	(4) Adjusted	(5) Base	(6) Adjusted	(7) Base	(8) Adjusted
Men								
Country of birth (reference: black American movers)								
White Americans	14.352***	14.050***	14.321***	14.237***	14.716***	14.633***	11.847***	9.779***
Black American nonmovers	2.106***	2.126***	1.211***	1.233***	1.790***	1.776***	1.532***	1.231***
Caribbeans	0.493*	0.265	1.412***	1.268***	1.330***	1.238***	0.782***	0.398***
Observations	346,254	346,254	446,490	446,490	717,531	717,531	1,304,753	1,271,023
Women								
Country of birth (reference: black American movers)								
White Americans	15.406***	14.198***	16.556***	15.649***	19.115***	18.616***	13.770***	11.290***
Black American nonmovers	2.076***	2.151***	1.623***	1.891***	2.428***	2.545***	1.808***	1.410***
Caribbeans	0.558**	0.269	0.454***	0.317*	0.130	0.021	0.078	0.412***
Observations	114,597	114,597	163,779	163,779	262,310	262,310	577,436	562,413

Source: Full count of the U.S. Census of Population for the New York Metropolitan Area from 1910 to 1940.

$*p < .05$; $**p < .01$; $***p < .001$

Table 4.4 *Regressions of Log(Weekly Earnings) for Black American,*
White American, and Caribbean-Born Adults, Ages Twenty-Five
to Sixty-Four, 1940

	1940	
	(1) Base	(2) Adjusted
Men		
Country of birth (reference: black American movers)		
White Americans	0.456***	0.459***
Black American nonmovers	0.101***	0.102***
Caribbeans	−0.056***	−0.043***
Observations	1,173,109	1,144,492
Women		
Country of birth (reference: black American movers)		
White Americans	0.626***	0.507***
Black American nonmovers	0.091***	0.079***
Caribbeans	−0.040***	−0.018
Observations	488,603	478,153

Source: Full count of the U.S. Census of Population for the New York Metropolitan Area, 1940.
$^*p < .05;$ $^{**}p < .01;$ $^{***}p < .001$

Much of the existing literature on nativity-based labor market disparities among blacks focuses on comparisons at a single point in time (for example, tables 4.1 to 4.3). Contemporary research on the labor market outcomes of immigrants suggests that as immigrants learn the nuances of the host labor market, their labor market outcomes improve.

Therefore, because tenure of U.S. residence is a unique determinant of immigrants' labor market profiles, researchers would ideally follow the same individuals across time to assess how immigrants' labor market outcomes change the longer they live in the United States. No historical or contemporary data source exists, however, that allows for this type of comparison. In a series of papers published in the 1980s and 1990s, George Borjas developed an approach that addresses some of the shortcomings in the extant literature.[22] Rather than tracking the same individuals over time, Borjas showed that by using repeated cross-sections from the U.S. census, it is possible to track the labor market trajectories of different arrival cohorts across census waves. For example, a researcher can use data from the 1910 U.S. census to observe the initial labor force participation rates of individuals who migrated between 1905 and 1909. This arrival cohort can then be assessed ten years later via the 1920 U.S. census, allowing for a comparison of the same group of individuals at two different time points with different U.S. tenures at each time period. Although mortality, return migration, and non-enumeration will impact the representativeness of arrival cohorts over time, to date this approach offers the best analysis of immigrants' labor market trajectories.

In the following analyses, I employ the strategy developed by Borjas to examine trajectories in labor force participation, employment, and occupational prestige for different black Caribbean immigrant arrival cohorts. Specifically, I use data from the 1910 to 1930 U.S. censuses, years that include immigrants' year of immigration, which are needed to construct measures of arrival cohort dynamics to analyze the labor market trajectories of different arrival cohorts from the Caribbean.

Figure 4.1 (labor force participation), figure 4.2 (employment), and figure 4.3 (occupational prestige) show the trajectories of immigrants who arrived from the Caribbean between 1900 and 1930. The results are based on the fully specified models, and the reference category is black American movers. Observing the gap between a particular arrival cohort and black American movers provides an estimate of how disparities between the two groups change as immigrants' tenure of U.S. residence increases. Collectively, the three figures show very modest changes between black American movers and arrival cohorts from the Caribbean across the survey years. Indeed, with the exception of occupational prestige, where there is evidence of very modest improvement the longer immigrants live in the United States, there no substantive improvement in labor force participation and employment as immigrants' tenure of U.S. residence increases.

So far, the analysis of labor market disparities during the early twentieth century confirmed the expectations derived in chapter 3. Across all outcomes studied, in most cases black immigrants from the Caribbean have similar or worse profiles than black Americans. These findings contradict prior research focusing on this time period that suggested that black Caribbean immigrants performed markedly better than black Americans in the labor market.[23] The only consistent, although very modest, advantage achieved by black immigrants was in the domain of occupational prestige. However, results from the 1940 census, the first census with information on earnings, suggest that black immigrants

Figure 4.1 *Trajectories of Labor Force Participation for Black American and Caribbean-Born Adults, Ages Twenty-Five to Sixty-Four, 1910–1930*

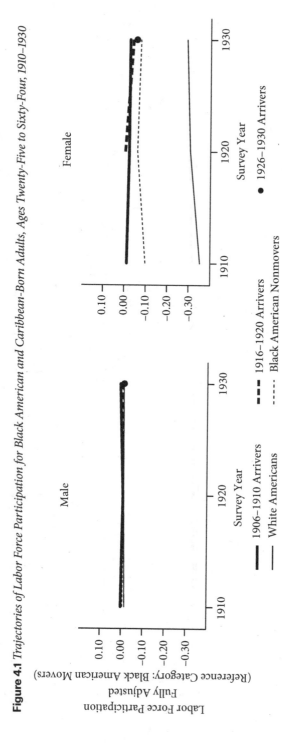

Source: Full count of the U.S. Census of Population for the New York Metropolitan Area from 1910 to 1930.

Figure 4.2 *Trajectories of Employment for Black American and Caribbean-Born Adults, Ages Twenty-Five to Sixty-Four, 1910–1930*

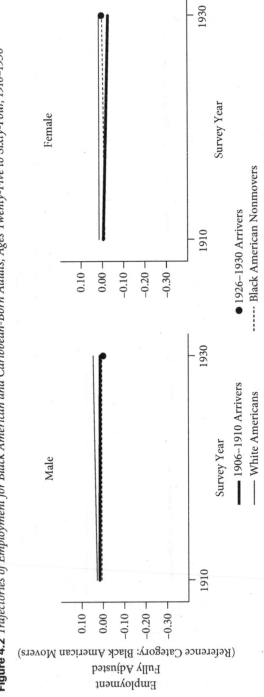

Source: Full count of the U.S. Census of Population for the New York Metropolitan Area from 1910 to 1930.

Figure 4.3 *Trajectories of Occupational Prestige for Black American and Caribbean-Born Adults, Ages Twenty-Five to Sixty-Four, 1910–1930*

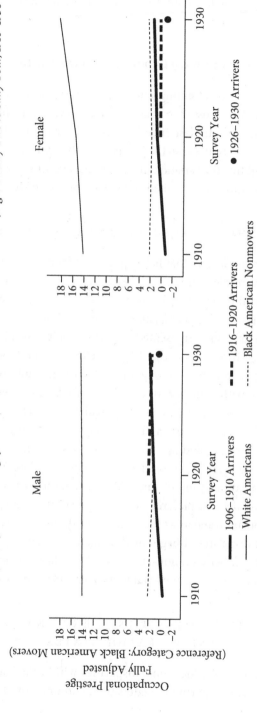

Source: Full count of the U.S. Census of Population for the New York Metropolitan Area from 1910 to 1930.

earned considerably less than both black American movers and black American nonmovers.

Contemporary Labor Market Disparities

I now focus on documenting contemporary (post-1980) disparities among blacks. As discussed in chapter 2, the growth of the black immigrant population over the last three decades has been marked by immense birth-country variation within the population. Therefore, I begin this section by highlighting the variation in educational attainment among black immigrants residing in the United States over the last thirty years.

SETTING THE STAGE: EDUCATION AND IMMIGRATION

Among the many factors that help explain the labor market success of contemporary immigrants in the United States, the most influential, after wealth and institutional factors such as discrimination, is educational attainment. The sociologists Alejandro Portes and Rubén Rumbaut argue that immigrants' skills, represented in part by their educational attainment, is one of three factors that largely determine the economic success of immigrant groups.[24] Among contemporary migrants to the United States, groups with a higher average level of education tend to have better labor market outcomes than groups with lower levels of educational attainment. For example, arrivals from countries such as India and South Korea—who have 15.9 and 14.3 mean years of education, respectively— have better aggregate labor market outcomes than Dominicans and Haitians, who have 10.3 and 11.2 mean years of education, respectively.

To provide a detailed picture of variation in years of schooling within the black population and to set the stage for the discussion of current-day labor market disparities, I begin by documenting disparities in educational attainment between non-Hispanic whites, black Americans, and black immigrants in the United States between 1980 and 2014.

EDUCATION DISPARITIES BY RACE, NATIVITY, AND MIGRATION STATUS

To contextualize the educational disparities within the black population, I begin by comparing the educational attainment of blacks and whites in the United States. As shown in table 4.5, in 2014, relative to black Americans and black immigrants, non-Hispanic white Americans had more years of schooling: on average, non-Hispanic whites had 13.75 years of education, while black Americans had 13.00 years and black immigrants had 12.47 years.[25] These overall levels, however, mask variation among black immigrants. Although most black immigrant country-specific groups had less education than white Americans, three groups had more education than white Americans: Nigerians (15.01 years), Kenyans (14.30 years), and Cameroonians (14.35 years).

Table 4.5 presents education levels for black Americans by domestic migration status (whether they had moved across state lines), revealing considerable variation among native-born blacks and the importance of selective migration for black Americans. Twenty-eight percent of black American movers had at least a college-level education compared to only 17 percent of black American nonmovers, a pattern that reveals a strong correlation between internal migration and education.

Table 4.5 also sheds light on educational disparities between black immigrants and black Americans. At the aggregate level, black Americans (13.00) have more education than black Caribbean immigrants (12.47) but less education than black African immigrants (13.24). There are significant differences, however, when these aggregate groups are partitioned by country of origin and domestic migration status. Relative to black American movers, immigrants from only five of the fourteen countries listed in table 4.5 had more mean years of education, but immigrants from twelve of the fourteen countries had more schooling than black American nonmovers. All the black immigrant subgroups with more mean years of education than black American movers hailed from sub-Saharan Africa, which highlights the stark differences in educational attainment between black immigrants from this region and those from the Caribbean. Indeed, among African immigrants, the mean level of education was 13.24 years and 36 percent had a college degree or more education; by contrast, among Caribbean immigrants, the mean level of education was 12.47 years and only 20 percent had a college education or more.

Several factors are likely to explain the educational disparities between black immigrants from the Caribbean and those from Africa. First, the high cost, both physical and economic, of moving from Africa serves as a significant barrier to migration for Africans of modest means and

Table 4.5 *Education Attainment of Adults Ages Twenty-Five to Sixty-Four, by Race and Country of Origin, 2014*

				Highest Educational Level (Proportions)		
	Mean Years	More Than College	College	Some College	High School	Less Than High School
Non-Hispanic white natives	13.75	0.13	0.23	0.25	0.34	0.05
Black Americans	13.00	0.07	0.13	0.30	0.41	0.09
Black movers	13.41	0.11	0.17	0.32	0.35	0.07
Black nonmovers	12.81	0.06	0.11	0.29	0.43	0.11
Black Caribbean immigrants	12.47	0.07	0.13	0.23	0.43	0.14
Haiti	11.94	0.04	0.09	0.26	0.41	0.20
Dominican Republic	11.39	0.03	0.11	0.16	0.45	0.25
Jamaica	12.78	0.07	0.15	0.22	0.45	0.12
Trinidad and Tobago	13.11	0.11	0.16	0.22	0.44	0.07
Guyana	12.91	0.08	0.14	0.21	0.51	0.05
Black African immigrants	13.24	0.15	0.21	0.26	0.27	0.11
Nigeria	15.01	0.30	0.33	0.22	0.13	0.02
Ethiopia	12.72	0.10	0.15	0.26	0.39	0.10
Ghana	13.55	0.14	0.23	0.21	0.35	0.06
Kenya	14.30	0.16	0.27	0.38	0.16	0.03
Liberia	12.99	0.10	0.15	0.32	0.36	0.08
Somalia	9.11	0.02	0.04	0.18	0.31	0.44
Cameroon	14.35	0.23	0.27	0.27	0.18	0.05
Sierra Leone	13.53	0.10	0.18	0.25	0.45	0.03
Sudan	12.72	0.15	0.13	0.24	0.32	0.16

Source: U.S. census and 2014 ACS.
Note: Survey weights applied.

thus restricts immigration flows to the more-educated members of these African countries. Second, a major driver of immigration from Africa in recent years has been the diversity visa lottery. Since the U.S. presidential election of 2016, the diversity visa lottery has been attacked by politicians arguing that the program is a vehicle for less talented individuals to immigrate to the United States. In an interview with *Fox News* on February 24, 2018, President Donald Trump stated:

> We need something to do with chain migration and something to do with visa lottery. I mean, we actually have lottery systems where you go to countries and they do lotteries for who comes into the United States. Now, you know they are not going to have their best people in the lottery, because they're not going to put their best people in a lottery. They don't want to have their good people to leave. . . . We want people based on merit. Not based on the fact they are thrown into a bin, and many of those people are not the people you want in the country, believe me.

In the case of immigrants from sub-Saharan African (and those from most other diversity-visa-eligible countries), this statement could not be further from the truth. The criteria for the diversity visa lottery are set by U.S. immigration law. To qualify for the diversity visa lottery, an individual must have completed at least a high school education or its equivalent, defined as successful completion of a twelve-year course of formal elementary and secondary education, or have two years of work experience within the past five years in an occupation that requires at least two years of training or experience to perform. Obtaining a twelve-year course of formal schooling is no trivial accomplishment in many sub-Saharan African countries. The mean years of schooling in most countries in sub-Saharan Africa is less than seven, highlighting that across countries in Africa eligible for the diversity visa lottery, such as Ghana, individuals with twelve years of schooling are a highly selected population. Moreover, diversity visa winners typically need to move within a year of being notified. Given the cost of moving from Africa, it is not surprising that the diversity visa winners who actually migrate to the United States typically have more than twelve years of schooling, with immigrant flows often representing the most-skilled members of the origin countries.

Third, relative to Caribbean migration, African migration is more recent. Because the Caribbean has experienced a more sustained period of migration than Africa, a greater proportion of Caribbean migrants moved using visas intended for individuals seeking to reunite with family; this group tends to be less educated than immigrants moving for economic reasons. In 2014, compared to immigrants from the Caribbean, a greater proportion of immigrants from Africa came to the United States using visas reserved for individuals with occupational skills needed in the country or using the diversity visa lottery.

Not all African immigrants, however, are highly educated. Among the African countries shown in table 4.5, Ethiopia, Somalia, and Sudan send immigrants with lower levels of educational attainment. Ten percent of immigrants from Ethiopia, 44 percent of immigrants from Somalia, and 16 percent of immigrants from Sudan have less than a high school education. Many of the individuals who have moved to the United States from these countries arrived as refugees. Research suggests that "initial waves of refugees tend to come from the higher socioeconomic strata, but as the movement continues, they are increasingly drawn from the popular classes. The decline in schooling tends to be faster when refugees originate in poor countries where the well-educated represent but a small proportion of the total population."[26] This pattern explains the low levels of education attainment for immigrants from Ethiopia, Somalia, and Sudan, countries where the mean level of education is very low and where only a small percentage of the population over age twenty-five has completed secondary education.

Education attainment is also significantly varied across the focal Caribbean countries. On average, immigrants from Jamaica have 12.78 years of education, immigrants from Guyana have 12.91 years of education, and immigrants from Trinidad and Tobago have 13.11 years of education. Immigrants from Haiti and the Dominican Republic have the lowest education levels of those from the Caribbean countries (11.94 years and 11.39 years, respectively). Two factors are likely to explain the low education levels of Haitian and Dominican immigrants. First, the high demand created by the economy of the United States, particularly in past decades, for low-wage labor in agriculture and other labor-intensive industries has stimulated and sustained underground flows of migrants from countries in close proximity to the United States, such as Haiti and the Dominican Republic, where employment prospects are less favorable and the cost of migrating to the United States is sufficiently low.[27]

Second, similar to countries such as Nigeria, Ghana, and Kenya, the Caribbean countries of Jamaica and Trinidad and Tobago have the facilities to train professionals at levels suitable for employment in the United States, but lack the ability to employ these individuals in jobs that offer the standard of living they desire.[28] This context helps explain the higher levels of education among immigrants from the English-speaking Caribbean. Both Haiti and the Dominican Republic, however, lack the educational institutions to educate a large fraction of their populations, which helps explain the low education levels of immigrants from these countries.

CHANGES IN THE EDUCATIONAL PROFILE
OF BLACK IMMIGRANTS, 1980–2014

In addition to understanding current disparities in education by race, nativity, and migration status, it is also important to highlight how the education levels of both black immigrants and black Americans have changed over time, because these shifts have affected changes in economic outcomes across time. To contextualize the trends in social and economic status, it is especially useful to examine how the education profile of the black immigrant population changed between 1980 and 2014 as the flow of black immigrants increased and shifted in composition, moving from a period dominated by Caribbean migration to a period dominated by African migration.

Table 4.6 shows changes in educational attainment for black immigrants and black Americans between 1980 and 2014 as well as changes in education for each country subgroup and each arrival cohort over the same period. For black Americans, the average years of schooling increased substantially, from 11.25 years of schooling in 1980 to 12.93 years in 2014, an increase of 1.68 years over three decades. This increase in education was especially pronounced among black movers, whose mean years of education increased by nearly two full years, compared to an increase of 1.63 years (from 11.10 in 1980 to 12.81 in 2014) among black nonmovers.

The educational profile of black immigrants has also changed in recent decades. The overall immigrant population (immigrants of all

Table 4.6 *Average Years of Schooling of Adults Ages Twenty-Five to Sixty-Four, by Nativity, Immigrant Arrival Cohort, and Census Year*

Group	Census Year			
	1980	*1990*	*2000*	*2010–2014*
White Americans	12.51	13.10	13.39	13.70
All black Americans	11.25	12.16	12.54	12.93
Black American movers	11.42	12.39	12.87	13.34
Black American nonmovers	11.11	12.02	12.37	12.74
Caribbean immigrants	11.50	11.57	12.04	12.45
Haiti	11.40	10.91	11.46	11.92
Dominican Republic	9.39	9.63	10.95	11.51
Jamaica	11.49	12.06	12.26	12.74
Trinidad and Tobago	11.84	12.25	12.53	12.94
Guyana	12.36	12.25	12.69	12.91
African immigrants	14.49	14.20	13.65	13.30
Nigeria	15.08	15.20	14.83	14.98
Ethiopia	14.35	13.23	13.17	12.95
Ghana	14.40	14.40	13.48	13.46
Kenya	15.17	14.78	14.45	14.29
Liberia	13.60	13.78	13.55	12.85
Somalia	13.89	13.90	10.44	9.95
Cameroon	14.62	14.84	14.74	14.27
Sierra Leone	14.50	14.35	13.59	13.17
Sudan	13.73	14.30	13.19	12.52
Immigrant cohort				
Pre-1970	11.89	12.18	12.65	13.36
1970–1974	11.90	12.38	12.78	13.36
1975–1979	11.59	12.31	12.78	13.05
1980–1984		11.84	12.53	12.92
1985–1989		11.64	12.45	12.86
1990–1994			12.30	12.73
1995–1999			12.40	13.01
2000–2004				12.79
2005–2009				12.54
2010–2014				12.50

Source: U.S. census and 2014 ACS.
Note: Survey weights applied.

Table 4.7 *Average Years of Schooling of Caribbean Immigrants Ages Twenty-Five to Sixty-Four, by Arrival Cohort and Census Year*

Cohort	Census Year			
	1980	*1990*	*2000*	*2010–2014*
Pre-1970	11.83	12.07	12.56	13.25
1970–1974	11.50	12.06	12.38	12.96
1975–1979	10.85	11.84	12.22	12.61
1980–1984		11.13	11.94	12.35
1985–1989		11.16	12.06	12.61
1990–1994			11.89	12.33
1995–1999			11.76	12.55
2000–2004				12.53
2005–2009				12.21
2010–2014				12.12

Source: U.S. census and 2014 ACS.
Note: Survey weights applied.

races and national origins) has seen a decline in education levels, but the mean years of schooling for new black immigrant arrival cohorts has increased over time. For example, table 4.6 shows that the mean years of schooling for the 1975–1979 cohort of black immigrants, upon arrival in the United States, was 11.59, compared to 12.40 years for the 1995–1999 arrival cohort and 12.50 years for the 2010–2014 cohort.

This overall increase in education among black immigrants obscures an important difference between the two regional groups: while early arrival cohorts of African immigrants had a much higher average level of education than early arrival cohorts of Caribbean immigrants (for example, 14.31 years compared to 10.85 years among members of the 1975–1979 arrival cohorts, respectively), the disparity in educational attainment between the two groups has narrowed for recent arrival cohorts. Tables 4.7 and 4.8 show changes in the educational profiles of arrival cohorts from the Caribbean and Africa. Table 4.7 indicates that, for Caribbean immigrants, mean years of education has increased steadily, albeit modestly, since 1980. The 1975–1979 cohort had 10.85 years of education, on average, just after arriving in the United States; in comparison, the 2010–2014 cohort had a mean of 12.12 years shortly after arrival, an increase of 1.27 years.

Table 4.8 *Average Years of Schooling of African Immigrants Ages Twenty-Five to Sixty-Four, by Arrival Cohort and Census Year*

	Census Year			
Cohort	1980	1990	2000	2010–2014
Pre-1970	14.48	15.41	14.87	15.34
1970–1974	14.74	15.00	15.02	15.08
1975–1979	14.31	14.92	15.13	14.87
1980–1984		14.31	14.40	14.62
1985–1989		13.20	13.88	13.78
1990–1994			13.24	13.54
1995–1999			13.06	13.55
2000–2004				13.11
2005–2009				12.85
2010–2014				12.73

Source: U.S. census and 2014 ACS.
Note: Survey weights applied.

A different pattern emerged for African immigrants during this period: the mean years of education for the most recent cohort from this group decreased between 1980 and 2014. For example, the 1975–1979 cohort from sub-Saharan Africa had 14.31 mean years of schooling just after their arrival in the United States. Ten years later, among members of the 1985–1989 arrival cohort, mean years of schooling had fallen by almost a full year, to 13.20 years, a pattern of decline that continued for African immigrants from the most recent arrival cohorts.

In summary, there is considerable variation in educational obtainment among black immigrants in the United States, and the educational profiles of black Americans, white Americans, and black immigrants have changed over time. Notably, mean years of education among black immigrants range widely, from 9.95 for immigrants from Somalia to 14.98 for immigrants from Nigeria in 2014. Despite this within-group variation, most groups of blacks, both native and immigrant, have lower educational attainment than white Americans. Indeed, only three immigrant subgroups had more education than white Americans in 2014: immigrants from Nigeria, Kenya, and Cameroon.

I have highlighted three meaningful divisions in educational attainment within the black population. First, among U.S.-born blacks, the educational profiles of movers are superior to those of nonmovers.

Second, educational attainment among black immigrants from sub-Saharan Africa is greater than that of immigrants from the Caribbean. Third, there is significant variation in educational attainment among immigrants from both the Caribbean and Africa. Among immigrants from the Caribbean, those from Haiti and the Dominican Republic have the lowest education levels, and immigrants from Jamaica, Trinidad and Tobago, and Guyana have higher education levels. Among immigrants from Africa, those from countries with large refugee populations, Somalia, Ethiopia, and Sudan, have less education. Black immigrants from Nigeria, Ghana, Cameroon, and Kenya, countries that have the capacity to train professionals but lack adequate labor market opportunities for highly trained individuals, have the highest education levels. In the following sections, I document disparities in labor force participation, employment, and earnings among blacks Americans, white Americans, and black immigrants.

Contemporary Disparities in Labor Market Outcomes

DISPARITIES IN LABOR FORCE PARTICIPATION
AMONG BLACKS: THE BASIC FACTS

Table 4.9 presents descriptive statistics of the study populations in the 2010–2014 time period. For several decades, researchers have attempted to answer the following question: do black immigrants have better labor market outcomes than black Americans? In terms of labor force participation, with a few exceptions, the answer is yes. Seventy-six percent of black American men participate in the labor force, compared to 87 percent of black Caribbean men and 90 percent of black sub-Saharan African men. Indeed, every national-origin group shown in table 4.9 has a greater labor force participation rate than both black and white Americans. Among black American men, labor force participation varies by internal migration status: black American movers have a higher labor force participation rate (79 percent) than black American nonmovers (75 percent). Large disparities exist between black immigrants and black American nonmovers, but the disparity between black American movers and black immigrants is considerably smaller, highlighting the importance of accounting for selective migration when studying labor market disparities among blacks in the United States.

Table 4.9 *Labor Force Participation Rate of Adults Ages Twenty-Five to Sixty-Four, by Race and Country of Origin, 2010–2014*

	Men	Women
Native whites	0.85	0.74
Black Americans	0.76	0.74
Black American movers	0.79	0.75
Black American nonmovers	0.75	0.74
All black immigrants	0.89	0.79
Black Caribbean immigrants	0.87	0.80
Haiti	0.87	0.79
Dominican Republic	0.86	0.72
Jamaica	0.88	0.84
Trinidad and Tobago	0.88	0.76
Guyana	0.87	0.83
Black African immigrants	0.90	0.78
Nigeria	0.90	0.82
Ethiopia	0.92	0.79
Ghana	0.92	0.82
Kenya	0.93	0.85
Liberia	0.92	0.85
Somalia	0.86	0.61
Cameroon	0.93	0.80
Sierra Leone	0.92	0.90
Sudan	0.90	0.61

Source: 2010–2014 ACS.
Note: Weighted values.

Among women, with the exception of women from Somalia, Sudan, and the Dominican Republic, every subgroup of women from the Caribbean and Africa has a greater labor force participation rate than both black and white American women. In contrast to the result for men, internal migration status produces no meaningful disparity in labor force participation among black American women.

Table 4.9 also highlights patterns that are often missed by studies that focus exclusively on disparities among blacks. First, white American women have a lower labor force participation rate (74 percent) than many subgroups of black immigrant women. Second, there is immense birth-country heterogeneity among black immigrants. Although there is almost no difference in labor force participation among men from the Caribbean, participation rates vary considerably among Caribbean women, with those from Jamaica and Guyana having the highest levels of labor force participation and those from the Dominican Republic the lowest. Similarly, while the table shows modest variation in labor force participation among men from Africa, the birth-country differences among African women are more dramatic. Approximately 78 percent of immigrant women from Africa are in the labor force. Those from Nigeria, Ghana, Kenya, Liberia, and Sierra Leone are significantly above the group average in labor force participation, while immigrant women from Somalia and Sudan are significantly below the group average.

STRAIGHTFORWARD EXPLANATIONS
FOR LABOR FORCE PARTICIPATION RATES

Figure 4.4 presents the results of linear probability models of labor force participation to determine whether the results in table 4.9 hold after accounting for a basic set of social and demographic characteristics, particularly education. As in the analysis of disparities in the early 1900s, the reference group in the models is black American movers, and I estimate two regression models for both men and women: a baseline model that accounts only for nationality and age and a second model (adjusted) that accounts for differences in work experience, education, English-language proficiency, marital status, residence in a metropolitan area, and state of current residence. The adjusted model for women also controls for the number of their own children and the number of children under the age of five in the household. Because the results are based on linear probability regression models of labor force participation, the coefficient for each country subgroup measures whether members of that group have a higher or lower probability of participating in the labor market than black American movers, the reference group.

To ease the interpretation of the many coefficients, the results are presented as plots. Two estimates are presented for each country group. The open circle represents estimates from the base model and the shaded circle represents estimates from the adjusted model. The line running through each estimate represents the confidence interval. Estimates to the right of the vertical line at zero means that the group is more likely to be in the labor force than black American movers

Figure 4.4 *Regressions of Labor Force Participation for Black American, White American, and Black Immigrant Adults, Ages Twenty-Five to Sixty-Four, 2010–2014*

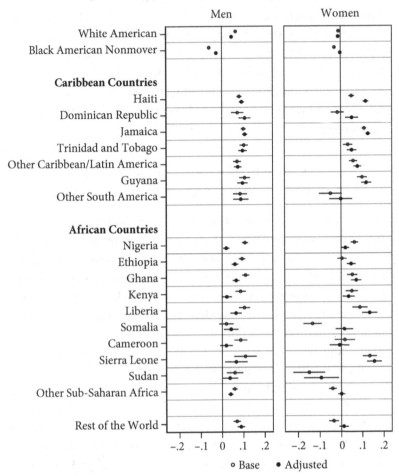

Source: 2010–2014 ACS.

Note: Reference category: black American movers.

(the reference group). Points to the left of the vertical line indicate that the group is less likely to be in the labor force than black American movers. Points where the circle or the confidence interval touches the vertical lines indicate that no statistically significant difference exists between the country group and black American movers. The greater the distance between the estimate and the vertical line, the greater the difference between black American movers and the subgroup in question. For brevity, the discussion focuses on the adjusted results.

Beginning with the results for men, the adjusted model in figure 4.4 shows that, relative to black American movers, the probability of being in the labor market is greater for white Americans and lower for black American nonmovers. Figure 4.4 shows that nearly all the coefficients in the adjusted model for men from both the Caribbean and Africa are to the right of the vertical line, indicating that, compared to black American movers, the probability of being in the labor force is greater for all black immigrant men.

Compared to the results for men, there is greater variation in labor force participation among women. The adjusted model indicates that white American women and women from Sudan are less likely to participate in the labor force than black American movers. The probability of being in the labor force for women from Somalia and Cameroon is statistically indistinguishable from the probability for black American movers. Compared to black American movers, the probability of being in the labor force is greater for all other subgroups of black immigrant women.

Given the significant disparities in educational attainment within the black population, the predictions from theories of labor migration (discussed in chapter 3) that jobs on the lowest rung of the educational distribution might be more attractive to less-educated immigrants than less-educated native populations, as well as the contextual differences in the meaning of education for less-educated individuals, it is important to examine variation in labor force participation among individuals by education level. Figure 4.5 shows results from two regression models: one for individuals with a high school education or less and another for individuals with at least a college education. The shaded circles show estimates for individuals with a high school education or less, and the open circles show estimates for individuals with at least a college education. All models account for differences in work experience, English-language proficiency, marital status, residence in a metropolitan area, and state of current residence. Models for women also control for the number of their own children and the number children under the age of five in the household.

Figure 4.5 shows that among men with at least a college education, there is no statistically significant difference between black American

Figure 4.5 *Regressions of Labor Force Participation for Black Americans, White Americans, and Black Immigrants, by Educational Attainment, Adults Ages Twenty-Five to Sixty-Four, 2010–2014*

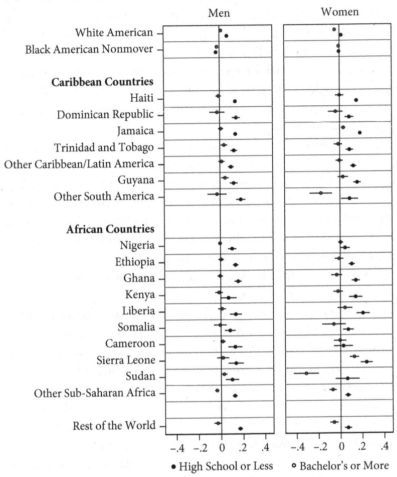

Source: 2010–2014 ACS.
Note: Reference category: black American movers.

movers and black immigrants from most of the focal sending countries. Similarly, among women with at least a college education, there is no statistically significant difference between black American movers and black immigrants from most of the countries in the Caribbean. However, among individuals with at least a college education, the probability of being in the labor force for two groups of African women is significantly different from that of black American movers: immigrants from Sudan have a lower probability of being in the labor force and immigrants from Sierra Leone have a greater probability.

Among individuals with a high school education or less, however, the estimates for immigrant men and women are all to the right of the vertical line, indicating that, relative to black American movers, the probability of being in the labor force is greater for these groups. Although several of the estimates for immigrants from Africa are statistically insignificant, the general pattern of results suggests that the immigrant advantage in labor force participation pertains primarily to individuals with fewer years of education.

Arrival Cohort Analysis

As with the results in figures 4.1 to 4.3, I employ the strategy developed by Borjas to examine trajectories in labor force participation for different black immigrant arrival cohorts as their tenure of U.S. residence increases. Specifically, I use data from both the 2010–2014 waves of the American Community Survey and the Integrated Public Use Micro Series (IPUMS) samples of the 1980, 1990, and 2000 U.S. censuses to analyze the trajectories of different subgroups of black immigrants. The available samples of the 1950 and 1970 U.S. censuses cover only 1 percent of the U.S. population, and the 1960 U.S. census covers 5 percent of the U.S. population. The black immigrant sample sizes during these years are insufficient to generate reliable estimates of labor market trajectories across arrival cohorts. As a result, while I document the profiles of black immigrants who arrived during the 1970s, shortly after the height of the civil rights movement, I do not use data from 1950 to 1970 because of small sample sizes.

Figure 4.6 shows the trajectories of labor force participation for white American men, black American movers (the reference group), and black American nonmovers. It also shows the trajectories of three arrival cohorts of black immigrant men, beginning when they had resided in the United States between zero and five years (the 1975–1979 arrival cohort beginning in 1980, the 1985–1989 arrival cohort beginning in 1990, and the 1995–1999 arrival cohort beginning in 2000). These curves illustrate both differences across immigrant arrival cohorts and the impact of tenure of U.S. residence for a given arrival

Figure 4.6 *Trajectories of Labor Force Participation, Men Ages Twenty-Five to Sixty-Four, 1980–2014*

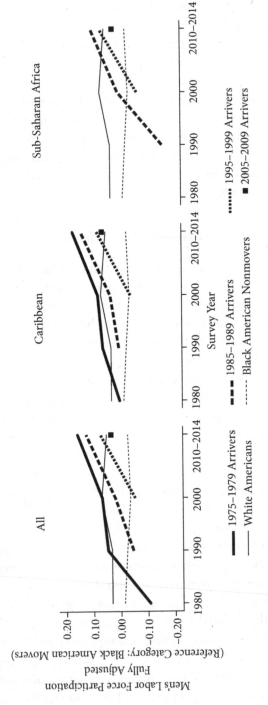

Source: U.S. census and ACS.

cohort. Figure 4.6 displays the labor force participation trajectories for all black male immigrants, black male immigrants from the Caribbean, and black male immigrants from Africa. The information pertaining to the native population is the same on all three graphs. The results shown in figure 4.6 adjust for a standard set of social and demographic characteristics. The graphs are based on a series of regression models for each period; the respective coefficients for each arrival cohort and all subgroups of native blacks are plotted for the respective period. A curve that hovers around zero indicates that there are no differences between that group and black American movers, the reference group.

The curves in figure 4.6 show that labor force participation for white American men was greater than the rate for black American movers from 1980 to 2014. For most of the focal period, compared to black American movers, the probability of being in the labor force was lower for black American nonmovers.

The graph for all black immigrants reveals that when they first arrived in the United States, compared to black American movers, each of the three arrival cohorts shown in figure 4.6 had a lower probability of being in the labor force. The earliest arrival cohort had the largest deficit relative to black American movers, while the most recent arrival cohort had the smallest deficit.

In the 2010–2014 time period, the 1975–1979 arrival cohort had resided in the United States between thirty-five and thirty-nine years, the 1985–1989 arrival cohort had resided in the United States between twenty-five and twenty-nine years, and the 1995–1999 arrival cohort had resided in the United States between fifteen and nineteen years. Figure 4.6 shows that in 2014, the 1975–1979, 1985–1989, and 1995–1999 arrival cohorts had a greater probability of being in the labor force than black American nonmovers, black American movers, and white Americans.

There is significant variation in labor force participation among Caribbean and African men. While the initial probability of being in the labor force for Caribbean men has remained relatively stable across the focal period, the estimates for African immigrants have varied considerably. Because few African immigrants arrived in the United States prior to 1990, I graph only estimates for the 1985–1989 and 1995–1999 arrival cohorts for this group. In 1990, the probability of being in the labor market was sixteen percentage points lower among the 1985–1989 arrival cohort from Africa compared to black American movers. By contrast, in 2000, the deficit was only seven percentage points for black African men who arrived between 1995 and 1999. Despite initial deficits, particularly among early arrivals from Africa, the probability of being in the labor force for every arrival cohort of men from Africa and the Caribbean eventually overtook or converged with that of white American men.

Figure 4.7 provides similar estimates for women. In stark contrast to the results for men, between 1980 and 2014, compared to black American movers, the probability of being in the labor force was lower or similar for white American women. Moreover, while the initial likelihood of participating in the labor force for women from Africa mirrors the pattern observed for men, the initial likelihood varies considerably among Caribbean immigrants. Upon arrival in the country, the probability of being in the labor market for the 1975–1979 and 1985–1989 arrival cohorts was greater than that of both groups of black Americans (movers and nonmovers) as well as that of white Americans. The 1995–1999 arrival cohort, however, had a lower probability of being in the labor force than black American movers when they first arrived in the United States. The arrival cohort variation in labor force participation among both Caribbean and African immigrant women highlights the degree of selectivity for both groups.

Because the regression models control for a standard set of social and demographic characteristics, including education, disparities across the groups are residual gaps that could be viewed as a measure of the degree of selectivity across arrival cohorts. For example, if the decision to move is highly correlated with factors such as motivation and wealth, factors that are not measured in the regression models, the arrival cohort coefficients suggest that earlier arrivals from the Caribbean are more positively selected than more recent arrival cohorts from the region. In contrast, the estimates for African men and women suggest that more recent arrival cohorts are more positively selected than earlier arrivals. Despite the variation across arrival cohorts, every arrival cohort of black immigrant women was substantially more likely to participate in the labor force than both black and white American women as their tenure of U.S. residence increased.

Figure 4.7 *Trajectories of Labor Force Participation, Women Ages Twenty-Five to Sixty-Four, 1980–2014*

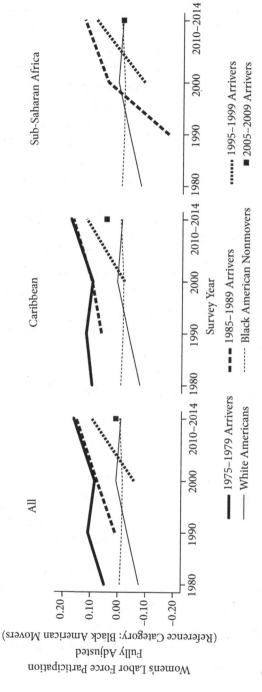

Source: U.S. census and ACS.

I next analyze trajectories of labor force participation across arrival cohorts by country of origin (see online appendix figure A4.1 [men] and figure A4.2 [women]).[29] Because the sample sizes for some groups are small, I estimate models for only the top five sending countries from the Caribbean—Haiti, the Dominican Republic, Jamaica, Trinidad and Tobago, and Guyana—and the top three sending countries from Africa: Nigeria, Ethiopia, and Ghana. Among men, while trajectories of labor force participation vary across countries to a certain degree, every arrival cohort from every country (except the earliest arrival cohort of men from the Dominican Republic) converges or slightly overtakes the labor force participation probabilities of white American men.

Among women, every arrival cohort of women from every country eventually overtakes the labor force participation rates of white American women. Mirroring the regional patterns, upon first arrival in the United States, early arrival cohorts from the Caribbean had higher labor force participation rates than more recent arrivals. Women from Africa followed the opposite pattern, with more recent arrival cohorts having higher labor force participation rates than earlier arrival cohorts.

Employment and Earnings

The results from the prior section show that most arrival cohorts of black immigrant men and women from each of the focal countries eventually surpass the labor force participation rates of both white and black Americans. I now turn to analyzing demand-side determinants of labor market success: employment and earnings.

THE BASIC FACTS: EMPLOYMENT

I start by presenting estimates of employment for the focal groups in the 2010–2014 time period. I define employment as the proportion of individuals who are in the labor force (that is, either currently working or looking for work) and are currently working. Table 4.10 shows that 85 percent of black Americans are employed compared to 90 percent of all black immigrants, 88 percent of black Caribbean immigrants,

Table 4.10 *Employment Rate of Adults Ages Twenty-Five to Sixty-Four,*
by Race and Country of Origin, 2010–2014

	Men	Women
Native whites	0.93	0.94
Black Americans	0.85	0.88
Black American movers	0.88	0.89
Black American nonmovers	0.84	0.87
All black immigrants	0.90	0.89
Black Caribbean immigrants	0.88	0.90
Haiti	0.87	0.87
Dominican Republic	0.89	0.87
Jamaica	0.88	0.91
Trinidad and Tobago	0.87	0.91
Guyana	0.89	0.91
Black African immigrants	0.92	0.89
Nigeria	0.92	0.92
Ethiopia	0.95	0.89
Ghana	0.92	0.90
Kenya	0.95	0.92
Liberia	0.89	0.91
Somalia	0.86	0.78
Cameroon	0.90	0.91
Sierra Leone	0.89	0.92
Sudan	0.92	0.78

Source: 2010–2014 ACS.
Note: Weighted values.

and 92 percent of African immigrants. Employment status, however, varies among black Americans by internal migration status, with 88 percent of black American movers being employed compared to 84 percent of black American nonmovers. Only immigrant men from the Dominican Republic and Guyana (both 89 percent) have an employment advantage, albeit a small one, over black American male movers. Men from Somalia have a lower employment rate than black American movers, and immigrants from Liberia, Cameroon, and Sierra Leone have a similar probability of being employed. All other country subgroups of African men are more likely to be employed than black American male movers.

Table 4.10 shows that, among women, 94 percent of white American women in the labor force are employed, a higher percentage than every subgroup of black women, native or immigrant. Mirroring the pattern among men, black American female movers are more likely to be employed than black American female nonmovers (89 percent and 87 percent, respectively). In contrast to the results for men, however, black American female movers and black immigrant women (collectively) have the same likelihood of being employed. Looking at the regional estimates, there is no substantive disparity in employment between women from the Caribbean and Africa. Among women from the specific sending countries, only those from Nigeria, Kenya, and Sierra Leone are substantially more likely to be employed than black American female movers (92 percent, 92 percent, and 93 percent, respectively).

STRAIGHTFORWARD EXPLANATIONS: EMPLOYMENT

To better understand the factors driving the disparities in table 4.10, figure 4.8 presents the results of linear probability models of employment status for both men and women. The base and adjusted models include the same set of controls as the models of labor force participation. I focus the discussion on the adjusted models.

As in the descriptive results, figure 4.8 shows that relative to black American male movers, the probability of being employed is greater for white American men and lower for black American nonmovers. The adjusted model also shows that men from only four of these fourteen countries—Ethiopia, Ghana, Kenya, and Sudan—are more likely to be employed than black American male movers. For all other subgroups of black immigrant men, the probability of being employed is similar to that of black American male movers.

Similar to the pattern among men, once a standard set of social and demographic characteristics is controlled, the probability of being in the labor force is greater for white American women compared to black American female movers. There is no statistically significant difference in the probability of being employed between black American female movers and nonmovers. Figure 4.8 shows that one subgroup of immigrant women from the Caribbean, Jamaican women, are more likely to be employed than black American female movers. Women

Figure 4.8 *Regressions of Employment for Black American, White American, and Black Immigrant Adults, Ages Twenty-Five to Sixty-Four, 2010–2014*

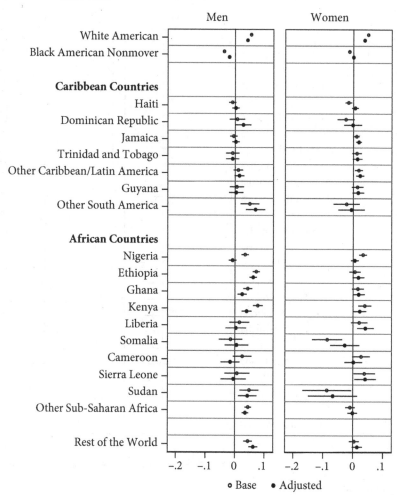

○ Base   ● Adjusted

Source: 2010–2014 ACS.

Note: Reference category: black American movers.

Figure 4.9 *Regressions of Employment for Black Americans, White Americans, and Black Immigrants, by Educational Attainment, Adults Ages Twenty-Five to Sixty-Four, 2010–2014*

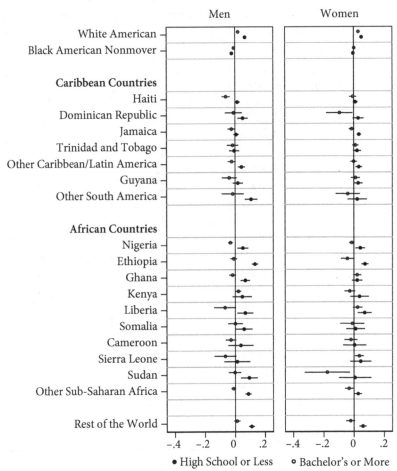

Source: 2010–2014 ACS.
Note: Reference category: black American movers.

from two country subgroups from sub-Saharan Africa—Liberia and Sierra Leone—are more likely to be employed than black American female movers.

Figure 4.9 shows the results of models partitioned by educational status. Similar to the results for labor force participation, among both men and women with at least a college education, immigrant women from Sierra Leone are the only subgroup that is more likely to be employed than black American female movers. Among immigrants with a high school education or less, however, men from six countries—the Dominican Republic, Nigeria, Ethiopia, Ghana, Liberia, and Sudan—are more likely to be employed than black American movers. Among women, individuals from Jamaica, Nigeria, Liberia, and Ethiopia are more likely to be employed than black American movers.

Similar to the labor force participation results, I estimate models that track changes in the probability of being employed across immigrant arrival cohorts (see online appendix figures A4.3 and A4.4). Among men, the results show that upon arrival in the United States, the probability of being employed for Caribbean men who arrived between 1975 and 1979 was similar to that of black American movers, and the probability of being employed for Caribbean men in the 1985–1989 and 1995–1999 arrival cohorts was lower than that of black American movers. Although men in the 1975–1979 arrival cohort experienced very little improvement in the probability of being employed as their tenure of U.S. residence increased, the relative probability of being employed for both the 1985–1989 arrival cohort and the 1995–1999 arrival cohort increased over time, with the probability for the 1985–1989 arrival cohort eventually converging with that of black American movers, and the probability of being employed for the 1995–1999 arrival cohort eventually overtaking the probability of black American movers but still falling short of the probability for white American men.

For the two arrival cohorts from Africa, both the 1985–1989 and 1995–1999 arrival cohorts were slightly more likely to be employed upon arrival in the United States than black American movers. Although the 1985–1989 arrival cohort experienced a slight decrease in the probability of being employed after residing in the United States for ten years, the 1995–1999 arrival cohort experienced an improvement, overtaking the employment probability of black American movers.

Among women from the Caribbean, upon arrival in the United States, the probability of being employed for the 1975–1979 arrival cohort and the 1995–1999 arrival cohort was lower than that of both black American movers and black American nonmovers. The probability of being employed for Caribbean women who arrived between 1975 and 1979 eventually converged with the employment probability of black American movers, and the employment probabilities of those in the two more recent arrival cohorts increased enough to eventually converge with the employment probabilities of white Americans.

Among women from Africa, relative to black American movers, the probability of being employed for both the 1985–1989 and the 1995–1999 arrival cohorts was lower when they first arrived in the United States. However, the probability of being employed for both cohorts eventually overtook the employment probabilities of black American movers.

I also analyze the employment trajectories for the five Caribbean and three African countries with large enough samples to power the cohort analysis (see online appendix figures A4.5 and A4.6). Among both men and women, at least one arrival cohort from each country, with the exception of men from Haiti, Trinidad and Tobago, and Nigeria, is projected to eventually converge with the employment rates of white Americans.

THE BASIC FACTS: EARNINGS

Turning to earnings, table 4.11 presents estimates of weekly earnings for white Americans, black Americans, and black immigrants collectively and by region of birth. As discussed in prior sections, several decades of research have attempted to answer the following question: do black immigrants, particularly those from the English-speaking Caribbean, have better labor market outcomes than black Americans? In terms of earnings, the descriptive data suggest that the answer varies considerably by birth country, with most black immigrant subgroups having lower weekly earnings than black American movers. Among men, black American movers earn approximately $941 per week, and only immigrants from Guyana, Nigeria, and Cameroon have higher average weekly earnings. Table 4.11 shows a similar pattern among black women: black American movers have weekly earnings of $793, and only immigrants from Nigeria earn more. With the exception of women from Nigeria, every subgroup of blacks, native or immigrant, has lower earnings than white Americans.

STRAIGHTFORWARD EXPLANATIONS: EARNINGS

Figure 4.10 examines the degree to which the disparities documented in table 4.11 are the result of disparities in observable characteristics

Table 4.11 *Weekly Earnings of Adults Ages Twenty-Five to Sixty-Four, by Race and Country of Origin, 2010–2014*

	Men	Women
Native whites	$1,263	$816
Black Americans	815	685
Black American movers	941	793
Black American nonmovers	747	635
All black immigrants	842	682
Black Caribbean immigrants	799	673
Haiti	683	577
Dominican Republic	700	455
Jamaica	829	720
Trinidad and Tobago	904	764
Guyana	951	750
Black African immigrants	881	692
Nigeria	1,141	908
Ethiopia	766	584
Ghana	921	731
Kenya	897	755
Liberia	836	581
Somalia	585	417
Cameroon	987	713
Sierra Leone	895	721
Sudan	682	457

Source: 2010–2014 ACS.
Note: Weekly earnings equals wage/salary income plus positive business income.
Weighted values.

that correlate with earnings. Figure 4.10 presents results from base and adjusted models of log(weekly earnings). Among men, the most striking disparity is between blacks in general and whites. White American men earn considerably more than black American movers and more than every subgroup of black immigrant men. The base model shows that only black immigrant men from Nigeria and Kenya have greater earnings than black American male movers. All other subgroups of immigrant men either earn less than or have similar earnings as black American movers. After accounting for a standard set of characteristics, no subgroup of black immigrants has greater earnings than black American movers.

Figure 4.10 *Regressions of Log(Weekly Earnings) for Black American, White American, and Black Immigrant Adults, Ages Twenty-Five to Sixty-Four, 2010–2014*

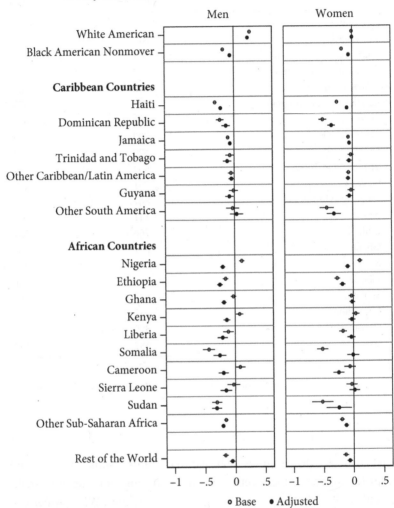

Source: 2010–2014 ACS.
Note: Reference category: black American movers.

Mirroring the results for men, in the adjusted model, black American female nonmovers earn less than black American female movers. Moreover, women from eight of the fourteen focal country subgroups included in the model earn significantly less than black American female movers; women from the remaining six country subgroups have comparable earnings. Figure 4.11 shows models partitioned by educational attainment. While prior tables show that black immigrants' advantage in labor force participation and employment is truncated among the least educated, figure 4.11 shows that the earnings gap between black American movers and nearly all subgroups of black immigrants is least pronounced among the least educated. This finding suggests that although less-educated immigrants are more likely to participate in the labor market or hold jobs than less-educated black Americans, they tend to hold jobs that offer lower remuneration.

EARNINGS ASSIMILATION: ARRIVAL COHORT EFFECTS

Given that time spent in the United States is a unique determinant of immigrants' earnings, figure 4.12 shows the earnings trajectories for three groups of men: white Americans, black American movers (the reference group), and black American nonmovers. The curves show that white American men earned at least 17 percent more than black American male movers in every period and that black American nonmovers earned 6 to 8 percent less than black American movers in every period. The graph for black immigrant men from the Caribbean reveals that every arrival cohort of Caribbean immigrant men earned significantly less (at least 19 percent less) than black American male movers when they first arrived in the United States. For the two earliest arrivals cohorts, after their second or third decade of U.S. residence, the earnings of cohort members had almost converged with those of black American male movers.

A strikingly different pattern emerges for men from sub-Saharan Africa. First, upon arrival in the United States, every black African arrival cohort earned significantly less than both black American movers and the parallel cohort from the Caribbean. Although the pace of earnings growth for both cohorts of African immigrants is considerably greater than the growth among Caribbean immigrants,

Figure 4.11 *Regressions of Log(Weekly Earnings) for Black Americans, White Americans, and Black Immigrants, by Educational Attainment, Adults Ages Twenty-Five to Sixty-Four, 2010–2014*

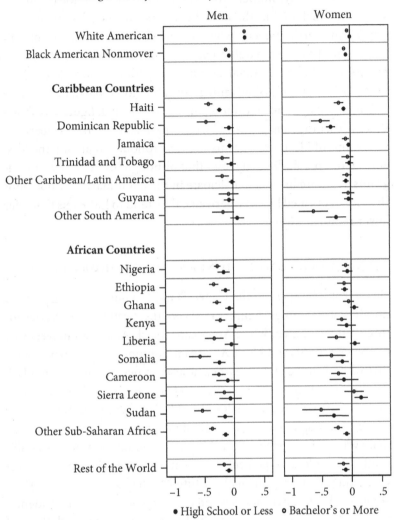

Source: 2010–2014 ACS.

Note: Reference category: black American movers.

Figure 4.12 *Trajectories of Log(Weekly Earnings), Men Ages Twenty-Five to Sixty-Four, 1980–2014*

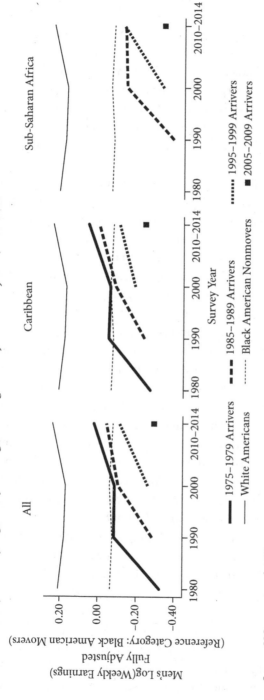

Source: U.S. census and ACS.

no cohort of African men overtook the earnings of black American male movers.

Figure 4.13 repeats the analysis of earnings assimilation for women. The Caribbean and African curves show that after accounting for observable characteristics, the two early arrival cohorts of women from the Caribbean surpassed the earnings of both black and white American women after residing in the United States for at least one decade, and their earnings continued to grow into the second decade of U.S. residence. Similarly, the graph for immigrants from sub-Saharan Africa shows significant growth as immigrants' tenure in the United States increased. Although both cohorts earned at least 30 percent less than black American female movers when they first arrived in the United States, the earnings of both cohorts converged with those of black female American movers and white American women after the cohorts had resided in the United States for a decade.

Figures 4.14 (men) and 4.15 (women) examine whether the patterns observed for the two regional subgroups hold for the specific sending countries in those subgroups. Again, owing to small sample sizes, I am able to provide country-specific analyses for only three African countries: Nigeria, Ethiopia, and Ghana. Among immigrants from the five Caribbean countries shown in figure 4.14, immigrant men from Jamaica and Guyana have similar earnings profiles. For both groups, the earnings of the 1975–1979 arrival cohort appeared to overtake the earnings of black American movers after the cohort had resided in the United States for approximately two decades. Immigrant men who arrived from Trinidad and Tobago between 1975 and 1979 also surpassed the earnings of black American male movers, although it took the group three decades to achieve this milestone. The earnings trajectories of immigrants from Haiti and the Dominican Republic are the two notable outliers on the graph among the Caribbean countries. Relative to immigrant men from Jamaica, Trinidad and Tobago, and Guyana, those from Haiti and the Dominican Republic had larger initial earnings deficits.

Among immigrant men from sub-Saharan Africa, none of the three arrival cohorts shown were able to overtake the earnings of black American movers. Although individuals from all three countries had large initial earnings deficits upon arrival in the United States, the deficit was most pronounced for immigrants from Ethiopia.

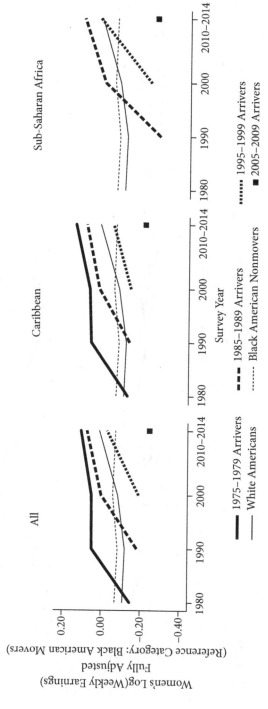

Figure 4.13 *Trajectories of Log(Weekly Earnings), Women Ages Twenty-Five to Sixty-Four, 1980–2014*

Source: U.S. census and ACS.

Figure 4.14 *Trajectories of Log(Weekly Earnings), Men Ages Twenty-Five to Sixty-Four, 1980–2014*

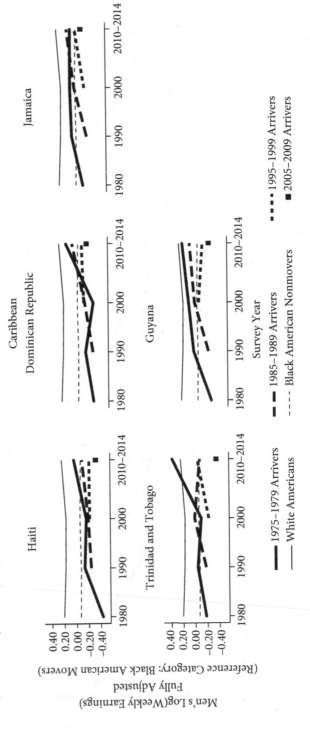

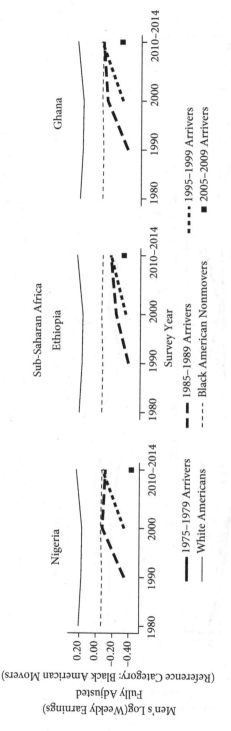

Source: U.S. census and ACS.

Figure 4.15 *Trajectories of Log(Weekly Earnings), Women Ages Twenty-Five to Sixty-Four, 1980–2014*

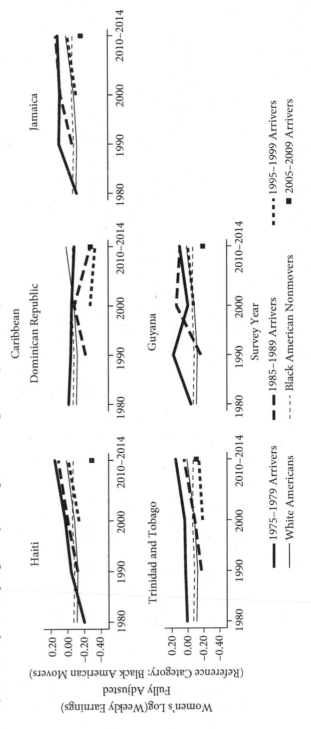

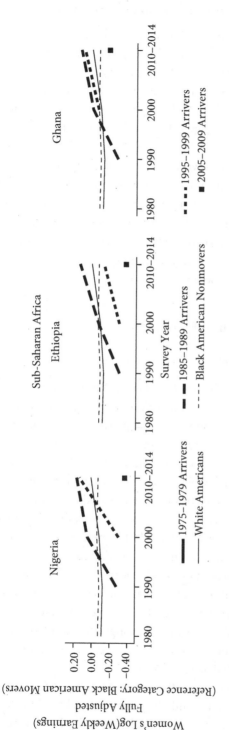

Source: U.S. census and ACS.

Even after two decades of U.S. residence, men who migrated from Ethiopia between 1985 and 1989 had lower earnings than black American nonmovers. Of the cohorts with the longest tenure of U.S. residence—immigrant men who arrived between 1985 and 1989 and between 1995 and 1999—only those from Nigeria and Ghana were able to converge with the earnings of black American nonmovers.

Figure 4.15 shows that almost all subgroups and cohorts of black Caribbean women experienced favorable earnings trajectories. With the exception of immigrants from the Dominican Republic, all black immigrant women in the 1975–1979 and 1985–1989 arrival cohorts overtook the earnings of white American women and black American female movers. Similarly, women in the 1985–1989 arrival cohort from all three African countries also exceeded the earnings of black American movers and white American women.

Chapter Summary

EARLY TWENTIETH-CENTURY RESULTS

Using data from the complete count (100 percent) of the 1910, 1920, 1930, and 1940 U.S. censuses of the New York metropolitan area, I provide the most complete and comprehensive analysis to date of disparities between black Caribbean immigrants and black Americans during the early twentieth century. I find no consistent evidence of labor market advantages favoring black Caribbean immigrants during this period, in contrast to accounts from qualitative studies.[30] Although several results pertaining to occupational prestige show a slight advantage for black Caribbean immigrants over black American movers, in most of these cases black American nonmovers had jobs with more prestige than the jobs held by both black American movers and Caribbean immigrants, which contradicts the idea of an immigrant advantage. Moreover, unlike the post-1980 results, estimates of changes in labor force participation and occupational prestige during the period reveal very modest improvements in labor market outcomes the longer immigrants lived in the United States.

The most robust and consistent disparities documented in this section are those between whites and all groups of blacks. With the exception of labor force participation (blacks typically had higher labor force participation than whites), whites had more favorable outcomes than blacks for all measures of labor market success. Further, these results persist after controlling for a standard set of characteristics known to predict labor market success, such as education and literacy. This pattern suggests that whatever degree of unobserved selectivity or cultural differences existed within New York City's black population in the early 1900s, these differences were not pronounced enough to overcome the enormity of racism during the period.

CONTEMPORARY RESULTS

Labor Force Participation

My review of the literature on labor migration in chapter 3 highlighted several mechanisms that might produce disparities in labor force participation between black immigrants and the U.S.-born. First, labor market opportunities in the United States compare favorably to those in the focal Caribbean and African countries. Consequently, immigrants, particularly less-educated immigrants, may have a more favorable view of U.S. labor market opportunities than the U.S.-born, which could lead to higher labor force participation rates.

The substantial improvement in living conditions associated with moving for black immigrants, as well as the factors outlined in the theories of labor migration discussed in chapter 3, suggests that the reservation wage of immigrants—the minimum wage required to induce individuals into the labor market—is considerably lower among many subgroups of black immigrants, particularly those with lower levels of education. Indeed, for less-educated Caribbean and African immigrants, even the worst-paying jobs in the United States offer greater financial opportunities than the jobs available in their home countries. At the same time, because the financial motives and family networks of U.S.-born individuals reside in the United States, Americans, black or white, would tend to consider many of the jobs held by immigrants to be dead-end employment. Consequently, less-educated black immigrants are likely to have higher labor market participation rates than black Americans.

To evaluate these propositions, I analyzed variation in labor force participation for black Americans, white Americans, and black immigrants, using data from the 2010–2014 American Community Surveys. The analyses produced four key findings. First, white American women had lower labor force participation rates than black American female movers, black American female nonmovers, and women in nearly every black immigrant subgroup studied. Second, for almost every country subgroup studied, as immigrants' tenure of U.S. residence increased, their labor force participation rates eventually surpassed those of black American movers. Third, the initial deficit in labor force participation (relative to black American movers) was larger among immigrants from sub-Saharan Africa than among Caribbean immigrants.

The analysis also produced a finding that has been missed in most prior studies on the labor market experiences of black immigrants: black immigrant men and women from most of the focal countries eventually surpassed the labor force participation rates of *both black and white* Americans.

Table 4.12 provides a set of indicators of social and economic well-being, including unemployment, homicide rates, gross national income, and poverty for the United States and the fourteen focal black immigrant-sending countries. Across these indicators, there are only a few instances in which the origin country has a better profile than the United States. For most indicator-country combinations, the well-being of individuals residing in the United States is considerably better than that of individuals residing in the black immigrant-sending countries. Moreover, the remittance data shown in table 4.12 indicate that the desire to achieve financial and family objectives at home motivates many immigrants. Remittances account for a significant share of GDP in Jamaica, the Dominican Republic, Guyana, Ghana, Haiti, and Liberia. In sum, a combination of insights from push-pull theories of labor migration, the new economics of labor migration theory, and world systems theory provides a more comprehensive framework for understanding the disparities in labor force participation between black Americans and black immigrants.

Employment

Employment captures not only an individual's desire to work but also supply-side factors that have an impact on labor market outcomes.

Table 4.12 *Origin-Country Social and Economic Characteristics*

Country	Gross National Income per Capita (2011 PPP$), 2015	Inequality in Income, 2015	Gini Coefficient, 2010–2015	Employment-to-Population Ratio, 2015	Unemployment Rate, 2015	Homicide Rate, 2010–2014	Remittances, Inflows (% of GDP), 2015	Net Migration Rate, 2010–2015	National Poverty Line, 2005–2014	PPP$1.90 a Day, 2005–2014
United States	53,245	27.0	41.1	58.8	5.3	3.9	0.04	3.2		
Trinidad and Tobago	28,049	21.9		60.5	3.8	25.9	0.45	-0.7		
Jamaica	8,350	30.1		56.0	13.7	36.1	16.86	-7.0	19.9	1.7
Dominican Republic	12,756	28.1	47.1	55.9	14.4	17.4	7.74	-3.0	32.4	2.3
Guyana	6,884	24.4		52.9	11.2	20.4	9.27	-7.2		
Ghana	3,839	31.7	42.8	72.1	6.3	1.7	13.16	-0.4	24.2	25.2
Kenya	2,881	33.1	48.5	60.9	9.2	5.9	2.46	-0.2	45.9	33.6
Nigeria	5,443	28.4	43.0	53.1	5.8	10.1	4.29	-0.4	46.0	53.5
Cameroon	2,894	23.1	46.5	72.5	4.6	2.7	0.84	-0.5	37.5	24.0
Haiti	1,657	48.4	60.8	61.7	6.9	10.0	24.73	-2.9	58.5	53.9
Sudan	3,846	—	35.4	41.6	13.6	6.5	0.18	-4.2	46.5	14.9
Ethiopia	1,523	9.5	33.2	78.4	5.5	8.0	1.01	-0.1	29.6	33.5
Liberia	683	22.7	36.5	58.4	4.2	3.2	31.21	-0.9	63.8	68.6
Sierra Leone	1,529	19.2	34.0	64.5	3.4	1.9	1.48	-0.7	52.9	52.3
Somalia	294	—	—	50.2	7.5	5.6	—	-7.9	—	—

Source: United Nations Development Program (UNDP) 2016 *Human Development Report.*

For example, labor market discrimination can produce disparities in employment between black Americans and black immigrants as well as between blacks and whites. Although discrimination also affects wages, denying individuals the opportunity to work is the first step in the discrimination process. If a hiring manager holds a negative perception of a minority group, he or she may simply refuse to hire members of the stigmatized group, creating employment disparities between stigmatized and nonstigmatized groups.[31] Therefore, while workers have some degree of agency over both labor force participation and employment, employment also captures differential patterns of discrimination.

My employment results produced several key findings. First, among men, black American nonmovers had lower employment rates than black American movers. Among women, however, black American movers and black American nonmovers had similar employment rates. Second, among men, the results from the 2010–2014 time period show that, compared to black American movers, black immigrant men from Ethiopia, Ghana, Kenya, and Sudan were more likely to be employed. All other groups of immigrant men had employment rates similar to those of black American movers. Among women in the 2010–2014 period, relative to black American movers, individuals from Jamaica, Liberia, and Sierra Leone were more likely to be employed. Models partitioned by educational attainment, however, revealed that any employment advantages accrued primarily to individuals with less than a high school education. Among individuals with at least a college education, there were fewer disparities among blacks.

For the eight countries where the data allowed me to track trajectories in employment over time for different arrival cohorts—Haiti, the Dominican Republic, Jamaica, Trinidad and Tobago, Guyana, Nigeria, Ethiopia, and Ghana—the results suggest that, with the exception of men from Nigeria, at least one immigrant arrival cohort, typically the post-1985 arrivals, from each subgroup eventually surpassed the employment rates of black American movers. The employment trajectories also show that the employment rates of black immigrant women who arrived after 1985 eventually converged with those of black American female movers. Indeed, several subgroups of black immigrant women included in this analysis were on track to surpass the employment rates of white American women.

Earnings

Although the vast majority of the research on labor market disparities among blacks focuses on earnings disparities between black Americans and black immigrants, the mechanism producing earnings disparities among blacks in many ways involves a more complex set of processes than the mechanisms producing disparities in labor force participation or employment. Along with differences in observable skills, earnings disparities reflect at least four additional factors: (1) patterns of labor market discrimination, which can vary between native and immigrant populations; (2) differential patterns of labor market clustering, such as ethnic niches and enclave employment; (3) challenges that individuals face finding a job at their skill level, which could lead to skills-occupation mismatches, particularly among highly skilled immigrants; and (4) differences in unobserved factors that make one group more productive than another.[32] Each of these factors complicate researchers' ability to isolate the exact mechanism producing earnings disparities among blacks.

The analyses in this section produced four major findings. First, using data from 2010–2014, after adjusting for a standard set of social and demographic characteristics, I find that white men earned nearly 20 percent more than black American male movers, and that no subgroup of black immigrant men earned more than black American male movers. Similarly, the models from the 2010–2014 time period show that, while black American female movers had similar earnings as white American women, most immigrant women had similar or lower earnings than both white American women and black American female movers.

The models of earnings trajectories show that for some cohorts of black Caribbean men, earnings converged with or slightly overtook the earnings of black American movers, while immigrant men from Nigeria, Ethiopia, and Ghana reached the earnings level only of black American nonmovers. In remarkable contrast, cohorts of women from Haiti, Jamaica, Trinidad and Tobago, Guyana, Nigeria, Ethiopia, and Ghana were on track to surpass the earnings of both black American women and white American women. Moreover, relative to black immigrants from non-English-speaking countries (Haiti, the Dominican Republic, and Ethiopia), those from English-speaking countries in Africa and the Caribbean experienced more rapid earnings growth.

Conclusion

In this chapter, I conducted a comprehensive and nuanced analysis of labor market disparities among blacks in the United States that revealed several macrolevel patterns. First, models using the complete count data from the U.S. Census of Population and Housing from 1910 to 1940, as well as samples from the U.S. Census of Population and Housing from 1980 to 2014, reveal that black American movers tend to have better outcomes than black American nonmovers across most outcomes and in most years, highlighting the strong correlation between moving and labor market outcomes for black Americans. Second, although some groups of black immigrants outperform black Americans movers, the labor market outcomes of black immigrants are more similar to those of black American movers than to those of black American nonmovers. Because the mover-nonmover comparisons allow me to hold constant factors associated with black Americans (such as culture) and to vary migration status, the results show that to some degree disparities between black Americans and black immigrants are driven by selective migration.

Third, black immigrants did not outperform black Americans in the U.S. labor market in the early twentieth century. Across nearly every focal outcome for the first four decades of the twentieth century, black immigrants had similar or worse outcomes than black American movers. This finding suggests that any differences between black immigrants and black Americans, observed or unobserved, were not large enough to produce meaningful labor market disparities between the two groups. Indeed, disparities among blacks did not emerge until the advent of legislative and institutional changes that made America a less overtly racist society.

Fourth, the most consistent immigrant advantage occurs in labor force participation and employment. For example, as immigrants' tenure of U.S. residence increases, the labor force participation rate of

nearly every black immigrant arrival cohort, for all the countries studied, eventually converges with or exceeds the rates of both black American movers and white Americans. Although there is more variation
in the employment results than in the labor force participation results,
many arrival cohorts of black immigrants, both men and women, are
on a path to overtake the employment rates of both black American
movers and white Americans. If scholars use the favorable labor force
participation and employment profiles of black immigrants to claim
that black Americans suffer from a cultural deficit (as has been done
in much of the extensive literature on nativity-based disparities among
blacks), they must also acknowledge that white Americans suffer from
a similar deficit. As shown earlier, these findings are clearly better
explained by differences in the benefits of low-skilled employment for
immigrants and natives.

Fifth, the chapter has highlighted a less-appreciated aspect of racial
disparities in labor market outcomes: gender. If black immigrants represent an economic success story, then the story is really about black
immigrant women. Black immigrant women from all focal countries
except the Dominican Republic surpass both black American female
movers and white American women in terms of earnings. Moreover,
black American female movers earn the same as or more than white
American women. The results show that all subgroups of immigrant
men earn less than white American men and that most earn less than
black American men, demonstrating that gender clearly stratifies labor
market outcomes in the United States. Research on occupational niches
highlights the gendered nature of work in the United States, with men
and women routinely holding jobs in different occupations and industries.[33] Given the significant occupational and industrial stratification along gender lines, the findings in this chapter suggest that black
women in general and black immigrant women in particular may face
a more welcoming labor market than black men—a difference that
shapes black immigrant women's context of reception and labor market outcomes.[34]

Lastly, in chapter 3 I argued that, among black immigrants, those
from Somalia, Sierra Leone, Sudan, Haiti, and the Dominican Republic experienced a negative reception context, which could lead to poor
labor market outcomes. The results provide partial support for this
claim. Although immigrants from these countries have employment

rates similar to those of immigrant groups that are theorized to experience a neutral context of reception, immigrants from Haiti, the Dominican Republic, Somalia, and Sudan have lower earnings. Moreover, compared to immigrants from the English-speaking Caribbean, the earnings growth profiles of immigrants from Haiti and the Dominican Republic are more modest. Because of small sample sizes, I am not able to track the earnings trajectories of immigrants from Somalia and Sudan. These findings provide partial support for the context-of-reception framework.

CHAPTER FIVE

ACHIEVING THE AMERICAN DREAM: PAST AND PRESENT HOMEOWNERSHIP DISPARITIES

Chapter 4 illustrated the considerable variation in labor market outcomes among blacks in the United States. Labor market disparities, however, are only one metric of overall economic well-being. Another major aspect of well-being is a group's wealth holdings.[1] In addition to providing individuals with financial reserves, wealth buffers and softens the impact of financial shocks, such as periods of unemployment and medical emergencies.[2] Wealth also allows individuals to take economic risks that could result in long-term financial rewards. For example, in addition to the incredible power of compound interest and equity growth that benefits those with more wealth, a person with greater wealth holdings may be more willing to start a new business or invest in education, both of which could result in favorable economic returns. Wealth impacts individuals' labor market prospects. During periods of unemployment, those with greater wealth may search longer for a job at their skill level rather than hastily taking a lower-level job, which could affect lifetime earnings and wealth accumulation.[3] Consequently, disparities in wealth among Americans contribute significantly to racial disparities in overall well-being.

A large literature documents significant and persistent racial disparities in wealth among Americans. In 1983, the median wealth of white families was eight times the median wealth of black families.[4] By 2013, this wealth gap had increased by 63 percent, with the median wealth of white families at $141,000 compared to $11,000 for black families.[5] A key factor driving wealth disparities between black and white Americans is homeownership.

Home equity comprises the bulk of the wealth portfolios of all but the wealthiest American families, regardless of race.[6] In 2017, home equity accounted for 92 percent of the personal net worth of African American homeowners and 58 percent of that of white homeowners.[7] It thus follows that racial differences in homeownership account for a large portion of the overall racial wealth gap between black and white Americans. Oliver and Shapiro document that the wealth gap between black and white Americans nearly tripled between 1984 and 2009.[8] The largest driver of the growth in that gap was years of homeownership, which translates into higher levels of home equity.

Although many in the real estate and lending industries argue that disparities in homeownership stem exclusively from the profit-maximizing decisions of firms—implying that blacks are less likely to own homes because they represent greater financial risk to lenders—studies have found that this gap in homeownership stems from racial discrimination. Research has shown that, dating back to the 1990s, racial disparities in mortgage approvals—a primary determinant of homeownership—persist even after controlling for the age of the home being purchased and borrower characteristics such as income.[9] Moreover, Sunwoong Kim and Gregory Squires showed that a lending institution's loan approval rates for black Americans increases as the proportion of minority employees within the institution increases.[10] Under the assumption that minority employees are less likely to discriminate against minority borrowers based on their race, this finding supports the argument that racial discrimination plays some role in producing differential patterns of homeownership between blacks and whites in the United States.[11]

Although a number of studies have shown that homeownership rates among blacks in the United States have historically been lower than those of whites, little is known about how patterns of homeownership vary among blacks by nativity.[12] In a descriptive study for the Pew Research Center, Monica Anderson has shown that, relative to both black Americans and all other immigrant groups, on average, black immigrants had the lowest rates of homeownership in 2013.[13] Subpopulation differences also exist among black immigrants, with those from the Caribbean exhibiting higher homeownership rates than those from Africa. These findings suggest that if not appropriately taken into account, changes in the composition of the black population could skew our understanding of the factors producing the black-white homeownership gap over time.

This chapter documents and contextualizes homeownership disparities among black Americans, white Americans, and black immigrants during both the pre– and post–civil rights eras. In chapter 3, I argued that two factors are responsible for any advantages achieved by black immigrants over black Americans: institutional changes that made the United States a less overtly racist society and selective migration. If this proposition holds, then homeownership disparities between black Americans and black immigrants should be smaller or nonexistent during the pre–civil rights era and emerge only after structural barriers were reduced. This chapter also continues my examination of the relative importance of selective migration in explaining differential patterns of well-being among blacks residing in the United States. I compare the homeownership rates of both black American movers and nonmovers to those of black immigrants from the fourteen primary black immigrant-sending countries.

Homeownership: What Do We Know?

HOMEOWNERSHIP AND IMMIGRANTS

Owning a home is a milestone that marks attainment of solid middle-class status for many American families. Among immigrants, home-ownership is also a marker of incorporation into the American mainstream and an indicator of a person's intention to remain in the United States.[14] The mere decision to purchase a home thus makes immigrant homeowners considerably different from immigrants who do not own their homes. A substantial literature highlights the difficulties faced by minority populations when purchasing a home (for example, housing discrimination), but immigrants face additional barriers to homeownership. Chief among these hurdles is the ability to speak English. Upon arrival in the United States, many immigrants speak little English, and that limits their access to lending institutions and real estate agents.[15] Additionally, a considerable proportion of the immigrant population, particularly those from less-developed countries, send remittances to family members in their home countries, reducing the amount of income available for home purchases in the United States.[16]

Upon arrival in the United States, many immigrants, particularly black immigrants, have lower earnings than similarly skilled Americans, a factor that could lead to lower homeownership rates. As immigrants learn the nuances of their new labor market, however, their earnings grow and, in some cases, converge with those of their native-born counterparts. As shown in chapter 4, the earnings growth profiles of immigrants vary considerably by arrival cohort, with earlier arrivals from the Caribbean and more recent arrivals from Africa having the best labor market outcomes.

Similar to immigrants' earnings, patterns of homeownership also vary by arrival cohort and time spent in the United States.[17] Borjas has identified a persistent decline in homeownership across successive immigrant arrival cohorts between 1980 and 2000 that has resulted in an increase in the homeownership gap between immigrants and natives.[18] He argues that this pattern is largely driven by national-origin shifts in the immigrant population over time. Specifically, he shows that more recent immigrant waves have lower homeownership rates than earlier arrival cohorts, resulting in growth in the homeownership gap between immigrants and natives in more recent time periods. Although the changing composition of the foreign-born population has resulted in a larger nativity gap in homeownership, homeownership rates of arrival cohorts tend to rise as their tenure of U.S. residency increases.[19]

HOMEOWNERSHIP, IMMIGRATION, AND RACE

Earlier research on homeownership among immigrants highlighted persistent racial gaps in homeownership across immigrant groups from different sending countries, with black immigrants exhibiting the lowest rates of homeownership.[20] The increase in homeownership for most immigrants typically associated with greater tenure of U.S. residence is less pronounced for black immigrants.

Prior research also has shown that homeownership varies among black immigrants by region of birth. Immigrants from the Caribbean exhibit higher rates of homeownership than black Americans, and immigrants from Africa exhibit lower rates than both of these groups.[21] To my knowledge, no studies exist that fully document national-origin differences among black immigrants from all of the primary sending countries.

THE ORIGINS OF RACIAL DISPARITIES IN HOMEOWNERSHIP IN THE UNITED STATES

Before analyzing disparities between black immigrants and black Americans, it is important to highlight the unique barriers that have hindered the ability of black Americans to become homeowners, factors that fundamentally shape homeownership disparities between black Americans and black immigrants. On the eve of emancipation from slavery, the vast majority of black Americans had no property. Remarkably, however, black Americans made considerable progress toward becoming homeowners in the decades after emancipation. In 1870, five years after slavery officially ended, approximately 8 percent of black Americans and 56 percent of white Americans owned homes.[22] By 2007, approximately 54 percent of blacks and 77 percent of whites owned homes.[23] To put this change in context, while homeownership among blacks increased by 600 percent between 1870 and 2007, it took black Americans nearly 140 years to make it to where white Americans were in 1870.[24]

According to economist William Collins and Robert Margo, homeownership rates, however, did not change evenly across the period. The vast majority of the narrowing of the racial gap occurred between 1870 and 1900.[25] In 1870, the probability of owning a home was forty-nine percentage points greater for white Americans than for black Americans. Remarkably, the homeownership gap had narrowed by twenty-five percentage points by 1900, thirty-five years after slavery officially ended. After this time, the gap between the two groups increased modestly between 1910 and 1920, and then narrowed between 1920 and 1940. Between 1940 and 1960, the homeownership gap between the two groups widened to twenty-seven percentage points, before declining to nineteen percentage points in 1980. During the Great Recession, the homeownership gap between black and white Americans once again widened, to twenty-three percentage points.[26]

Several factors are responsible for changes in the black-white gap in homeownership from 1870 to the present. Collins and Margo have found that the majority of the decrease between 1870 and

1910—almost two-thirds—resulted from the rise in homeownership among blacks rather than from decreases in homeownership among whites.[27] This improvement was largely driven by the post–Civil War accumulation of human capital among black Americans. When slavery ended in the United States, most black Americans were illiterate, particularly those residing in the South. By 1900, only 50 percent of black Americans were illiterate.[28] These gains in human capital, along with modest changes in occupational status, helped some black Americans accumulate property, including homes. The remaining one-third of the reduction in the homeownership gap between black and white Americans between 1870 and 1900 resulted from a decline in homeownership among whites, many of whom were moving out of agriculture into urban employment.[29]

The stagnation of the gap between white and black Americans between 1910 and 1940 coincided with the onset of the Great Migration. The first wave of the Great Migration began around 1916 and lasted until 1930; during that period, approximately 1.6 million people moved from mostly rural areas to northern industrial cities.[30] In addition to escaping the harsh conditions of the American South, the hope of obtaining better jobs and more favorable living conditions motivated many black Americans to leave their agricultural occupations in search of urban jobs, primarily in the North.[31]

Conditions in northern cities, however, were not conducive for black Americans to become homeowners. Jobs in urban areas paid more than those in the rural South, but property prices were also higher, a factor that had a dampening effect on homeownership among both blacks and whites moving to urban areas during the early twentieth century.[32] Along with higher prices, black Americans faced additional barriers to homeownership. High levels of racial discrimination in the labor market, combined with limited housing options for blacks in many urban cities, confined them to poor-quality homes in racially segregated and densely populated neighborhoods.[33]

Both the rise in unemployment and the drop in personal income during the Great Depression resulted in increases in home and farm foreclosures between 1930 to 1940, which led to a decline in homeownership rates for both black and white Americans.[34] To aid Americans recovering from the Great Depression, President Franklin Roosevelt created a number of new programs designed to help the millions facing the risk of foreclosure and to help families purchase their first homes. As part of President Roosevelt's New Deal, his administration created the Home Owners' Loan Corporation (HOLC), whose primary goal was to purchase existing mortgages at risk of defaulting and then amortize the mortgages over longer terms and with lower interest rates. Scholars have argued, however, that these benefits were denied to blacks and promoted segregation.[35]

Because of the favorable lending conditions, longer terms, and lower interest rates relative to conventional lenders, HOLC administrators wanted to ensure that the homes associated with the mortgages they were purchasing maintained their value over time. To achieve this goal, "HOLC created color-coded maps of every metropolitan area in the nation, with the safest [in terms of risk of default] neighborhoods colored green and the riskiest colored red. A neighborhood earned a red color if African Americans lived in it, even if it was a solidly middle-class neighborhood of single-family homes."[36] This practice would eventually become known as "redlining." According to Richard Rothstein, "while HOLC did not always decline to purchase homes in neighborhoods colored red, HOLC's method of evaluating risk negatively impacted the likelihood that the HOLC would purchase a mortgage and put the federal government on record as judging that African Americans, simply because of their race, were poor risk."[37]

The Federal Housing Administration (FHA) was also developed during the Great Depression to help individuals purchase their first home. When the FHA was established, the implementation of the program benefits also disproportionately benefited white Americans and became a mechanism for residential segregation. Similar to HOLC, the FHA also judged the risk of homes based on a neighborhood's racial composition. According to the FHA's *Underwriting Manual* in 1935, "If a neighborhood is to retain stability it is necessary that properties shall continue to be occupied by the same social and racial classes. A change in social or racial occupancy generally leads to instability and a reduction in values."[38] According to Rothstein:

> Because the FHA's appraisal standards included a whites-only requirement, racial segregation now became the official requirement of the federal mortgage insurance program. The FHA judged that properties would probably be too risky for insurance if they were in racially

mixed neighborhoods or even in white neighborhoods near black ones that might possibly integrate in the future.[39]

Moreover, the Veterans Administration (VA) relied on the FHA underwriting policies when it began to guarantee mortgages for returning servicemen after World War II. Because the FHA and VA used race as a marker of risk, entire suburbs were constructed after World War II for the near-exclusive benefit of white Americans.[40]

In addition to the biased policies of these federal programs, the benefits associated with the GI Bill were also administered in a manner that hindered the ability of blacks to purchase homes. After World War II, rather than having the benefits of the GI Bill administered through a federal agency, returning servicemen were required to obtain benefits at the state level.[41] To obtain loan benefits, servicemen had to work with local banks, which meant that many blacks had to obtain benefits in the South under Jim Crow laws and from whites committed to maintaining the status quo. Studies have found that black veterans were systematically denied benefits, including access to loans through the GI Bill that could be used to purchase homes.[42] Indeed, research suggests that the deliberate exclusion of black Americans from the benefits of the GI Bill and other federal programs that helped white Americans obtain homes since the 1930s was one of the central drivers of widening racial disparities in wealth and general well-being in the post–World War II era.[43] In short, the practice of "redlining," unequal access to a range of federal programs that promoted homeownership, restrictive covenants that prevented blacks from buying homes in white neighborhoods, and many resulting externalities associated with segregation help explain the widening of the homeownership gap between black and white Americans between 1940 and 1960.

Although the exact mechanism causing the gap to narrow between 1960 and 1980 is unclear, the change coincided with a period of intense regulatory efforts to eliminate racial discrimination in housing. The 1968 Fair Housing Act and the 1977 Community Reinvestment Act were both designed to curtail discrimination in housing and lending.[44]

The gap in homeownership between blacks and whites stagnated from 1980 to 1990, but it began to widen once again after 1990. Research analyzing post-1990 loan application data has suggested that despite the federal regulatory efforts of the late 1960s and 1970s, black applicants are still approximately 80 percent more likely to have a loan application rejected than white applicants.[45] Moreover, a disproportionate number of subprime loans were issued to minorities in the lead-up to the Great Recession.[46]

This section has provided a brief history of the historical dynamics that have influenced black homeownership rates during the pre- and post–civil rights eras. Slavery, Jim Crow, segregation, and biased federal policies hindered the ability of black Americans to purchase homes during the twentieth century. Moreover, blacks in northern cities were frequently exposed to violence when they attempted to buy homes in areas outside of the black ghettos.[47] Although the first wave of black Caribbean immigrants migrating to the United States during the early twentieth century experienced difficulties similar to those of black Americans when they attempted to obtain housing, the vast majority of black immigrants arrived in the United States after 1965. To be sure, blacks continue to experience difficulties purchasing homes, but the terrain is more navigable than in the past, when racial discrimination was the de jure policy of the federal government.[48] These structural shifts provide the background for understanding disparities in homeownership between black and white Americans and among blacks in the twenty-first century. In the absence of exclusionary policies, the homeownership rate of blacks most likely would be closer to that of white Americans.

With this background in place, the following section provides original estimates of disparities in homeownership among white Americans, black Americans, and black immigrants. As in the prior chapter, I begin by showing disparities during the early twentieth century using full count U.S. census data for New York City from 1910 to 1940.

Analysis of Disparities in Homeownership in the Pre- and Post-Civil Rights Eras

ANALYSIS OF DISPARITIES IN THE PRE–CIVIL RIGHTS ERA

Table 5.1 shows homeownership rates from 1910 to 1940 for the New York metropolitan area. As expected, across each survey year, white Americans have higher homeownership rates than black Americans,

Table 5.1 *Homeownership for White Americans, Black Americans, and Black Immigrants from the Caribbean in New York City, Adults Ages Twenty-Five to Sixty-Four, 1910–1940*

	Census Year			
Group	*1910*	*1920*	*1930*	*1940*
White Americans	18%	19%	28%	21%
All black natives	5	5	8	5
Native black movers	3	4	7	4
Native black nonmovers	10	7	13	9
Caribbean	1	2	6	7

Source: Full count of the U.S. Census of Population for the New York Metropolitan Area from 1910 to 1940.

regardless of migration status, and higher rates than black immigrants from the Caribbean. In 1910, 18 percent of white Americans were homeowners. By 1930, just prior to the height of the Great Depression, 28 percent of white Americans in New York were homeowners, a 55 percent increase over the twenty-year period. Between 1930 and 1940, the percentage of homeowners among white Americans fell by seven percentage points to 21 percent, showing the dramatic impact of the Great Depression on white Americans in New York.

Homeownership among black American movers, black American nonmovers, and black immigrants from the Caribbean followed similar patterns to that of white Americans during this period. For example, the percentage of black American nonmovers in New York who were homeowners increased by three percentage points between 1910 and 1930, from 10 percent to 13 percent. After 1930, homeownership among black American nonmovers fell by four percentage points, to 9 percent in 1940.

In contrast to the small disparities between black American movers and nonmovers I documented in chapter 4, homeownership varies considerably between the two groups in every census year, although the gap between the two groups narrows over time. In 1910, compared to black American movers, homeownership was seven percentage points greater for black American nonmovers. In 1940, the gap narrowed to five percentage points. Unfortunately, this data source does not contain information on the length of residence for domestic movers.

Disparities among blacks by migration status probably reflect the adjustment needed for movers to become acclimated to the city, find suitable employment, and navigate obstacles related to residential segregation. Moreover, most of the movers in New York City were from southern states and most likely brought with them little capital that could be used to purchase property.

Similar to the findings in chapter 4, despite substantial literature chronicling the success of black immigrants from the Caribbean in obtaining property in New York during the early twentieth century, the actual record paints a much different picture. In 1910, only 1 percent of black immigrants from the Caribbean were homeowners—seventeen percentage points less than white Americans, nine percentage points less than black American nonmovers, and two percentage points less than black American movers. Homeownership increased considerably, however, among immigrants between 1910 and 1940, from 1 percent to 7 percent. Indeed, in 1940, a higher percentage of blacks from the Caribbean were homeowners than were black American movers, 7 percent versus 4 percent; however, this immigrant group still fell short of the homeownership percentage achieved by black American nonmovers (9 percent). Interestingly, although the patterns are opposite of the labor market findings, where the movers tended to do better than the nonmovers, the outcomes of black immigrants from the Caribbean are more similar to those of black American movers than to those of black American nonmovers; this finding is likely to reflect the difficulties faced by all black migrants in obtaining homes during this period. Moreover, the lower levels of homeownership among black movers is consistent with the corresponding differentials in income and occupational prestige reported in chapter 4.

To determine whether the outcomes in table 5.1 result from observable differences between the two groups, table 5.2 presents estimates from linear probability regression models of homeownership. Two models are estimated in each year. First, I present a base model that controls only for age differences across the four groups, with black American movers serving as the reference group. Second, I present an adjusted model that controls for age, whether the head of the household is female, citizenship, household size, the number of household members under the age of eighteen, marital status, literacy (1910 to 1930 samples), and education (1940 sample).

Table 5.2 *Regressions of Homeownership for Black American, White American, and Caribbean-Born Adults, Ages Twenty-Five to Sixty-Four, 1910–1940*

	1910		1920		1930		1940	
	(1) Base	(2) Adjusted	(3) Base	(4) Adjusted	(5) Base	(6) Adjusted	(7) Base	(8) Adjusted
Country of birth (reference: black American movers)								
White Americans	0.131***	0.119***	0.138***	0.128***	0.205***	0.201***	0.168***	0.149***
Black American nonmovers	0.049***	0.052***	0.031***	0.036***	0.058***	0.062***	0.063***	0.058***
Caribbeans	0.001	-0.014*	0.008***	0.023*	-0.008***	0.005	-0.016***	-0.011**
Observations	387,975	387,975	519,102	519,102	815,515	815,515	1,155,616	1,124,205

Source: Full count of the U.S. Census of Population for the New York Metropolitan Area from 1910 to 1940.

$*p < .05; **p < .01; ***p < .001$

Similar to the descriptive results, in every census year, relative to black American movers, the probability of being a homeowner was greater for white Americans and black American nonmovers. Focusing on the adjusted model in each year, compared to black American movers, except in 1920, when the probability of owning a home was greater for black immigrants from the Caribbean, the probability of being a homeowner for black immigrants from the Caribbean was either similar or lower.

My final analysis of homeownership during the early twentieth century examines the homeownership trajectories of blacks from the Caribbean. Similar to labor market outcomes, it probably takes immigrants time to become familiar with the housing market in the new destination. After an adjustment period, we might expect the homeownership rates of black immigrants to improve and eventually overtake those of black Americans. The 1940 U.S. census does not contain data on immigrants' year of arrival in the United States. Fortunately, however, this information is available from 1910 to 1930, which allows me to implement the Borjas approach discussed in chapter 4.[49]

Figure 5.1 shows the homeownership trajectories of two cohorts from the Caribbean when they first arrived in the United States, the 1906–1910 arrival cohort in 1910 and the 1916–1920 cohort in 1920. The curve for the 1906–1910 arrival cohort, the group with the longest tenure of U.S. residence, ranging from twenty to twenty-four years in 1930, shows very modest changes in homeownership as their time in the United States increases. Although the probability of being a homeowner for immigrants who arrived between 1916 and 1920 was slighter greater than that of black American movers when they first arrived in the United States, by 1930 the probability of being a homeowner for members of this cohort was lower than that of black American movers. Moreover, across the time period, relative to black American movers, both immigrant arrival cohorts tended to have lower homeownership rates than black American nonmovers.

The findings from this section are clear: in New York City during the early twentieth century, black immigrants from the Caribbean had homeownership rates lower than or similar to those of black Americans. This finding suggests that whatever cultural disposition or degree

Figure 5.1 *Trajectories of Homeownership, Adults Ages Twenty-Five to Sixty-Four, 1910–1930*

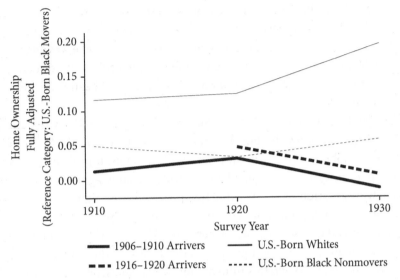

Source: Full count of the U.S. Census of Population for the New York Metropolitan Area from 1910 to 1930.

of selection there was among black immigrants during this period was not meaningful enough to generate any advantages for black Caribbean immigrants.

ANALYSIS OF DISPARITIES IN THE POST–CIVIL RIGHTS ERA

The data used to analyze homeownership disparities between black Americans and black immigrants come from the 1980–2000 U.S. censuses and the 2010–2014 American Community Surveys. As stated earlier, the available samples of the 1950 and 1970 U.S. censuses comprise only 1 percent of the U.S. population, and the 1960 U.S. census comprises 5 percent of the U.S. population. The black immigrant sample sizes during these years are insufficient to generate reliable estimates, particularly for the analysis of homeownership trajectories, which this section relies on heavily. As a result, while I document the homeownership profiles of black immigrants who arrived during the 1970s, shortly after the height of the civil rights movement, I do not use data from 1950 to 1970 because of small sample sizes.

Table 5.3 presents descriptive statistics for white Americans, black Americans (movers and nonmovers), and black immigrants by region of birth and country of birth. In 2014, 71 percent of white Americans owned the home in which they resided. The table also shows that 39 percent of black Americans owned their homes, with a modest difference between black American movers (41 percent) and black American nonmovers (38 percent). Although the percentage of all black immigrants who owned their homes (40 percent) is comparable to the percentage among black American movers, significant disparities in

Table 5.3 *Homeownership Rates by Race and Country of Origin, 2010–2014*

	Homeownership Rate
Native whites	0.71
Black Americans	0.39
Black American movers	0.41
Black American nonmovers	0.38
All black immigrants	0.40
Black Caribbean immigrants	0.46
Haiti	0.44
Dominican Republic	0.25
Jamaica	0.51
Trinidad and Tobago	0.46
Guyana	0.51
Black African immigrants	0.34
Nigeria	0.52
Ethiopia	0.35
Ghana	0.32
Kenya	0.33
Liberia	0.37
Somalia	0.12
Cameroon	0.29
Sierra Leone	0.39
Sudan	0.24

Source: 2010–2014 ACS.
Note: Weighted values.

homeownership exist among black immigrants: 46 percent of Caribbean immigrants owned their homes compared to 34 percent of immigrants from Africa.

Table 5.3 also highlights subgroup differences in homeownership among black immigrants by presenting descriptive statistics for the largest sending countries in each region. Consistent with the patterns highlighted in prior chapters, with the exception of immigrants from the Dominican Republic, every subgroup of Caribbean immigrants was more likely to own a home than black Americans (collectively). Immigrants from English-speaking Caribbean countries—Jamaica and Guyana—had the highest rates of homeownership. In contrast to the results for immigrants from the Caribbean, with the exception of immigrants from Nigeria, table 5.3 shows that every subgroup of African immigrants had a lower or similar probability of owning a home than black Americans, with immigrants from Somalia and Sudan having the lowest rate of homeownership.

To determine whether the descriptive results in table 5.3 hold after accounting for differences in demographic and socioeconomic status, figure 5.2 shows results from a set of linear probability models of homeownership. The results are presented as plots. I begin with the base model, which shows differences in homeownership between black American movers and black immigrants, only making adjustments for age differences across the groups. Black American non-movers were slightly less likely to own their home than black American movers. Among black immigrants, those from Jamaica, Guyana, and Nigeria were more likely to own their home than black American movers. All other black immigrant subgroups were less likely, or similarly likely, to own a home than black American movers, with immigrants from Somalia and the Dominican Republic having the largest deficits in homeownership.

The adjusted model for figure 5.2 shows disparities in homeownership after accounting for a standard set of social, demographic, and economic characteristics. In addition to age, the adjusted model includes controls for sex of the head of household, citizenship, veteran status, household size, number of household members younger than eighteen, number of household members older than sixty-four, English-language proficiency, marital status, education, household income, residence in a metropolitan area, and U.S. region of residence. Although

Figure 5.2 *Regressions of Homeownership for Black American, White American, and Black Immigrant Adults, Ages Twenty-Five to Sixty-Four, 2010–2014*

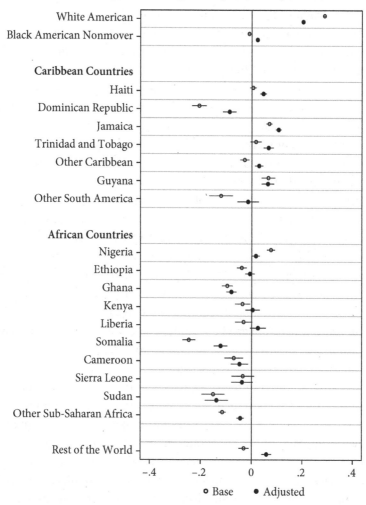

Source: 2010–2014 ACS.
Note: Reference category: black American movers.

controlling for these characteristics reduces the magnitude of the gap between black American movers and white Americans, white Americans maintain a substantial advantage (nineteen percentage points) over black American movers as well as over the black immigrant subgroups. Including the controls in the adjusted model reverses the direction of the disparity between black American movers and nonmovers, with black American nonmovers being two percentage points more likely to own their home than black American movers.

Controlling for social, demographic, and geographic characteristics increases the magnitude of most black immigrant coefficients. Black immigrants from every Caribbean subgroup except the Dominican Republic were more likely to own their home than black American movers. By contrast, no sub-Saharan Africa subgroup of immigrants was significantly more likely to own their own homes than black American movers.

As with labor market outcomes, prior studies have shown that time spent in the United States has a positive impact for immigrants on the likelihood of owning a home. To account for this factor, figure 5.3 examines whether the favorable homeownership trajectories of black immigrants hold across arrival cohorts for immigrants from the primary sending countries. The figure shows trajectories after controlling for social, demographic, and geographic characteristics. Similar to the plots of earnings in chapter 4, each point plotted on the graph represents differences between an arrival cohort and black American movers at a particular point in time. The initial point on each of the arrival cohort curves represents the gap between that cohort and native black movers within the first five years of arrival. Zero indicates parity with black American movers, the reference group.

Similar to the results in chapter 4, figure 5.3 shows that after controlling for a standard set of social, demographic, and economic characteristics, white Americans were more likely to own a home than every subgroup of blacks, immigrant or native. In every period since 1980, there are modest differences between black American movers and black American nonmovers. Focusing on the results for the entire immigrant sample, after one decade of U.S. residence, members of all three arrival cohorts converged with the homeownership probabilities of black American movers. After two decades of U.S. residence, members of the 1975–1979 and 1985–1989 arrival cohorts overtook the homeownership probabilities of black American movers. The general pattern documented for all black immigrants also holds for the subgroup of black immigrants from the Caribbean. In contrast, black African immigrants who arrived in 1985–1989 saw very modest growth in homeownership during their first ten years of U.S. residence. The probability of being a homeowner for this cohort increased

Figure 5.3 *Trajectories of Homeownership, Adults Ages Twenty-Five to Sixty-Four, 1980–2014*

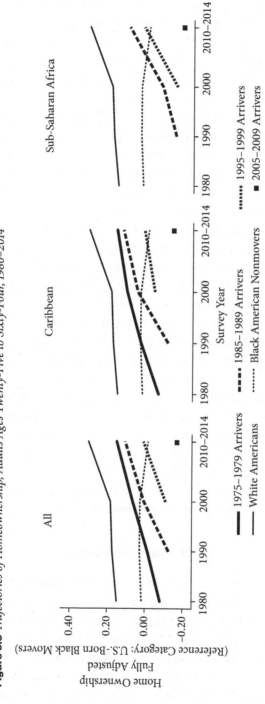

Source: U.S. censuses and ACS.

substantially and overtook the homeownership probabilities of black American movers after their second decade of U.S. residence. Similarly, among members of the 1995–1999 arrival cohort, individuals from Africa had the fastest growth in the probability of being a homeowner, converging with the homeownership probabilities of black American movers after one decade of U.S. residence.

Figure 5.4 shows adjusted plots for the five primary sending countries from the Caribbean and the three primary sending countries from Africa. Across the country groups, every arrival cohort from every major sending country was, on average, less likely to own a home than native black movers when they first arrived in the United States. On average, immigrants from the Dominican Republic, Nigeria, Ethiopia, and Ghana had the largest initial deficits in the probability of being a homeowner upon arrival in the United States. Arrival cohorts from Jamaica and Trinidad and Tobago had the smallest initial deficits. The 1975–1979 arrival cohort is the earliest shown in figure 5.3. By 2010–2014, when members of this cohort had resided in the United States for more than thirty years, the homeownership probabilities for arrivals from every country in the Caribbean except the Dominican Republic had overtaken or converged with the homeownership probability of native black movers. Similarly, the homeownership probabilities of the earliest arrival cohort from Africa, those who arrived between 1985 and 1989, had either overtaken or converged with the homeownership probabilities of native black movers by their second decade of U.S. residence. Immigrants in this cohort from Nigeria and Ethiopia had steeper trajectories than those from Ghana. No arrival cohort from any country appears likely to converge with the homeownership probabilities of white Americans.

Chapter Summary

The analyses in this chapter lead to several key insights. First, despite variation among blacks, between 1910 and 2014 all groups of blacks had lower homeownership rates than white Americans. Second, contrary to accounts from prior studies, between 1910 and 1940, compared to black American movers and black American nonmovers residing in the New York metropolitan area, black immigrants from the Caribbean living in New York tended to have a lower probability of owning a home.

Figure 5.4 *Trajectories of Homeownership, Adults Ages Twenty-Five to Sixty-Four, 1980–2014*

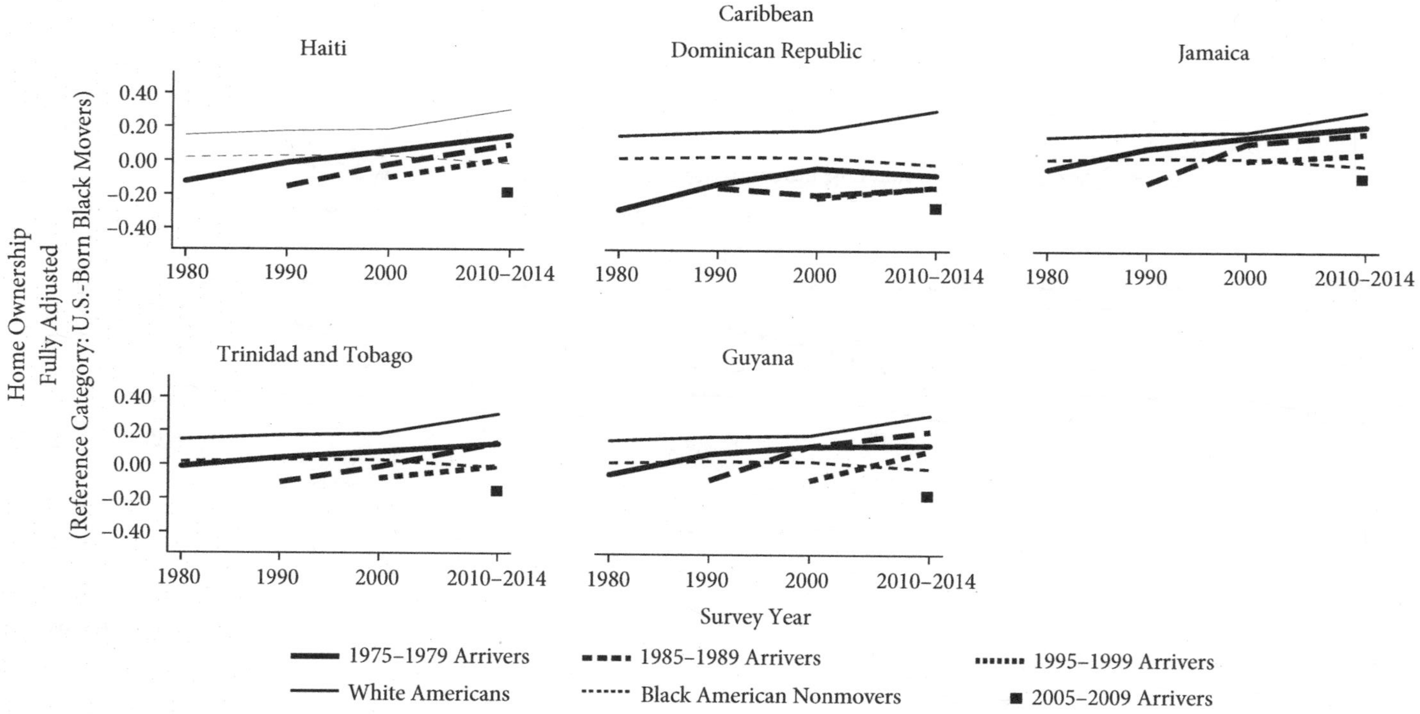

Source: U.S. censuses and ACS.

(continued)

Figure 5.4 (*continued*)

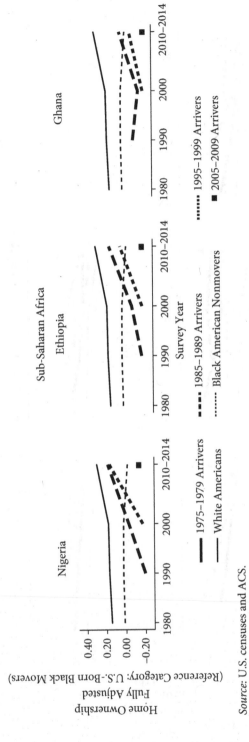

Source: U.S. censuses and ACS.

During this period, time spent in the United States had almost no impact on the probability of becoming a homeowner for Caribbean immigrants. Third, during the early twentieth century, compared to black American movers, black American nonmovers had a greater probability of owning a home.

Fourth, I detected no statistically significant difference between black American movers and black American nonmovers in the probability of owning a home between 1980 and 2014.

Fifth, without exception, the contemporary results show that every black immigrant arrival cohort had a lower probability of owning a home than black Americans within their first five years of arrival in the United States. The homeownership probabilities of every black immigrant arrival cohort, however, improved as their tenure of U.S. residence increased. With the exception of immigrants from the Dominican Republic, black immigrants from the 1975–1979, 1985–1989, and 1995–1999 arrival cohorts all overtook or converged with native blacks in their homeownership rates. The rate of homeownership convergence varied among black immigrant groups. For example, all three arrival cohorts from Jamaica overtook the homeownership rates of native black movers within their first decade of U.S. residence. In contrast, among immigrants from Nigeria, the 1985–1989 arrival cohort required two decades to overtake the homeownership rate of native black movers. Nigerian immigrants in the 1995–1999 arrival cohort overtook the homeownership rates of native black movers within ten years of arriving in the United States. Lastly, I found modest initial differences in homeownership across arrival cohorts of black immigrants from any country. These results have several implications for the study of nativity differences in homeownership among blacks.

Dominicans, Somalians, and Sudanese had the least favorable homeownership profiles among black immigrants in the United States, underscoring the negative reception context faced by members of these groups. As noted in chapter 3, black Caribbean and African immigrants from all of the focal sending countries, being more highly educated than individuals who remain in their countries of origin, are highly selected on both education and social class. Consequently, black African and Caribbean immigrants may be able to take advantage of aspects of their social class background to navigate the home-buying process in the United States.

The results also suggest that migrating to the United States during the post–civil rights era had a significant impact on the ability of Caribbean immigrants to become homeowners. Focusing on Caribbean immigrants, the different homeownership patterns in the 1910–1940 period versus the 1980–2014 period indicate that the favorable homeownership profiles for the group are unique to the contemporary period. Research has shown that blacks from the Caribbean who migrated to the United States between 1910 and 1940 were positively selected on education and occupational characteristics.[50] Numerous studies have also claimed that because of their entrepreneurial spirit, black immigrants from the Caribbean in New York City were able to find avenues to purchase homes even during an era of intense racial discrimination.[51] My analysis of homeownership during the early twentieth century provides no evidence to support such claims. Indeed, the homeownership rates of all blacks were lower than those of white Americans.

Comparisons that strictly focus on the contemporary period fail to illuminate how de jure housing discrimination and systematic exclusion from a range of federal programs hindered black Americans' ability to become homeowners.[52] The homeownership rates of black Americans would be considerably higher if they had had the same access to the range of federal programs—FHA programs, VA benefits, and the GI Bill—that promoted homeownership among whites. Indeed, homeownership rates among black Americans improved and the gap between black and white Americans narrowed after the passage of federal policies aimed at eliminating housing discrimination.[53]

The legacy of past barriers to homeownership are still reflected in the outcomes of black Americans, which have translated into lower levels of intergenerational wealth accumulation and a sustained period of racial segregation.[54] Discrimination persists in the housing market, but compared to the pre–civil rights era, conditions have improved. These improvements provide an easier path for black immigrants—many of whom are positively selected on education and social class—to become homeowners.

In addition to the relatively favorable home-buying environment, the favorable homeownership profiles of black immigrants also suggest that the group has greater access to the financial information and resources needed to purchase a home, particularly in the form of down payments and access to lending institutions. Chapter 4 showed that upon arrival in the United States, immigrants have lower earnings than black Americans. However, some black immigrants, particularly immigrant women, surpass the earnings of black American movers the longer they live in the United States. This could allow such immigrant families to save for a down payment to purchase a home. Relative to black Americans, however, black immigrants may also have greater demands on their incomes. Nearly all black immigrants come from less-developed nations, and these groups remit millions of dollars to their origin countries each year, a factor that could hinder their purchasing power. Therefore, it is unclear whether the favorable earnings profiles of some black immigrants allow them to achieve higher rates of homeownership than native blacks.

Although research suggests that the wealth holdings and debt levels of black Americans and black immigrants are comparable, there is little information on immigrant wealth holdings at origin.[55] Despite the popular myth that immigrants comprise the poorest members of the origin society, it takes resources to move.[56] Because many black immigrants tend to come from the higher social classes, many of them are likely to have been property owners in their origin countries. Although I cannot examine this claim with available data, it is possible that black immigrants are able to leverage wealth obtained in their origin countries to purchase homes in the United States. Moreover, even if immigrants are not able to directly transfer home-country wealth to the United States, their wealth holdings in other countries could place them in a better wealth position than that of black Americans, allowing them to take greater financial risks. In general, wealthier individuals take more financial risks, both because they have the resources and because they have a financial cushion to rely on if investments fail. Among immigrants who own homes in the Caribbean, for example, returning to their birth country may be a reasonable option if investments in the United States fail, a factor that may increase their risk tolerance and the likelihood that they will purchase a home in the United States.

Their coethnic communities are another potential source of capital for immigrants seeking to purchase a home. Studies suggest that some black immigrants have developed informal credit networks to satisfy the credit and capital needs of coethnics. One type of credit network is the rotating savings and credit association, which aids immigrants in acquiring the capital needed to purchase a home.[57] Rebecca Tesfai notes that

> credit-pooling groups may compensate for black immigrants' lower credit and social capital than the U.S.-born, helping them attain the capital necessary to purchase a home. Given the necessity of an ethnic social network for the formation of credit-pooling groups, Caribbean immigrants, the larger black immigrant group, may be better able to use these informal savings associations to finance home purchases. In addition to having a larger population, Caribbean immigrants are also more highly concentrated than African-born; nearly 60 percent of Caribbean immigrants live in just three metropolitan areas. Africans are more dispersed; however, there are large populations in New York and Washington, D.C., that have led to the formation of substantial African ethnic enclaves.[58]

Research also suggests that the geographic clustering of immigrants increases the likelihood that they will benefit from the assistance of coethnic real estate agents.[59] Such clustering could help them avoid the discriminatory practices of financial institutions and agents.[60]

In summary, while the data used in this chapter make it impossible to determine the actual mechanism leading to the favorable home-ownership profiles of black immigrants, cultural differences between the two groups are unlikely to be the primary drivers of the disparities. If this were the case, black immigrants would have obtained higher homeownership rates in both the pre– and post–civil right eras. Given that disparities only emerged in the post–civil rights era, the findings suggest that institutional changes that reduced the degree of discrimination in the U.S. housing market were the conditions needed for the disparities between black Americans to emerge.

The findings in this chapter also have clear demographic implications. If immigration from the Caribbean and sub-Saharan Africa persists in the coming decades, interracial homeownership disparities between blacks and whites in general might improve during a period of worsening conditions for black Americans. In the coming decades, researchers will need to examine whether changes in racial disparities in homeownership and wealth result from changes in the composition of the black population (for example, immigration) or from improvements in the social conditions faced by blacks residing in the United States.

PART III

EXPANDING THE DISCUSSION

CHAPTER SIX

HEALTH DISPARITIES

Some of the most consequential disparities between black and white Americans appear in the domain of health and mortality.[1] Compared to white Americans, black Americans experience more chronic conditions, are more likely to be overweight or obese, self-report lower ratings of overall health, and have worse mortality profiles.[2] Relative to white Americans, blacks also have a greater likelihood of being diagnosed with most cancers, and among those diagnosed with cancer, black Americans are more likely to die from the condition than their white counterparts.[3]

The disparities in health and mortality between white and black Americans begin in infancy.[4] In 2015, approximately 5 out of every 1,000 white American infants died before their first birthday, compared to approximately 11.7 per 1,000 black babies. Thus, strikingly, black American babies are more than twice as likely to die before their first birthday than white American babies. Although research has shown that education is highly correlated with a range of social and economic outcomes, with more-educated individuals enjoying higher life expectancy, lower morbidity, and greater earnings, surprisingly, education seems to do very little to narrow the infant mortality gap between white and black American infants. In a 2018 study with my coauthor Tiffany Green, we use the 1998–2002 Linked Birth-Infant Death Cohort Data to show that while only 2.85 per 1,000 white American infants whose mothers had at least a bachelor's degree died within their first year of life, 8.76 per 1,000 infants of similarly educated black American women died within their first year of life, more than three times the rate for white American infants.[5] Indeed, infants born to the most highly educated black American mothers faced a greater risk of dying before their first birthday than infants born to white mothers with less than a high school education (8.53 per 1,000 versus 8.76 per 1,000). This gap implies that while educational attainment decreases the risk of infant mortality among black American mothers—the infants of black American mothers with a bachelor's education had a lower mortality rate than the infants of black American mothers with less than a high school education—gaining additional education does nothing to close the black-white gap in infant mortality among mothers with a similar level of education.

Disparities in mortality between white and black Americans persist throughout adulthood.[6] Life expectancy at birth is an estimate of the average number of years a baby born in a given year can expect to live given the mortality risks faced by individuals across the age distribution. According to estimates from the Centers for Disease Control and Prevention's *National Vital Statistics Reports,* in 2015 life expectancy at birth was 75.1 for black Americans and 78.7 for white Americans, a difference of 3.6 years. The racial gap was higher for men (4.5 years) than for women (3.0 years).

Like the more heavily studied Hispanic immigrant population, black immigrants, on average, have better health outcomes than U.S.-born blacks. Relative to black Americans, black immigrants have more favorable self-reported health profiles, experience better infant and child health outcomes, and exhibit lower rates of disability, obesity, and adult mortality.[7] Prior studies also show that black immigrants from Africa have better health profiles than black immigrants from the Caribbean, but few researchers have delved into these differences.

As documented in prior chapters, even among immigrants from the Caribbean and Africa, the vastly different conditions in their home countries to which black immigrants are exposed prior to coming to the United States could lead to significant variation in their postmigration health and health trajectories. Consequently, we know little about which countries are driving the favorable health profiles of the aggregate black immigrant population.

Similar to the labor market literature, most studies on the health of black immigrants (and immigrants more generally) tend to compare the health profiles of black immigrants to representative samples of black Americans. Such comparisons, as shown in prior chapters, can produce misleading inferences about the exact mechanism responsible for disparities between the two groups. The analyses in this chapter address the limitations in the extant literature by estimating health models for black American movers and nonmovers, white Americans, and the fourteen focal black immigrant subgroups, using twenty years of data (1996 to 2016) from the U.S. March Current Population Survey (CPS).

What Do We Know about Health Disparities between Native and Immigrant Populations?

Research suggests that immigrants tend to arrive in the United States with a health advantage over their native-born counterparts, a phenomenon termed the "healthy immigrant effect."[8] Researchers have attributed this effect to two primary factors: selective migration and cultural buffering. Explanations based on cultural buffering suggest that health and mortality differences between immigrants and U.S.-born individuals stem from immigrants' relatively low tendency to smoke, consume alcohol, use illicit drugs, or be overweight or obese compared to similar members of the U.S.-born population. This explanation also implies that the positive culture that initially helps produce better health and lower mortality rates among immigrants erodes as they acculturate and begin to adopt the negative health behaviors and lifestyles common within the United States.[9]

Explanations of the healthy immigrant effect based on selective migration propose that good health is highly correlated with factors that drive people to move across country lines. These factors include age, differences in the value of skills across countries, education, and unobserved factors such as drive and motivation.[10] For example, Cynthia Feliciano shows that immigrants to the United States from almost all regions of the world tend to be more highly educated than people in their countries of origin who do not migrate.[11]

In spite of the relatively consistent evidence that immigrants have a health and mortality advantage over members of the U.S.-born population, another body of research suggests that these findings are driven in part by poor data that do not properly capture the impact of the return migration of less healthy immigrants to their countries of origin.[12] For example, the sociologists Alberto Palloni and Elizabeth Arias show that the mortality advantage achieved by Hispanic immigrants is exhibited only among foreign-born Mexicans and foreign-born Hispanics other than Cubans and Puerto Ricans.[13] Moreover, these authors largely attribute the mortality advantage among Mexican immigrants to the out-migration of less-healthy individuals back to Mexico. Other work in this area suggests that although return migration accounts for some of the observed health advantage of Hispanic immigrants, this factor alone does not erase that advantage.[14]

Health outcomes among immigrants tend to eventually converge toward the health outcomes of their racial-ethnic counterparts in the United States. One possible explanation for the erosion in immigrant health associated with time in the United States is exposure to racism and discrimination as well as other negative social, economic, and environmental factors that have a detrimental effect on the health of U.S. minority groups.[15] One area where these risk factors are present is in the provision of health services.[16] Thomas LaVeist, Robert Sellers, and Harold Neighbors, for example, show that blacks are more likely than whites to report discrimination in both access to health services and provision of health services.[17] These authors have further determined that blacks are 50 percent less likely than whites to receive invasive treatment for coronary disease.[18] James Collins, Shou-Yien Wu, and Richard David find a correlation between mothers reporting health discrimination and very low birth weights of their children.[19] Indeed, the legacy of segregation and Jim Crow—under which black Americans were forced to live in underinvested neighborhoods with poor-quality schools and were denied access to proper medical care—helps to explain some of these disparities.[20]

What Do We Know about the Health of Black Immigrants?

The existing literature shows that black immigrants have better birth outcomes, lower mortality rates, lower morbidity rates, and more favorable physical health than black Americans.[21] Across some indicators of health, black immigrants seem to be more similar to white Americans than to black Americans.[22] Heather Antecol and Kelly Bedard also document that, like other immigrant groups, black immigrants arrive in the

United States with better initial health than black Americans.[23] However, they also find that even after twenty years in the United States, black immigrants maintain their health advantage over black Americans.[24] These results are a significant departure from the standard pattern of initial favorable health and subsequent declines in health experienced by other immigrant groups.

Other studies suggest, however, that there may be distinct patterns of health and health assimilation among black immigrants from different regions of the world.[25] Regional heterogeneity in health among black immigrants may be explained in part by conditions in their countries of origin.[26] Indeed, the population health literature shows that early-life conditions play an important role in health and mortality differences in the United States.[27] Thus, black immigrants who faced health conditions similar to those of black Americans in early life might have health and mortality profiles that mirror those of black Americans, while those who were less disadvantaged early in life may exhibit healthier profiles later in life.

In an effort to explain heterogeneity in health among black immigrants, Jen'nan Ghazal Read and Michael Emerson stress the importance of the racial context of black immigrants' countries of origin.[28] According to their "racial context of origin" hypothesis, black immigrants who face racism and discrimination in their countries of origin similar to that faced by blacks born in the United States should have health outcomes that mirror those of U.S.-born blacks. In particular, they hypothesize that the healthiest groups of black immigrants should come from Africa and South America (minority-white regions). They find empirical evidence that supports their hypothesis. After black immigrants from Africa and South America, immigrants from the West Indies (a racially mixed region) report the second-best health. Black immigrants from Europe (a majority-white region) tend to report the worst health. Although not using this theoretical framework, Irma Elo, Neil Mehta, and Cheng Huang also find this general racial-context-of-origin pattern among black immigrants across several health measures.[29]

With this chapter, I contribute to the developing literature on the health profiles of black immigrants. My analyses serve as a starting point for further examination of health heterogeneity among black immigrants, including studies that take into account the importance of immigrant origin contexts. Chapter 3 showed that the social and economic costs of migrating from a country in Africa might make African immigrants even more positively selected than immigrants from South America or the West Indies, for whom the costs of moving to the United States are presumably lower. Chapter 4 illustrated that income and education levels, health conditions, and social practices vary across countries of origin. Therefore, health differences between immigrants and the U.S.-born and among different groups of immigrants might stem from varying health, economic, and social conditions across sending countries.

Previous work on the health of black immigrants is limited in two important ways. First, although researchers have found evidence of region-of-birth variation in health among black immigrants, few studies have looked at birth-country variation in health among black immigrants. As a result, existing work has not evaluated whether health-related factors in countries of origin are driving the health outcome differences among black immigrant groups in the United States.

Second, most studies on the health of black immigrants (and immigrants more generally) tend to compare the health profiles of black immigrants to representative samples of natives. Such comparisons, however, could produce misleading estimates of the effect of selective migration and culture in producing health disparities between native and immigrant populations. Using data on immigrants in the United States and nonmigrants in immigrants' birth countries, researchers have shown that some immigrant subgroups are positively selected on good health.[30] In other words, the people who choose to emigrate tend to be among the healthiest in their countries of origin. Although such studies are likely to provide the best estimates of the degree of health selection among immigrants, reliable health data are unavailable for many origin countries, particularly less-developed countries in Africa and Central America. To address this data limitation, as in prior chapters, I argue that black American movers are a more appropriate comparison group for evaluating nativity differences in health than representative samples of the entire black American population.[31] That is, if the underlying unobserved characteristics associated with selective migration are similar for both immigrants and the U.S.-born, then changing the reference group to U.S.-born movers should produce more accurate estimates of the immigrant health advantage. In turn, this methodological change should diminish the unexplained gap that researchers often attribute to characteristics unique to immigrants' origin countries (for example, immigrant culture).

The analyses in this chapter address the limitations in the extant literature by estimating health models for black Americans and black immigrants using data from the 1996 to 2016 waves of the U.S. March Current Population Survey. This data source contains a much larger sample of black immigrants than the National Health Interview Survey and includes data on black immigrants' country of birth. Consequently, I can analyze the exact countries driving the health advantage for black immigrants from the Caribbean and Africa. An additional advantage of the March Current Population Survey is that the data allow me to partition the U.S.-born sample by internal migration status. I can thus determine whether migration is also correlated with good health for the U.S.-born population.

THE HEALTH MEASURE

The March Current Population Survey is one of the few nationally representative data sources that contains data on black immigrants' exact country of birth. The primary limitation of the survey, however, is that it contains only one health question: self-rated health (SRH). Survey respondents were asked to rate their current health as excellent, very good, good, fair, or poor. Following conventions in the health literature, the five-point scale is dichotomized into a "good" versus "poor" health outcome measure. Individuals who report fair or poor health are assigned a one, and individuals who report any of the other rating categories receive a zero.

To readers who are unfamiliar with social science research on health, self-rated health may seem like a rather imprecise measure of health. SRH, however, is a strong predictor of subsequent morbidity and mortality at every cut point. That is, individuals who report their health as poor are more likely to die during a follow-up period than individuals who report their health as fair, and individuals who report their health as good are more likely to die during a follow-up period than individuals who report their health as very good or excellent.[32]

Although studies have shown a strong correlation between self-rated health and subsequent mortality, there are limitations to SRH as an objective measure of health. First, the predictive strength of poor SRH on mortality increases with length of stay in the United States among Hispanic immigrants.[33] Furthermore, among all populations, there may be reporting heterogeneity. In other words, the correlations between SRH and mortality and between SRH and health status as measured by biomarkers have been found to vary by socioeconomic status (SES).[34] These differences may be due to cultural or linguistic understandings of health.[35] For example, imagine that wealthier individuals compare themselves to relatively healthier peers, and individuals of low SES have lower expectations for health given the lower average health profiles of their peers. Then low-SES individuals might rate themselves higher (more optimistically) and high-SES individuals might rate themselves lower, leading to an underestimate of health disparities.[36]

In one study, Jennifer Beam Dowd and Megan Todd used anchoring vignettes to test for differences by SES, race-ethnicity, and other characteristics.[37] They found that, compared to whites, Hispanics demonstrated more optimistic thresholds for health reporting at low levels of severity and more pessimistic or equal thresholds at higher levels of severity. It is also possible that Hispanics are more likely than whites to include social and mental health in their ratings of general health.[38]

The March Current Population Survey can be administered in English or Spanish. Recent research suggests that estimates of fair or poor health among Hispanics who speak only Spanish may be biased owing to the translation in the survey of the Spanish word for "fair" as "regular," which has a more positive connotation. The result may be overuse of the fair/poor health category.[39]

Given that most black immigrants report speaking English well, this translation limitation is not a concern in my analyses. In addition, prior research suggests that the aforementioned limitations of data from the March Current Population Survey and the use of SRH as an indicator of health are also mitigated in studies modeling the health of a specific immigrant group, which I do in this chapter. Certainly, more specific health outcomes, such as obesity or chronic conditions, could provide greater insights into variation in health among black immigrants.

Table 6.1 *Proportion Reporting Fair or Poor Health, by Race and Country of Origin, 1996–2016*

	Men	Women
Native whites	0.11	0.11
Black Americans	0.19	0.20
Black American movers	0.14	0.17
Black American nonmovers	0.19	0.20
All black immigrants	0.10	0.12
Black Caribbean immigrants	0.12	0.14
Haiti	0.12	0.13
Dominican Republic	0.13	0.21
Jamaica	0.13	0.10
Trinidad and Tobago	0.11	0.12
Guyana	0.11	0.22
Black African immigrants	0.08	0.08
Nigeria	0.08	0.06
Ethiopia	0.07	0.08
Ghana	0.08	0.05
Kenya	0.06	0.07
Liberia	0.06	0.10
Somalia	0.07	0.06
Cameroon	0.04	0.08
Sierra Leone	0.10	0.06
Sudan	0.14	0.02

Source: 1996–2016 March Current Population Surveys (CPS).
Note: Weighted values.

Unfortunately, no existing data set containing these measures has sufficient observations for black immigrants by birth country to model differences across the black immigrant population. My findings using SRH as an objective measure of health should be interpreted within the context of these limitations.

THE BASIC FACTS

Table 6.1 shows descriptive statistics for white Americans, black Americans by internal migration status, and black immigrants, as well as for men and women. The table highlights a reality that may be well known to those familiar with the current state of racial health disparities in the United States. Only 11 percent of white American men reported their health as fair or poor, compared to 19 percent of black American men. Similar to the findings in prior chapters, a smaller percentage of black American male movers (14 percent) reported their health as fair or poor than black American male non-movers (19 percent). Black immigrant men collectively (10 percent) had a significantly lower probability of reporting fair or poor health than black American men (19 percent). Indeed, the percentage of black immigrant men reporting fair or poor health is comparable to that of white American men (11 percent). Table 6.1 also shows that black immigrant men from Africa were less likely to report their health as fair or poor than black Caribbean immigrant men, highlighting the potential influence of selective migration among black immigrants from Africa. The table shows a similar pattern for women.

Table 6.1 shows some degree of health variation among immigrants from the Caribbean, particularly Caribbean women. Between 11 percent and 13 percent of Caribbean men from each of the focal Caribbean countries reported their health as fair or poor. Immigrant men from Jamaica and the Dominican Republic had the highest proportion of respondents reporting fair or poor health, and males from Guyana and Trinidad and Tobago had the lowest. The probability of reporting poor health ranges from 21 percent among immigrant women from the Dominican Republic to 10 percent among immigrant women from Jamaica.

Table 6.1 shows similar variation among immigrants from Africa, with women from Liberia (10 percent) and men from Sudan (14 percent) having the highest proportions of individuals reporting their health as fair or poor. Women from Sudan (2 percent) and men from Cameroon (4 percent) were the least likely to report fair or poor health.

STRAIGHTFORWARD EXPLANATIONS

Figure 6.1 presents health models that document country-of-origin differences in self-reported health among working-age adults. To

Figure 6.1 *Regressions of Fair or Poor Health for Black American, White American, and Black Immigrant Adults, Ages Twenty-Five to Sixty-Four, 1996–2016*

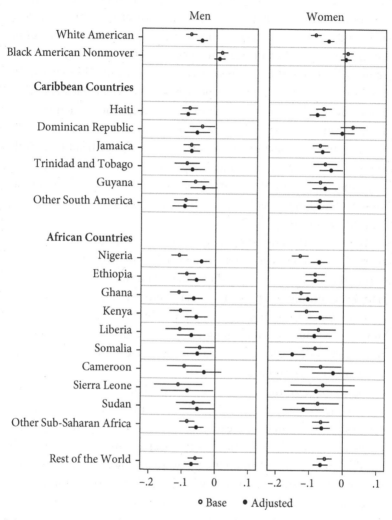

Source: 1996–2016 March CPS.
Note: Reference category: black American movers.

provide a set of baseline results, the base model shows estimates of fair or poor health status for men and women controlling for age differences across the populations. The probability of reporting fair or poor health was six percentage points lower for white American men and seven percentage points lower for white American women compared to black American movers, the reference group. For both men and women, there is no statistically significant difference in the probability of reporting fair or poor health between black American nonmovers and black American movers. Except for women from the Dominican Republic and Sierra Leone, who show no statistical differences in the probability of reporting fair or poor health, all of the estimates for black immigrants in figure 6.1 are to the left of the vertical line, suggesting that nearly every subgroup of black immigrants was less likely to report their health as fair or poor compared to black American movers.

The adjusted model in figure 6.1, which controls for age, education, marital status, region of current residence, and metropolitan area status, shows that adjusting for social and demographic differences between native and immigrant populations has a modest impact on disparities between black immigrants from the Caribbean and black American movers. By contrast, controlling for these factors results in a modest reduction in the health advantage for most black African immigrants, particularly African men.

Figure 6.2 examines the impact of time spent in the United States on the health profiles of black immigrants. Because of sample size issues, I am unable to examine individual birth-country differences and can only document differences for immigrants from the Caribbean and those from Africa. Figure 6.1 suggests that the health of black immigrant men and women is fairly comparable. Consequently, I combine men and women into a single model, which improves the duration estimates. Figure 6.2 presents graphs from health assimilation models for black immigrants from the Caribbean and Africa.

Relative to immigrants who have been in the United States between zero and five years, among immigrants from the Caribbean, time spent in the United States is associated with worsening health profiles. By contrast, the figure shows that the health of African immigrants improves the longer they live in the United States.

Figure 6.2 *Health Disparities among Black Immigrants by Duration of U.S. Residence, Adults Ages Twenty-Five to Sixty-Four, 1996–2016*

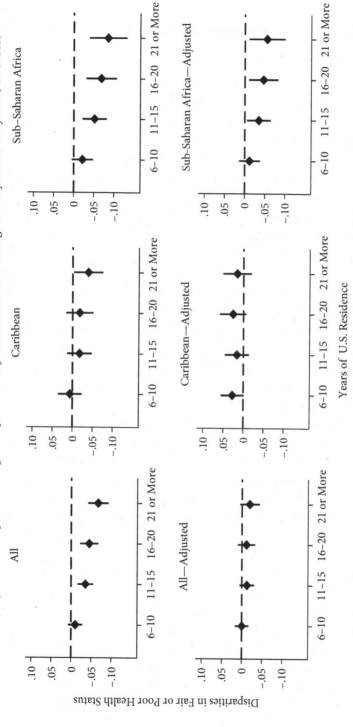

Source: 1996–2016 March CPS.
Note: Reference group: immigrants with zero to five years of U.S. residence.

Discussion and Conclusion

The analyses in this chapter produced several key findings. Black American movers are less likely than nonmovers to report their health as fair or poor. This disparity is largely explained, however, by differences in social and demographic characteristics. The analyses in this chapter consistently showed that most national-origin groups of black immigrants exhibit more favorable health than both black American movers and nonmovers, particularly upon arrival in the United States. Because I lack data with which to compare the health profiles of black immigrants to individuals in their home countries, I cannot definitively claim that black immigrants are more positively selected on health than black American movers. Given that the costs and risks associated with international migration are significantly greater than the costs and risks associated with domestic migration, however, it is reasonable to expect that black immigrants may be more positively selected on health than black American movers.[40] These findings are also likely to be driven by black Americans' greater exposure to discrimination and racism in the U.S. context, both historical and contemporary, which has been shown to negatively impact both the physical and mental health of U.S. blacks.[41]

The analyses also uncovered variation in immigrant health by duration of U.S. residence. The data suggest that the health of African immigrants appears to improve with increased duration in the United States. A somewhat different pattern emerged for Caribbean immigrants. Among Caribbean immigrants, time spent in the United States was associated with worse health. However, the most prevalent pattern shown in the data was very favorable health among black immigrants relative to the health of both black American movers and nonmovers.

The findings in this chapter also have clear demographic implications for how researchers understand health disparities in the United States, particularly disparities between blacks and whites. In 2016, the racial gap in life expectancy at birth was at its lowest level ever, 3.5 years. This means that a white baby born in 2016 could expect to live on average three and a half years longer than a black baby born in the same year. Life expectancy at birth has steadily improved for blacks over the last two decades. To date, no study has examined the degree to which improvements in the mortality profiles of blacks, particularly those residing in northeastern states with large black immigrant populations, results from improving social conditions, particularly conditions for black Americans, or simply from immigration. The findings in this chapter suggest that if researchers do not account for black immigration, health disparities researchers examining regional variation in health may arrive at misleading conclusions regarding the factors responsible for changes in racial health disparities.

CHAPTER SEVEN

FORMING UNIONS AND CROSSING RACIAL-ETHNIC BOUNDARIES

The underlying focus of U.S. immigration policy since the late 1880s has been the country's ability to absorb the social and cultural differences brought by new waves of immigrants.[1] The immigration laws in the late nineteenth century were designed to limit the flow of immigrants, particularly Chinese immigrants. Since that time, policymakers have been concerned that the cultural differences brought by new waves of immigrants might fundamentally alter the social fabric of America, generating social conflict and competition for jobs. When such conflict and competition occurs, it can lead to the creation of ethnic populations with limited ability to assimilate into the American mainstream. In other cases, the distinctiveness of immigrant groups eventually fades across generations, leaving the sociocultural landscape of American society unchanged. Sociologists consider rates of intermarriage, particularly intermarriage with white Americans, a primary marker or proxy of an immigrant group's social integration.[2]

During the 1920s, when most immigrants hailed from southern and eastern Europe, scholars observed high levels of in-group marriage among European immigrants and their descendants.[3] When immigrants overwhelmingly marry others of the same national origin, it signals a significant level of the larger society's hostility toward group members and their lack of social integration.[4] If we imagine a world where 1920s patterns of in-group marriage continued into the 2000s, eastern and southern European ethnic identity would have remained a salient feature of America's ethno-racial landscape.[5] By the 1960s, however, intermarriage among Americans of European descent had increased beyond the levels observed just forty years prior, and educational attainment rather than ancestry had become a stronger correlate of marriage choice.[6] Indeed, among Americans of European descent, out-marriage had become the dominant trend.[7]

Data on contemporary immigrants' marriage patterns show a similar trend occurring among immigrants who arrived during the 1990s and the 2000s. As of 2017, data from the American Community Survey show that individuals of Latin American ancestry were the largest racial-ethnic population residing in the United States, and that individuals of Asian ancestry represented the fastest-growing immigrant population. These trends highlight a strong shift in U.S. immigration since the 1920s. Indeed, the Immigration Act of 1924 nearly banned immigration from Asia and highly restricted Mexican immigration. In addition to the demand for highly skilled labor, the increase in Asian immigration highlights the dramatic easing of racial tensions toward Asian immigrants. During the 1920s, many Americans viewed the phenotypic distinctiveness of Asian individuals as unmalleable and the groups' sociocultural practices as fundamentally incompatible with those of the United States.[8] If the attitudes motivating the harsh restrictions on Asian immigration in the 1920s had continued, contemporary Asian immigrants and their descendants would display castelike patterns of in-group marriage.[9] In contrast to these predictions, data from the 2014–2015 American Community Survey show that roughly 30 percent of married Asians in the United States have a white American partner. Moreover, despite the harsh political rhetoric surrounding immigration from Latin America, particularly Mexico, 26 percent of newlywed Hispanic men and 28 percent of newlywed Hispanic women in the United States have a different-race spouse, with most marriages occurring between Hispanics and white Americans.[10]

Intermarriage patterns in the United States between whites and both Asians and Hispanics signify fading social distance between the groups and white Americans' increasing tolerance of the social and cultural distinctions displayed by Asian and Hispanic populations.[11] These trends have developed despite previous periods of racial animus against Asian immigrants and the heated anti-immigrant political discourse surrounding immigration from Latin America, particularly during the 1990s and into the 2000s.

In striking contrast to patterns of intermarriage found among Asians and Hispanics, intermarriage between blacks and whites remains relatively low in the United States. In 2017 the Pew Research Center issued the report "Intermarriage in the U.S. 50 Years after *Loving v. Virginia*," a title referencing the 1967 U.S. Supreme Court case that legalized marriages across racial lines throughout the country. The report documents a sharp increase in interracial marriages since the late 1960s. In 1967, approximately 3 percent of new marriages occurred between individuals of different races. By 2015, that figure had increased to 17 percent. Most intermarriages, however, occurred between white Americans and either Asians or Hispanics. Fewer than 12 percent of intermarriages were between blacks and whites. These marriage patterns led the sociologists Jennifer Lee and Frank Bean to argue that the black-white color line that has historically characterized U.S. racial stratification no longer holds.[12] Instead, they argue, the country's color line has shifted to a new binary: blacks and nonblacks.

In *The Diversity Paradox,* Lee and Bean capture the extent of black exceptionalism embedded in the intermarriage market. They quote a twenty-four-year-old woman born to a white mother and a Mexican father:

> I was never brought up to hate or dislike black people, but if I dated a black man, my white side of the family and Mexican side of the family would disown me. And they've made it very clear. My dad told me if I ever brought a black guy home, he would kill him, and my grandma told me if I ever brought a black man home that she would kill me. As long as he wasn't black. Never said anything about any Asians or Indians or Pakistani, nothing. As long as he wasn't black.[13]

In the same chapter, a second-generation Chinese woman who married a black American explains that her immigrant parents opposed her marriage because they believed that it would close off opportunities for her to move up in society:

> Of course, within our U.S. society there's a pecking order where whites are at the top of the socioeconomic ladder, and then probably Asians, and Latinos, and then blacks, and then I don't know where Native Americans fall—in there somewhere. So I think their concern was— what did they say?—"We've worked so hard to give you all these opportunities, to open doors to you, and now you are marrying

someone African American and those doors are going to close." Her African American husband added, "Yeah, you're limiting yourself." And she continued, "Because of the prejudice that exists in our society, and the racism that exists in our society."[14]

Both of these quotes underscore that despite the increased racial and ethnic diversity of American society generated largely by immigration from Latin America and Asia, color-coded race remains an impermeable social barrier.

Few studies, however, have examined the degree to which these social barriers vary among the diverse black immigrant population. Research suggests that highly educated black Americans have higher intermarriage rates than those with fewer years of schooling.[15] Although many black immigrant subgroups, particularly those from sub-Saharan Africa, have higher levels of education than the average black American, their education levels do not translate into higher levels of intermarriage. Indeed, highly educated black immigrants have lower rates of intermarriage than other highly educated racial minorities.[16] Prior studies also have produced mixed results concerning whether black immigrants are more likely to intermarry than black Americans. Suzanne Model and Gene Fisher found that unions between West Indians and white Americans occur more regularly than marriages between black and white Americans.[17] However, using data from the 2000 U.S. census, Christie Batson, Zhenchao Qian, and Daniel Lichter show that, relative to black Americans, black Puerto Ricans and black immigrants from the West Indies and Africa have lower rates of intermarriage and cohabitation with white Americans. The authors conclude that "if intermarriage is our measure, social distance between whites and all groups of blacks is wide in the United States."[18] They also show that, despite the surprisingly low numbers of interracial marriages, more marriages occur between black immigrants and black Americans than between black immigrants and white Americans. These findings further highlight the significance of color-coded race in American society.

Despite the significant contributions of prior work on intermarriages among blacks in the United States, few studies have examined the full range of variation in intermarriage within that population. Indeed, the most influential studies in the area examine only variation in intermarriage between white Americans and two regional subgroups of black immigrants: those from the Caribbean and those from Africa. There is probably significant variation, however, in intermarriage among immigrants from these two regions. For example, three Caribbean countries, Trinidad and Tobago, Guyana, and the Dominican Republic, have large immigrant flows, and all three countries also have large mixed-race populations. Unions are frequently formed between members of the Afro-descendant groups and both the South and East Asian populations in Trinidad and Tobago, and the mestizo (or mixed-race) population is the largest racial-ethnic group in the Dominican Republic. By contrast, Haiti and Jamaica have relatively racially homogenous populations. Given this variation in marriage norms across Caribbean countries, generated in part by differences in the racial composition of these countries, intermarriages may occur more frequently among black immigrants from Trinidad and Tobago, Guyana, and particularly the Dominican Republic, and less frequently among immigrants from Haiti or Jamaica.

Moreover, marriage customs vary considerably among black African immigrants, particularly along religious lines. Sudan, Somalia, and Sierra Leone have large Muslim populations. By contrast, Christians account for the largest religious group in the other major black immigrant-sending countries in sub-Saharan Africa: Nigeria, Ghana, Ethiopia, Kenya, Liberia, and Cameroon. Thus, in addition to skin shade, religion may play a significant role in producing marriage patterns among black African immigrants. Additionally, as documented in chapter 3, across the primary sending countries, black immigrants face different reception contexts, patterns of economic incorporation, and degrees of selectivity. I paint a more comprehensive portrait of the marriage landscape for black immigrants in the United States in this chapter by documenting patterns of intermarriage, intramarriage, and endogamy among white Americans, black Americans, and the major black immigrant country groups. The chapter continues my analytic strategy of examining disparities between black American movers and nonmovers to disentangle the relative importance of selective migration in producing disparities among blacks in the United States.

Marriage Patterns

Before analyzing differential patterns of inter- and intramarriage, I provide context for understanding these patterns by highlighting the unique factors that shape the family structure of black Americans.

I also provide current estimates of differences in marriage patterns across the groups.

THE HISTORY OF RACIAL DISPARITIES IN MARRIAGE

A large literature documents marriage disparities between black and white Americans since the late 1800s. In 1880, 57 percent of black American households were composed of married couples, compared to 67.3 percent of white Americans, a difference of ten percentage points.[19] Although the racial gap in marriage has fluctuated since the 1880s, it remained relatively stable for close to eighty years.

Around 1960, however, both groups experienced a significant decrease in the proportion of married individuals, with a more dramatic decrease among black Americans.[20] In 1940, 49.4 percent of black American households were composed of married couples, compared to 66.0 percent of white American households, a difference of 16.6 percentage points.[21] By 1960, the marriage gap between the two groups had increased to 21.7 percentage points, growing to 24.0 percentage points by 1980. In 2014, among adults age twenty-five or older, approximately 61 percent of both white American men and women were married, compared to 40 percent of black American men and 31 percent of black American women (author's calculation), a gap of twenty percentage points for men and thirty percentage points for women.

Several factors help explain changes in the marriage gap between black and white Americans. In terms of demographic mechanisms, this gap was driven primarily by a more rapid decline in the proportion of married blacks rather than a significant increase in marriage among white Americans. Moreover, before 1960, the age at first marriage and the proportion of ever-married women were similar for both black and white American women.[22] These figures have changed considerably, however, since the 1960s. Using data from 1979 to 1986, Lichter and his colleagues found that only about 50 percent of black American women were expected to marry by age twenty-eight, compared to nearly 80 percent of white women.[23] Moreover, by 2010, black American women were waiting about four years longer than white American women to get married. These changes partly explain disparities in marriage patterns between black and white women.

In addition to changes in both marriage formation and the mean age at first marriage for black and white Americans, racial disparities in marital stability have also changed since the 1960s. The percentage of ever-married black women who are currently married and living with their first husband at midlife (age forty to forty-four)—in other words, black women who have not divorced or separated and whose husband has not died by midlife—lagged almost twenty percentage points behind that of white women of the same age from the 1930s to the 1960s.[24] By 2012, however, this gap had increased to nearly thirty percentage points.[25] According to Kelly Raley, Megan Sweeney, and Danielle Wondra, this change was driven by at least two factors: mortality rates and divorce rates. First, compared to white American men, on average black American men lived 6.3 fewer years in 1960 and 8.0 fewer years in 1970. Second, although both white and black divorce rates increased between 1940 and 1980, the increase was more pronounced for black women. Moreover, as Raley, Sweeney, and Wondra note:

> Whites and blacks of all classes have experienced delays in marriage, but declines in the proportion ever married at age 40–44 also appeared first for blacks with low levels of education. By 1980, we began to see an educational divergence in family patterns for whites. First, the college-educated saw declines in divorce, while those without college maintained high levels of divorce. More recently, whites with the lowest levels of education are beginning to experience delays in marriage relative to college-educated women, and an increased proportion are likely to never marry.[26]

Thus, some of the social mechanisms affecting the marriage patterns of black Americans also changed the marriage probabilities of whites, but these changes occurred earlier and had a more dramatic impact on black marriage patterns.

Although no single factor explains the widening of the marriage gap between white and black Americans since the 1960s, research has converged on several social mechanisms that are likely to have helped drive divergent marriage patterns between the two groups. First, high levels of unemployment among men in poor urban areas reduced the number of marriageable black men.[27] In the 1970s, at the tail end of the Great Migration, manufacturing in the United States began to significantly decline, and the trend continued throughout the 1970s and 1980s. This economic restructuring had a devastating impact on employment for black American men. Across working ages, black American men often faced unemployment rates that were two to three times those of white American men.[28] Because employment is strongly correlated with men's ability to marry, black American men's high jobless rates combined with black American women's low rates of intermarriage led to a decline in marriage among blacks.

Raley, Sweeney, and Wondra also note that "women tend to marry partners who have accumulated at least as much education as they have."[29] Over the last several decades, the educational attainment of both black and white women has outpaced that of black and white men, respectively, a factor that limits the pool of desirable marriage partners for both groups of women.[30] Because the education gap between men and women is larger for blacks than for whites, this factor has had a stronger impact on marriage rates among blacks.[31]

A third notable factor explaining disparities between the two groups is incarceration rates. The 1970s marked the beginning of a dramatic and rapid increase in the imprisonment rate in the United States. Bruce Western has noted that,

> on any day for the fifty years from 1925 to 1975, about a hundred Americans out of a hundred thousand—just one-tenth of 1 percent of the population—were in prison. From 1975, the imprisonment rate began to rapidly increase. By 2003, the share of the population in prison had increased every year for twenty-eight years, standing at nearly half of 1 percent at the beginning of the new century.[32]

The massive rise in the prison population was not equally distributed across the U.S. population. In 1980, approximately 0.6 percent of white American men were in prisons, compared to 5.2 percent of black American men. By 2008, 1.8 percent of white American men were in prisons, compared to 11.4 percent of black American men.

These disparities are even more pronounced among less-educated individuals.[33] Among men with less than a high school education in 1980, 2.4 percent of white American men were in incarcerated, compared to 10.6 percent of black American men. By 2008, 12 percent of white American men with less than a high school education were incarcerated, compared to 37.2 percent of black American men.[34] The high incarceration rate of less-educated black men helps explain the significant decline in marriage rates and the rise in marital instability among less-educated blacks. Kerwin Kofi Charles and Ming Ching

Luoh estimate that in a given marriage market, defined by race, location, and age, increases in incarceration are negatively associated with female ever-married rates.[35] However, the association varies considerably by race. Among blacks, the increase in male incarceration between 1980 and 2000 accounts for a reduction of somewhere between 13 and 27 percent in black female ever-married rates. Although the absolute rate and the change in the incarceration rate were lower for white men, Charles and Luoh's findings suggest that the change in white male incarceration actually accounts for a greater share of the change in the ever-married rates among white American women.[36]

Lastly, while differential mortality rates between blacks and whites, particularly black men, impacted the number of intact marriages among blacks in midlife, the generally higher mortality from homicide for black American men also had a significant impact on the number of marriageable black men.[37] In 1960, the age-adjusted death rate from homicide for white American men was 3.9 per 100,000 residents. By 1970, the death rate from homicide for white men had increased to 7.2 per 100,000, and then to 10.4 per 100,000 by 1980, after which it declined for the next thirty-five years. Among black American men, in 1960, the age-adjusted death rate from homicide was 42.3 per 100,000 residents. By 1970, that rate had increased to 78.2 per 100,000 before declining to 69.4 per 100,000 in 1980. Similar to the pattern for white men, the death rate from homicide among black American men decreased from 63.1 per 100,000 to 35.4 per 100,000 in 2015, which is lower than the death rate from homicide that prevailed in the 1960s (42.3 per 100,000). Moreover, the increase in the death rate from homicide during the 1970s and 1980s was experienced most pronouncedly among men between the ages of twenty-five and thirty-five—prime marriage age. A similar pattern is seen among whites in the same age range. Indeed, while the percentage increase in the homicide rate was actually larger for white American men between the ages of twenty-five and thirty-five between 1960 and 1970 (119 percent for white men versus 79 percent for black men), the absolute number of deaths had a significant effect on the number of marriageable black men.

This brief history of marriage disparities between black and white Americans highlights some of the barriers to marriage faced by black Americans and less-educated white Americans and also provides background for understanding the context in which intermarriage and intramarriage occur in the United States. In particular, the high unemployment rates, high rates of incarceration, and high homicide rates have had a negative impact on the supply of marriageable black American men in general, creating a scenario where black women, particularly more-educated black women, face significant difficulties in finding husbands.

Because many immigrants marry before migrating to the United States, it is impossible to determine the mechanisms that produce disparities between black immigrants and black Americans. Despite this limitation, studying the marriage patterns of black immigrants can illuminate the impact of black immigration on national estimates of marriage for U.S. blacks in general.

CONTEMPORARY MARRIAGE PATTERNS

Table 7.1 shows marriage patterns for white Americans, black Americans (as well as the subgroups of movers and nonmovers), and black immigrants (as well as the Caribbean and African immigrant subgroups), based on data from the 2010–2014 waves of the American Community Survey. The marriage variable is defined as couples who are currently married with their spouse either present or absent.[38] The table shows a pattern that is very familiar to most demographers but may surprise laypeople: 61 percent of white American males ages twenty-five to sixty-four were married, compared to just 40 percent of black American males, a difference of twenty-one percentage points. With respect to domestic migration status, black American movers were substantially more likely to be married than black American nonmovers (47 percent and 36 percent, respectively). Despite modest differences in marriage rates among black immigrant men by region of birth, both African and Caribbean black immigrants were more likely to be married than either black Americans collectively or black American movers. Indeed, the marriage rates of both African and Caribbean immigrant men were more similar to those of white American men than those of black American men.

Table 7.1 reveals even larger racial disparities in marriage among women than among men. The marriage rate for white American women (62 percent) was double the rate for black American women (31 percent). The data in table 7.1 also further highlight the significance of selective

Table 7.1 *Proportion Married, by Race and Country of Origin, Adults Ages Twenty-Five to Sixty-Four, 2010–2014*

	Men	Women
Native whites	0.61	0.62
Black Americans	0.40	0.31
Black American movers	0.47	0.36
Black American nonmovers	0.36	0.28
All black immigrants	0.63	0.53
Black Caribbean immigrants	0.63	0.48
Haiti	0.64	0.53
Dominican Republic	0.57	0.44
Jamaica	0.62	0.46
Trinidad and Tobago	0.63	0.50
Guyana	0.67	0.51
Black African immigrants	0.63	0.60
Nigeria	0.73	0.70
Ethiopia	0.59	0.57
Ghana	0.62	0.56
Kenya	0.63	0.60
Liberia	0.57	0.51
Somalia	0.68	0.56
Cameroon	0.58	0.57
Sierra Leone	0.59	0.54
Sudan	0.59	0.75

Source: 2010–2014 ACS.
Note: Weighted values.

migration in generating differential marriage patterns among black Americans: 36 percent of black American female movers were married, compared to only 28 percent of their nonmoving counterparts. Marriage patterns also differ among black immigrant women, with women from Africa being more likely to be married (60 percent) than women from the Caribbean (48 percent). An even more significant pattern is that black immigrant women were far more likely to be married than black American women: more than half of all black immigrant women (53 percent) were married, compared to 36 percent of black American female movers and 28 percent of black American female nonmovers.

As shown throughout this book, black immigrants are far from a monolithic population. Even among immigrants from Africa and the Caribbean, there is considerable variation by country of origin. Table 7.1 also shows marriage patterns for immigrants from the focal Caribbean sending countries. The share of married individuals ranges from 67 percent (Guyana) to 57 percent (Dominican Republic) among Caribbean men and from 53 percent (Haiti) to 44 percent (Dominican Republic) among Caribbean women. For both men and women, every subgroup of Caribbean immigrants was more likely to be married than black American movers (47 percent of male movers and 36 percent of female movers). Table 7.1 shows similar variation in marriage rates among immigrants from Africa, with the percentage of married individuals ranging from 73 percent among Nigerian men to 57 percent among Liberian women. Further, like the Caribbean immigrant subgroups, every subgroup of African men and women had a higher marriage rate than black American movers.

Not surprisingly, marriage patterns vary considerably by age, socioeconomic status, urban or rural residence, and state of residence.[39] To examine how these factors impact marriage patterns in the United States, figure 7.1 presents results from linear probability regression models of marriage. Two regression models are estimated for men and women: a base model that includes adjustments for age differences across the subgroups, and an adjusted model that includes controls for age, education, metropolitan area status, and state of current residence.[40]

The results of the base model show that, compared to black American movers, the probability of being married was sixteen percentage points higher for white American men and twenty-eight percentage points higher for white American women. Among black Americans, the probability of being married was nine percentage points lower for male nonmovers and six percentage points lower for female nonmovers. Despite the substantial variation in marriage patterns among black immigrants, the probability of being married was universally higher for black immigrants than for black American movers in the base model.

The adjusted model shows that even after controlling for a standard set of social and demographic characteristics, compared to black

Figure 7.1 *Regressions of Marriage for Black American, White American, and Black Immigrant Adults, Ages Twenty-Five to Sixty-Four, 2010–2014*

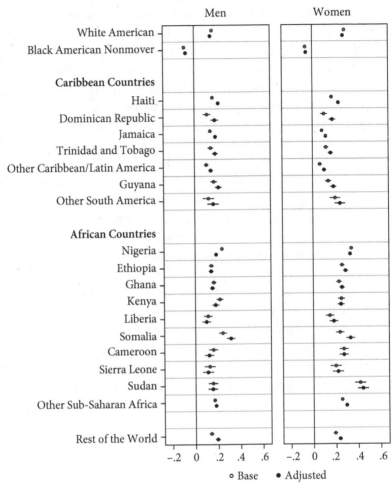

Source: 2010–2014 ACS.
Note: Reference category: black American movers.

American movers, the probability of being married was higher for all black immigrant subgroups. This snapshot of marital status shows that marriage patterns among black immigrants differ considerably from those of black American movers. In the next section, I extend the analysis of marriage differences by examining marriage trajectories among the black population between 1980 and 2014.

MARRIAGE TRAJECTORIES OVER TIME

As discussed earlier in the chapter, over the past several decades, marriage rates have declined for both blacks and whites in the United States. Figures 7.2 to 7.5 illustrate this trend for white Americans, black Americans, and black immigrants. Although the proportion of adults who are married has been consistently higher for white Americans than for black Americans (both movers and nonmovers), between 1980 and 2014, marriage declined significantly for all three groups. Looking first at changes among men, figure 7.2 shows that the proportion of white American men who were married dropped by eighteen percentage points, from 79 percent in 1980 to 61 percent in 2014. This change is dramatic, but the decline was even larger among black American men. The share of married black American nonmovers and movers declined by 40 percent and 27 percent, respectively.

During the same period, marriage also declined among women. Figure 7.3 shows that 76 percent of white American women were married in 1980, but by 2014 only 62 percent were married, an eighteen-percentage-point reduction. The proportion of married black American women has been consistently larger among movers. Moreover, the gap between movers and nonmovers has increased over time among black American women: in 1980, 47 percent of nonmovers and 49 percent of movers were married, a gap of only two percentage points. By 2014, only 28 percent of nonmovers and 36 percent of movers were married. This difference of eight percentage points marks a fourfold increase in the marriage gap over the thirty-four-year period.

Seventy-one percent of black immigrant men were married in 1980, compared to 63 percent in 2014, an eight-percentage-point reduction. Thus, immigrants saw a slower pace of decline in marriage rates than any of the three American subgroups of men (whites, black movers, and black nonmovers). These trends vary, however, across the two primary sending regions of black immigrants. While marriage declined by 13 percent among Caribbean men (from 73 percent to 63 percent) between 1980 and 2014, there was almost no change among African men during this period—approximately 61 percent were married in 1980 compared to 63 percent in 2014. A slightly different pattern unfolded among female black immigrants. In 1980, 56 percent of all

Figure 7.2 *Marriage Trends for Men, Ages Twenty-Five to Sixty-Four, 1980–2014*

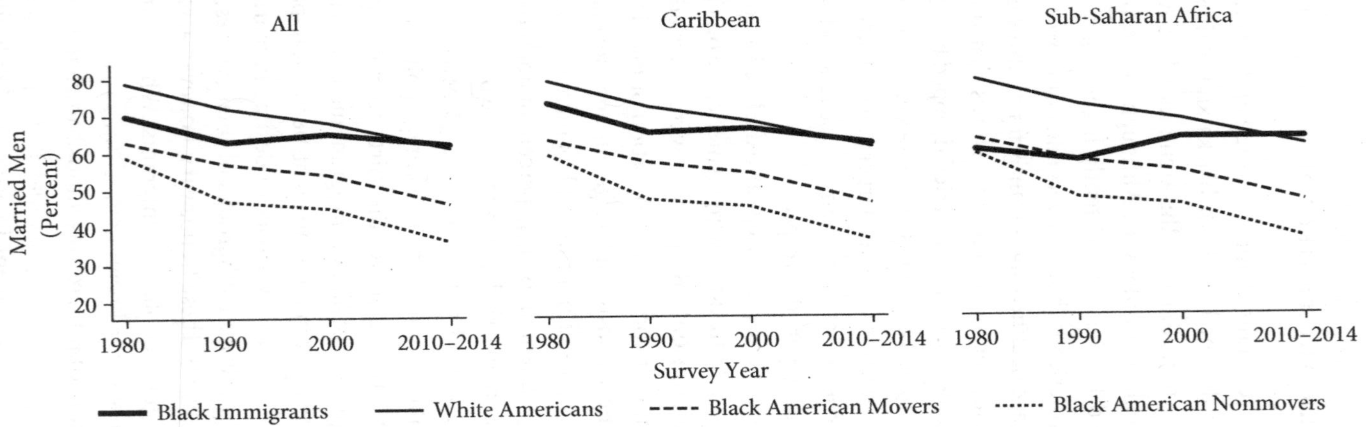

Source: U.S. census and ACS.

Figure 7.3 *Marriage Trends for Women, Ages Twenty-Five to Sixty-Four, 1980–2014*

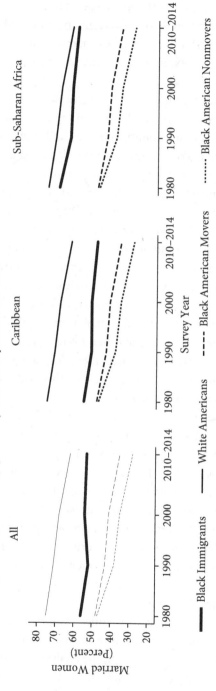

Source: U.S. census and ACS.

black immigrant women between the ages of twenty-five and sixty-four were married, compared to 53 percent in 2014. Although African women have consistently had higher marriage rates than Caribbean women, both groups experienced similar declines in marriage during the focal period.

Figures 7.4 and 7.5 illustrate the degree of heterogeneity in marriage trends between 1980 and 2014 among men and women from eight immigrant-sending countries in the Caribbean and Africa.[41] For example, in 1980, marriage rates among black immigrant men from the Caribbean varied by only eight percentage points, the smallest proportion of married men being from the Dominican Republic (69 percent) and the largest proportion from Guyana (77 percent). Among African male immigrants in the same year, marriage rates ranged from 39 percent among Ethiopian immigrants to 63 percent among Ghanaians. All subgroups of men from the Caribbean experienced declines in marriage between 1980 and 2014. Among Africans, men from Ghana saw a very modest decline in marriage during this period (one percentage point), while rates increased among men from Nigeria and Ethiopia. By the 2010–2014 period, immigrant men from Nigeria were more likely to be married than white American men; despite the modest decline among Ghanaian men, marriage rates for this group had converged with those of white American men.

Figure 7.5 shows that women experienced slightly different marriage trajectories than men, although some general patterns hold for both groups. With the exception of immigrants from Ethiopia, all other subgroups of black immigrant women saw a modest decline in the proportion of married individuals over the period. The marriage patterns of Caribbean immigrants were more like those of black American movers than white Americans and black American non-movers. In contrast, the marriage patterns of immigrant women from sub-Saharan Africa, particularly women from Nigeria and Ghana, resembled those of white American women more than those of female black American movers.

The trend analysis confirms findings from prior studies: marriage has declined among both black Americans and white Americans over the last thirty-four years. However, the analysis also shows that marriage trajectories vary dramatically within the U.S. black population. Black Americans as a whole are less likely to be married than black

Figure 7.4 *Marriage Trends for Men, Ages Twenty-Five to Sixty-Four, 1980–2014*

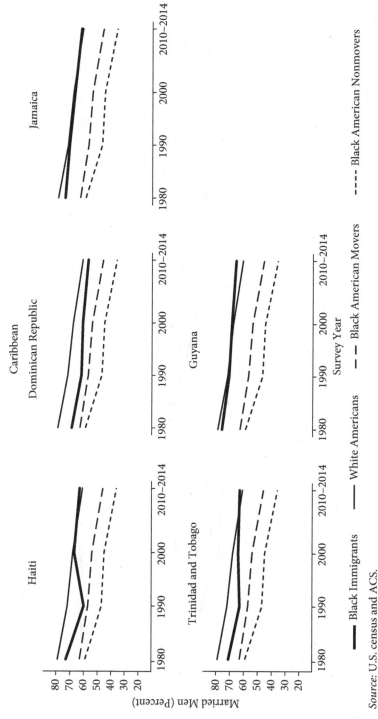

Caribbean

Source: U.S. census and ACS.

(continued)

Figure 7.4 (*continued*)

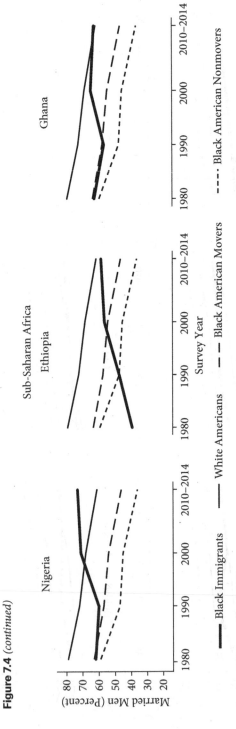

Source: U.S. census and ACS.

Figure 7.5 *Marriage Trends for Women, Ages Twenty-Five to Sixty-Four, 1980–2014*

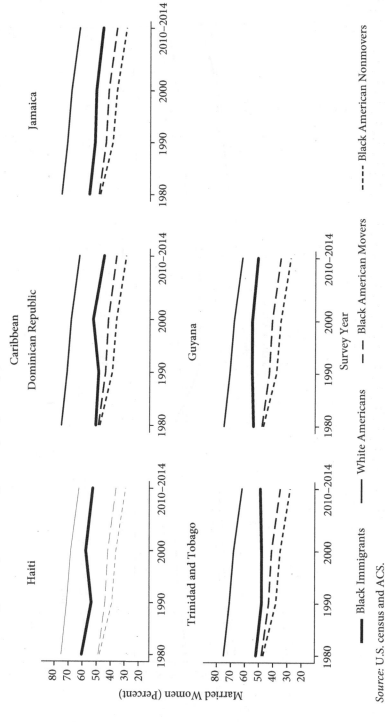

Caribbean

Source: U.S. census and ACS.

(continued)

Figure 7.5 *(continued)*

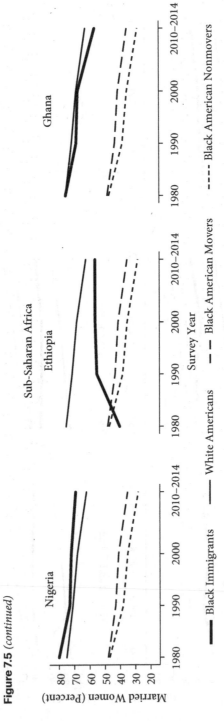

Source: U.S. census and ACS.

immigrants. Moreover, black immigrants' marriage trajectories are more similar to those of black American movers and white Americans than to those of black American nonmovers.

SECTION SUMMARY

The goal of this section was to highlight notable changes in marriage patterns among the black population in the United States. The trends outlined here are familiar to many demographers. During the last four decades, marriage declined significantly among both black and white Americans. As with prior outcomes, migration seems to play a significant role in shaping patterns of marriage among black Americans. Among both men and women, compared to black American nonmovers, black American movers were more likely to be married across the focal period.

The trend analysis in this section shows that research that implicitly assumes that changes in marriage patterns among blacks stem from changes in the social position of black Americans tells only part of the story. With a few exceptions, black immigrants have been more likely to marry than black Americans, both movers and nonmovers, over the last thirty-four years. This trend has put upward pressure on marriage rates for the entire black population. With this background in place, I now turn to analyzing patterns of union formation among blacks.

Determinants of Intermarriage

Although sociologists consider intermarriage to be a marker of social distance between native and immigrant populations, several proximate factors also influence the proclivity of groups to cross racial boundaries when making marriage decisions. For example, intermarriage patterns vary considerably by gender, social and economic status, and race.[42] In the marriage market, potential mates often stereotype black men as both more masculine and sexually potent than white and Asian men, characteristics that could make them more attractive in the out-marriage market.[43] Conversely, relative to nonblack women, black women are stereotyped as either more aggressive or forceful, as well as less ladylike, than white, Hispanic, and Asian women, qualities that reduce their attractiveness in the out-marriage market.[44] Patterns of inter-marriage provide evidence that such biases are salient in the marriage market. Although blacks are far less likely to out-marry than both Asians and Hispanics, black men are more likely to out-marry than black women. Moreover, Asian women are far more likely to marry white men than Asian men are to marry white women. The extant lit-erature suggests that black American, African, West Indian, and Puerto Rican men are all more successful in obtaining nonblack partners than their female counterparts.

The maintenance of class homogamy and upward mobility also influence intermarriage. In marriage markets with few in-group mem-bers, individuals may decide to cross racial boundaries to obtain a spouse of similar class status.[45] Moreover, intermarriage often involves a status exchange: for example, an economically advantaged racial minority (such as a high-income black American man) marries a less affluent person in a more favored racial group (for example, a white American women). In such scenarios, the favored racial group member exchanges his or her racial status for upward economic mobility and the racial minority exchanges economic status for greater acceptance in the dominant society.[46]

Some aspects of the local marriage market also impact patterns of intermarriage.[47] Intermarriages occur more frequently among immi-grants living in areas where few conationals or coethnics reside. Lower intermarriage rates prevail in areas with constant immigrant flows. Continual flows of immigrants into a particular geographic area gen-erate a steady supply of potential coethnics or conational marriage partners, a phenomenon often referred to as "immigrant replenish-ment."[48] Indeed, the sociologists Kate Choi and Marta Tienda argue that the characteristics associated with the marriage market, such as group size, rather than individual traits explain a larger share of panethnic differences in intermarriage.[49] The authors suggest that the limited supply of coethnics in a marriage market is a primary deter-minant of intermarriage decisions and provide evidence to support this claim regarding the importance of marriage market characteris-tics in producing patterns of intermarriage for Asian and Hispanic. However, they find that, among blacks, individual characteristics, such as social and economic status, are more important determinants of marriage choice than marriage market characteristics. These findings again highlight the unique position of blacks in the marriage market.

The Analytic Plan

To determine whether the patterns observed for black Americans hold for the various subgroups of blacks, I document variation in intermarriage by region of birth, country of birth, and internal migration status within the black population of the United States. I also examine the influence of the following key demographic, social, and economic characteristics known to influence the probability of intermarriage: education, state of current residence in the United States, metropolitan area status, English proficiency, and earnings.

The extant literature suggests that the determinants of first marriages differ substantially from the determinants of subsequent marriages. Moreover, the stock of individuals in the United States who are unmarried includes individuals who were formerly married. To account for these factors, I restrict my analysis of intermarriage to individuals in their first marriage and individuals married less than five years. Although the data allow for an analysis of only newly married individuals—those who married within the last year—such a restriction would limit my ability to examine variation in intermarriage across the primary sending countries. Restricting the sample to individuals married for less than five years creates a large enough analytic sample to study subgroup heterogeneity within both the Caribbean and African samples, while also minimizing the influence of divorce and mortality on marriage.

The relative timing of marriage and immigration creates an additional methodological problem. Many immigrants marry before moving to the United States. Given that some black immigrants come from racially homogenous societies, they are unlikely to intermarry before immigrating to the United States. To address this exposure issue, I further restrict the analytic sample to individuals who married after arriving in the United States. Most chapters in the book have included trend analyses of the focal outcome, but because the data needed to produce the precise estimates of intermarriage patterns are available only for after 2008, the analysis in this chapter is limited to the 2010–2014 time period.

Table 7.2 *Proportions Intermarried, Intramarried, or in Endogamous Marriages of Black Americans and Black Immigrants, Adults Ages Twenty-Five to Sixty-Four, 2010–2014*

	Intermarried		Intramarried		Endogamous	
	Men	Women	Men	Women	Men	Women
Black Americans	0.14	0.06	0.05	0.06	0.74	0.85
Black American movers	0.17	0.08	0.06	0.08	0.69	0.81
Black American nonmovers	0.12	0.05	0.05	0.05	0.77	0.87
All black immigrants	0.10	0.07	0.21	0.16	0.57	0.66
Black Caribbean immigrants	0.06	0.04	0.21	0.18	0.60	0.66
Haiti	0.02	0.01	0.13	0.05	0.81	0.91
Dominican Republic	0.03	0.07	0.07	0.15	0.68	0.60
Jamaica	0.09	0.05	0.27	0.28	0.53	0.57
Trinidad and Tobago	0.12	0.03	0.31	0.27	0.39	0.41
Guyana	0.08	0.03	0.17	0.16	0.63	0.64
Black African immigrants	0.11	0.08	0.20	0.11	0.59	0.72
Nigeria	0.10	0.05	0.35	0.14	0.50	0.76
Ethiopia	0.02	0.05	0.03	0.06	0.92	0.82
Ghana	0.18	0.03	0.21	0.08	0.56	0.82
Kenya	0.25	0.22	0.22	0.21	0.45	0.55
Liberia	0.04	0.06	0.17	0.00	0.63	0.90
Somalia	0.02	0.01	0.02	0.05	0.9	0.86
Cameroon	0.09	0.03	0.10	0.04	0.72	0.81
Sierra Leone	0.00	0.00	0.06	0.17	0.80	0.66
Sudan	0.02	0.00	0.04	0.08	0.76	0.81

Source: 2010–2014 ACS.
Note: Weighted values.

THE BASIC FACTS

Table 7.2 shows patterns of intermarriage (defined as marriages between white Americans and blacks of any nationality), intramarriage (defined as marriages between black Americans and black immigrants), and endogamy for black Americans, black immigrants (defined as marriage among blacks from the same birth country), and white Americans.

Like the general portrait of marriage, table 7.2 highlights systematic differences in intermarriage across the black population. Among married men, black American men were more likely to have a white spouse than black immigrants from either the Caribbean and Africa.

Indeed, 14 percent of married black American men had a white American spouse, compared to 10 percent of black immigrants. The panel also highlights the importance of selective migration for understanding differential patterns of intermarriage among black Americans. Seventeen percent of married black American male movers and 12 percent of married black American male nonmovers had a white spouse; this five-percentage-point difference represents a larger intermarriage gap than the general gap between black American men and black immigrant men of four percentage points.

In contrast to the many patterns previously documented in this book showing that black American movers and black immigrants have similar outcomes, black immigrants from both the Caribbean and Africa had a lower probability of being intermarried than black American movers. Indeed, with 6 percent of Caribbean men and 11 percent of African men having a white spouse, black immigrant men had intermarriage rates that are more comparable to those of black American nonmovers.

Consistent with prior research documenting the gendered nature of intermarriage among blacks, in striking contrast to the finding for black men, only 6 percent of married black American woman and 7 percent of black immigrant women had a white spouse. The descriptive results for women also highlight the importance of selective migration in intermarriage among black American women: married black American female movers (8 percent) were more likely to have a white spouse than married black American female nonmovers (5 percent).

Table 7.2 also shows that while endogamy, or marriages among immigrants from the same country, is the dominant trend for black immigrants, a significant share of black immigrant men and women marry black Americans. Indeed, while only 10 percent of married black immigrant men had a white spouse, 21 percent were married to black American women. Similarly, 7 percent of black immigrant women married white American men, but 16 percent married black American men. Among immigrant women from the two primary sending regions, Caribbean immigrants were more likely than African immigrants to marry black Americans. Men from the Caribbean and Africa had roughly the same probability of marrying a black American woman. Men from both the Caribbean and Africa, however, were more likely than women from these regions to marry black Americans.

The regional patterns paint only a partial picture of variation in intermarriage among blacks. Table 7.2 shows that greater variation exists among both Caribbean and African immigrants than between the two regional groupings. Although only 6 percent of married Caribbean men had a white spouse, intermarriage estimates vary from 2 percent among Haitian men to 12 percent among men from Trinidad and Tobago. Immigrant men from Jamaica (9 percent) and Guyana (11 percent) had similar intermarriage rates. Immigrant women showed similar disparities: fewer than 1 percent of Haitian women had a white spouse, compared to 7 percent of women from the Dominican Republic.

Intramarriage also varies greatly among Caribbean men and women. Only 13 percent of men from Haiti and 7 percent of men from the Dominican Republic had a black American spouse. By contrast, 27 percent of married Jamaican men and 31 percent of married men from Trinidad and Tobago had a black American spouse. Like Caribbean men, women from Haiti had the lowest rates of intramarriage, and women from Jamaica and Trinidad and Tobago had the highest.

Table 7.2 shows that intermarriage rates vary more among immigrants from Africa than among immigrants from the Caribbean. Immigrants from Somalia, Ethiopia, Sierra Leone, and Sudan, the four African countries in the analysis with large Muslim populations at origin, had the lowest rates of intermarriage, and immigrants from Kenya had the highest.

Patterns of intramarriage also vary among African immigrants. Most notable are the patterns of intramarriage for immigrant men from Nigeria, Ghana, and Kenya, with 35 percent, 21 percent, and 22 percent of the population, respectively, marrying black American women. These three groups also highlight the gendered nature of intramarriage among African immigrants. Only 14 percent of Nigerian women, 8 percent of Ghanaian women, and 21 percent of Kenyan women had a black American spouse. These descriptive results underscore the considerable heterogeneity in intermarriage and intramarriage among African immigrants, with some subgroups of African men being significantly more likely than their female counterparts to marry white and black Americans.

STRAIGHTFORWARD EXPLANATIONS

Social, demographic, and structural factors affect the likelihood of marrying a different-race spouse. Figure 7.6 shows in slightly more formal fashion some of the relationships presented in table 7.2 by providing estimates of intermarriage from linear probability models. Figure 7.6 evaluates the relationship between marriage partner choice and nativity, net of important determinants of marriage and intermarriage: age, education, place of residence, metropolitan area status, English-language proficiency, and annual earnings. The base model for each sex simply tests the statistical significance of the descriptive results shown in table 7.2 controlling for age differences across the populations. The adjusted model shows disparities in the probability of being intermarried after accounting for social and demographic characteristics.

The base model results for both men and women confirm the substantive results illustrated in the descriptive table: except for women from Kenya, all other subgroups of black immigrants were either less likely or similarly likely to marry white Americans as black American movers, the reference group. The adjusted model also shows that despite significant differences in social and demographic characteristics, particularly education and region of residence, accounting for these factors has no substantive impact on disparities in intermarriage among blacks. Indeed, the results in the base and adjusted models are remarkably similar.

Figure 7.7 estimates the same models for intramarriage. The estimates in this figure are based only on black immigrants, with Jamaican immigrants, the largest black immigrant subgroup, as the reference group for all models. The estimates are consistent with those presented in the descriptive results. The base model shows that immigrant men from Haiti, the Dominican Republic, Ethiopia, Somalia, Sierra Leone, and Sudan were less likely to intramarry than Jamaican men. All other subgroups of immigrant men had a similar likelihood of being intramarried as Jamaican immigrants. With the exception of women from Haiti, who were less likely to have a black American spouse, all other subgroups of black Caribbean women were equally likely to marry

Figure 7.6 *Regressions of Intermarriage for Black Americans and Black Immigrants, Adults Ages Twenty-Five to Sixty-Four, 2010–2014*

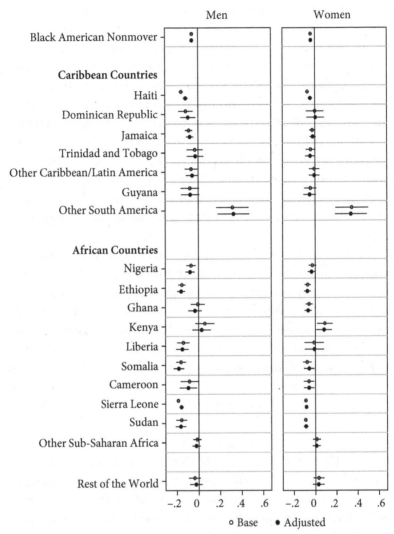

Source: 2010–2014 ACS.
Note: Reference category: black American movers.

Figure 7.7 *Regressions of Intramarriage for Black Immigrants, Adults Ages Twenty-Five to Sixty-Four, 2010–2014*

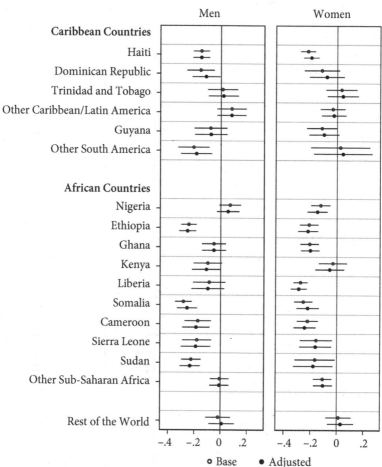

Source: 2010–2014 ACS.
Note: Reference category: Jamaica.

black American men as Jamaican women were. Although the probability of being intramarried was similar for Jamaican and Kenyan women, all other subgroups of black African women were less likely to marry black American men than Jamaican women.

The last set of results presented in this chapter relate to endogamy (figure 7.8), defined as marriages among blacks from the same birth country. The reference group for these regression models is black

Figure 7.8 *Regressions of Endogamy for Black Americans and Black Immigrants, Adults Ages Twenty-Five to Sixty-Four, 2010–2014*

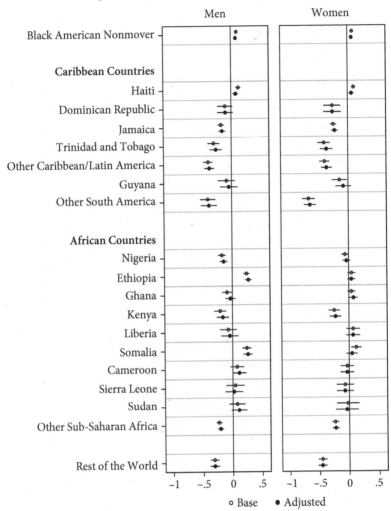

Source: 2010–2014 ACS.

Note: Reference category: black American movers.

American movers. Focusing on the adjusted models, among black Americans, both men and women, movers have a greater probability of being in an endogamous union than nonmovers. Figure 7.8 shows that patterns of endogamy vary considerably among immigrants from the Caribbean and those for Africa.

The pattern is similar for immigrants from the Caribbean, both men and women. Compared to black American movers, in-group marriages are more likely among immigrants from Haiti. The data suggest that immigrants from Jamaica, Trinidad and Tobago, and the Dominican Republic (although slightly insignificant for immigrant men from the Dominican Republic) are less likely to be in an endogamous marriage than black American movers.

Among immigrants from sub-Saharan Africa, patterns of endogamous unions vary to some degree by sex. Among men, compared to black American movers, immigrants from Nigeria and Kenya are less likely to marry coethnics, whereas immigrants from Ethiopia and Somalia are more likely to do so. There is no statistically significant difference in the probability of marrying a coethnic between black American movers and immigrants from Ghana, Cameroon, Sierra Leone, and Sudan. After controlling for a standard set of social and demographic characteristics, with the exception of immigrants from Kenya (who are less likely to marry coethnics), the probability of marrying a coethnic is similar for black American movers and all other subgroups of black African women.

Chapter Summary

Scholars consider intermarriages, particularly marriages between ethnic minorities and white Americans, to be a barometer of the degree of social integration within the country. Intermarriage rates reflect the strength of racially and ethnically based barriers to the formation of intimate social relationships and often signal the erosion of native hostilities toward minority group members.[50] Asian and Hispanic immigrants are good examples of such societal shifts. These groups have experienced harsh treatment in the United States, through both immigration policy and acts of racial violence, yet Asian and Hispanic immigrants are now the primary drivers of patterns of intermarriage within the country. At the same time, however, marriages between blacks and whites in the United States remain stubbornly low, signaling the persistence of the hard boundaries associated with blackness in the nation. Although prior studies have documented intermarriage trends for U.S.-born blacks and whites, relatively few have examined the dynamics among both the immigrant and native black populations or explored the degree of birth-country variation within the black immigrant population.

The analyses in this chapter produced several key findings. First, relative to black Americans, black immigrants are less likely to marry white Americans. Second, among black Americans, those who move across state lines are more likely than nonmovers to marry whites. Third, this is the first study to my knowledge that uses data for the primary sending countries of black immigrants from both the Caribbean and Africa to reveal the remarkable variation in inter- and intramarriage among black immigrants from these regions. Among immigrants from the Caribbean, those from Haiti are the least likely to marry whites or black Americans—and thus the most likely to be in an endogamous relationship—and those from Jamaica and Trinidad and Tobago are more likely to out-marry, particularly with black Americans. Among immigrants from Africa, those from Somalia, Sierra Leone, Sudan, and Ethiopia are the least likely to marry Americans, either black or white. Among African American immigrants, individuals from Nigeria, Ghana, and Kenya are more likely to out-marry, particularly with black Americans. Fourth, among black immigrants from the Caribbean and Africa, black men are more likely to out-marry than their female compatriots. These findings raise two important questions for understanding differential patterns of intermarriage among blacks in the United States.

1. *Why are black American movers more likely than black American nonmovers to marry white Americans?*

The findings in this chapter highlight the importance of unobserved forms of selectivity and potentially contextual differences in the places where black American movers tend to reside. Like international migrants, domestic migrants are probably positivity selected on observed characteristics that produce more favorable labor market outcomes. Although I account for some of these factors, unobserved factors such as early life social context (for example, attending a majority-white college), soft skills, and social class may also play a role in producing the higher intermarriage rate among black American movers. Moreover, although most black American movers reside in the South, the data used in this chapter do not allow me to evaluate neighborhood or workplace context. Such factors might produce differences in the types of people with whom black American movers and black American nonmovers come in contact, and that may influence patterns of intermarriage.

2. *What are the implications of these results for understanding the iconic color line in the twenty-first century?*

Findings from the analyses in this chapter provide support for a model of marital assimilation along the color line, with all groups of blacks significantly less likely to marry white Americans than they are to marry other blacks, regardless of nationality. Keep in mind that the intermarriage patterns documented in this chapter relate to immigrants who were unmarried when they arrived in the United States. Given this, the results also highlight that despite the popular rhetoric about the salience of the black American underclass, relative to black Americans, the social distance from whites is greater among Haitian and African immigrants who come from Muslim-majority countries. Again, these results are likely to reflect Haitian immigrants' low levels of educational attainment and the harsh political context that met them upon arrival in the United States. In chapter 3, I argued that, among black immigrants, those from countries with large Muslin populations (Somalia, Sierra Leone, Sudan, and Ethiopia) are more likely to face a negative reception context. Although the low intermarriage rates among immigrants from these countries probably reflect Muslim marriage customs, they also reflect hostility among Americans toward members of these groups. Consequently, while both the black-white and black-nonblack color lines remain salient features of American society, in the coming decades Haitians and African Muslim immigrants may find themselves furthest away from these imaginary color lines.

CHAPTER EIGHT

CONCLUSION

After researching the social integration of black immigrants for several years, I observed two major gaps in the extant literature. First, despite the rapid growth of the population, no studies had provided a detailed analysis of how black immigration has changed patterns of stratification among blacks in the United States. Over the last four decades, black immigration has increased by more than 2,000 percent, and immigrants hailing from the Caribbean and Africa have changed the face of cities throughout the country. Indeed, in some states, such as Minnesota and Washington, black African immigrants are now one of the primary drivers of growth in the overall black population. The most influential studies on black immigrants, however, were conducted during the 1980s and 1990s using data drawn almost exclusively from Caribbean immigrants in New York City. No prior study has provided a comprehensive portrait of the new diversity of the black population in the twenty-first century.

Second, I became increasingly unsatisfied by studies purporting to develop theoretical frameworks to explain disparities between black Americans and black immigrants that were inconsistent with the data or failed to account for broader immigration-related dynamics. For example, black immigrants rarely outperformed black Americans in the labor market before 1940, and even in recent years they usually outperform black Americans only after residing in the United States for several decades. Despite studies extolling the achievements of black immigrants during the early twentieth century, my empirical analysis finds very modest differences between the two groups during this period. Consequently, any useful theoretical framework explaining disparities between black Americans and black immigrants must explain why the favorable outcomes of black immigrants are limited almost exclusively to the post–civil rights era.

This book achieves three goals. First, I provide a comprehensive framework for understanding nativity-based economic disparities among blacks in the United States. For several decades research has argued that cultural differences between black Americans and black immigrants explain disparities between the two groups.[1] My research, however, challenges this view and shows that selective migration, the unique benefits of U.S. employment for immigrants, and the advantages associated with migrating to the United States during the post–civil rights era provide a more complete explanation for the documented economic disparities between the two groups. Second, I highlight how black immigration has changed the composition of the U.S. black population and examine the impact of these changes on how scholars and policymakers understand the primary factors underlying fluctuations in black-white disparities. Third, I paint a detailed portrait of inequality within the black population across a range of outcomes in the hope of providing the research community with a rich set of empirical facts that offer the necessary context to frame debates on sources of racial disparities in the twenty-first century.

Key Findings and Implications

GOAL 1: UNDERSTANDING DISPARITIES BETWEEN BLACK AMERICANS AND BLACK IMMIGRANTS

Across many outcomes, some groups of black immigrants have more favorable profiles than their black American counterparts. For several decades, researchers have debated whether culture, discrimination, or selective migration explains these disparities. This literature has produced many useful findings, but it has several limitations. First, most prior studies use the incorrect reference group when making comparisons between black Americans and black immigrants. Black immigrants are a self-selected group of movers. Research shows that compared to residents of their home countries, immigrants tend to have higher levels of education, wealth, and motivation. Consequently, comparisons between black immigrants and all black Americans very well may lead to misleading inferences regarding the mechanisms that produce disparities between the two groups.

Throughout the book, I show that black American movers, individuals who have moved away from the state of their birth, are a more appropriate reference group to use when trying to disentangle the relative importance of the mechanisms theorized to produce disparities between black Americans and black immigrants. Analytically, partitioning black Americans by migration status holds race constant and varies migration. Consequently, if the outcomes of black immigrants result from their status as *movers* rather than from their status as *immigrants*, there should be some convergence in the social outcomes of black immigrants and black American movers.

Throughout the book, I show that the outcomes of black immigrants are more like those of black American movers than those of black American nonmovers, a finding that suggests that the favorable outcomes of some black immigrants derive, at least in part, from processes associated with selective migration. Relative to black American nonmovers, black American movers are more educated, have better labor market outcomes, are more likely to marry and intermarry, and have more favorable health profiles. Although the outcomes of black immigrants are more like those of black American movers than those of black American nonmovers, in many cases black immigrants obtain substantial advantages over black American movers. This suggests that while selective migration is important, it does not completely explain disparities between the two groups.

I highlight a second, less-appreciated mechanism explaining the disparities between the two groups: arrival during the post–civil rights era. Since emancipation, black Americans have endured generations of state-sanctioned exclusion from various apparatuses of upward mobility. The legacy of discriminatory policies throughout the United States, particularly in the South, has created a social context in which a large share of black Americans reside in segregated and disadvantaged neighborhoods, attend underperforming and poorly funded schools, and are the victims of predatory policing that has led to the incarceration of generations of black men. Most black immigrants do not share this history with black Americans.

A sizable number of black immigrants, particularly those from the Caribbean, migrated to the United States during the first three or four decades of the twentieth century, but most black immigrants migrated to the United States during the post-1965 era, a period marked by relatively unprecedented access to opportunities for social mobility for minorities and women. After many years of protests and legal battles, the U.S. Congress passed several civil rights laws that helped make the United States a less overtly racist society across many domains of social life, including education, housing, and access to jobs. Moreover, in the years following the passage of landmark civil rights legislation, the implementation of affirmative action programs in government, education, and parts of the private sector further aided the social mobility of minorities in general and also of women. These programs and legislative victories did not eliminate discrimination, but they did provide avenues of upward mobility for previously disenfranchised groups.

Although it is difficult to produce specific causal estimates, the available data support the conclusion that changes in civil rights laws were one of the mechanisms that produced disparities between black American movers and some black immigrants. Using 1910–1940 data from the full (100 percent) census for New York City, the home of most black immigrants (who hailed primarily from the Caribbean) during the pre-1965 period, I show that black immigrants, while having more education and skills than individuals residing in the Caribbean during the period, show very few differences from black Americans. Contrary to claims in qualitative studies conducted during the 1930s that there were significant cultural differences between the two populations, these differences (if they actually existed) were not enough to overcome the salience of discrimination and racism experienced by all blacks during the early twentieth century.[2] It was only after some of these structural barriers had been removed that black immigrants (later cohorts) were able to generate some advantages over black Americans.

Although research suggests that both black immigrants and black Americans suffer from contemporary forms of discrimination, with some evidence that black Americans experience higher levels of discrimination, the legacy of prior discriminatory policies is reflected more acutely in the outcomes of black Americans. Many black Americans continue to live in highly segregated neighborhoods and attend underperforming schools, factors that are major hurdles to accessing good jobs, developing skills, and maintaining good health.[3] Although many black immigrants hail from countries ranking poorly on measures of social well-being, these social factors are not fully reflected in the outcomes of a selected group of migrants. For example, the mean level of education in Nigeria, the country sending the most African immigrants to the United States, was six years in 2015. Nigerian immigrants in the United States, however, have fifteen mean years of schooling, more than twice that of the population of their origin country. This discrepancy in education suggests that first-generation Nigerian immigrants residing in the United States disproportionately represent the upper social classes of an impoverished nation, where 53.5 percent of residents lived on less than $2 a day in 2014.

Among Nigerians who migrated to the United States as adults, it is possible that this highly selected population had access to more resources and opportunities to develop skills (that is, better education systems) than the average member of the black American population. In summary, the findings here suggest that the ability to obtain skills and resources at origin (selectivity), combined with migrating to the United States during arguably the best (though not a perfect) racial climate that has ever existed in the United States (historical context), sets the stage for some groups of black immigrants to achieve some social and economic advantages over black Americans.

I am not arguing that black immigrants do not experience discrimination, nor am I arguing that all black immigrants experienced the same post-1965 context. For example, the U.S. government has historically taken a restrictive stance toward immigration from Haiti, which in turn has produced native hostility toward the group, making it difficult for Haitians to become fully incorporated in the United States. Moreover, large waves of post-1990 immigrants to the United States arriving from Muslim-majority countries were exposed to social environments and state policies hostile to their origin country and their religion (for example, the Muslim ban proposed by President Trump's administration in 2016), and this factor could have a significant impact on their social integration. Although it is difficult, and beyond the scope of this book, to examine the nuanced factors that produce variation across seven different outcomes for fourteen different immigrant populations, I argue that not sharing the same pre-1965 history as the vast majority of black Americans creates the possibility for some groups of highly selected black immigrants to achieve greater social and economic status than black Americans.

GOAL 2: DISPARITIES AMONG BLACKS

This project highlights how black immigration has changed the demographic makeup of the U.S. black population. In 1960, less than 1 percent of the country's black population was foreign-born. By 2017, that number had increased to approximately 10 percent, a 900 percent increase over a fifty-seven-year period. In addition to decreasing the share of blacks who descend from American slaves, the growth of the black immigrant population has also increased overall birth-country diversity among U.S. blacks. Black immigrants hail from countries all over the world, particularly the Caribbean and Africa. Again, I underscore that black immigrants are not a monolithic group and that in the coming decades a more diverse black population will determine the social and economic trajectories of black America.

Indeed, in many ways my analyses show that the term "black immigrant" is meaningless in many contexts. With a few exceptions, I find that few patterns hold for all black immigrants. For example, black immigrants from the Caribbean have more favorable home-ownership profiles than immigrants from Africa. However, black immigrants from the Dominican Republic are less likely to own homes than blacks from the English-speaking Caribbean or Haiti. Similar degrees of heterogeneity can be found across all of the outcomes examined. These patterns highlight that researchers must collect data and analyze the outcomes of black immigrants at the country level, an exercise that will improve our understanding of how the social and economic conditions of black immigrants will change in the coming decades.

GOAL 3: BLACK-WHITE DISPARITIES

A large literature documents that black Americans trail their white counterparts on nearly every measure of social and economic well-being.[4] Prior to this book, less was known about whether similar patterns existed for black immigrants. My analyses show that black immigration has complicated our understanding of black-white disparities in the United States. When viewed in the aggregate, some social and economic outcomes among black immigrants resemble those of black Americans. In 2014, on average, white Americans had 13.75 mean years of education, more than the mean years of education for black Americans (13.00) and black immigrants collectively (12.98). These aggregate statistics, however, mask important variation among black immigrants. Although the mean education level of all the focal Caribbean countries was lower than that of white Americans, black Africans from Nigeria (15.01), Kenya (14.30), and Cameroon (14.35) had more mean years of schooling than white Americans.

Similarly, in 2014, 71 percent of white households owned the home in which they resided, compared to 39 percent of black Americans and 40 percent of black immigrants. Among black immigrants, however, 46 percent of Caribbean immigrants and 34 percent of African immigrants were homeowners. Indeed, except for immigrants from the Dominican Republic, all the focal Caribbean countries had higher homeownership rates than black Americans. By contrast, while African immigrants experienced a significant increase in homeownership as their tenure of U.S. residence increased, the simple descriptive statistics show that, among Africans, only immigrants from Nigeria had higher homeownership rates than black Americans.

In some outcomes, black immigrants not only look different from black Americans but also show patterns similar to or more favorable than those of white Americans, the most notable example being patterns of health. Indeed, nearly all of the focal black immigrant subgroups reported similar or more favorable health profiles than both white and black Americans.

These complex patterns have implications for the measurement of black-white disparities in the United States. From studies of health to analyses of labor market outcomes, researchers tend to aggregate all blacks, regardless of nativity, when examining racial disparities and explaining changes in social outcomes among blacks. As the black immigrant population grows, these new arrivals will play an increasingly important role in determining the well-being of the U.S. black population. In other words, immigration could drive many of the changes in social well-being among blacks in the United States. My analyses of marriage, education, labor participation, homeownership, and health provide evidence for these predictions.

Because the black immigrant population is still relatively small—approximately 10 percent of the overall black population—black immigration currently plays a limited role in driving racial disparities at the national level. This is not the case, however, in the Northeast, where black immigrants comprise more than 30 percent of the black population. These arrivals are already driving changes in the social profiles of the regional black population. If current immigration policies and patterns of selectivity continue, black immigration could eventually influence national estimates for the entire U.S. black population. Black immigrants accounted for more than 20 percent of the growth in the black population during the first fourteen years of this century. This pace could increase in the coming decades and lead researchers to overlook the historical importance of measuring and tracking disparities between black and white Americans.

To be sure, black immigrants suffer from contemporary forms of racism and discrimination in the United States. Despite black immigrants' higher median education levels, the analysis highlights that they tend to trail white Americans along most measures of social and economic well-being. In addition, the legacy of slavery and institutional racism during the Jim Crow era is still reflected in the social outcomes of black Americans.[5] Given the long history of oppression experienced by black Americans, researchers must systematically disaggregate the black populations when studying U.S. disparities.

Key Limitations

Throughout this book, I have examined disparities between blacks and whites, and among blacks by nativity, in the United States. Like most studies, this book contains a range of nuanced limitations that I have attempted to highlight across the chapters. Two limitations, however, cut across chapters: the invisibility of incarcerated black Americans, particularly men, across the United States, and the complexities of reporting racial identity among Dominicans.[6]

THE MASS INCARCERATION OF BLACK MEN

Although I have highlighted the importance of mass incarceration elsewhere in this book, here I want to further explain why recognizing this phenomenon is important for understanding my findings. In 1980, the incarceration rate for black men between the ages of twenty and thirty-four was 5.2 percent, compared to 0.6 percent for white men. By 2008, the incarceration rate for black men had climbed to 11.4 percent, compared to 1.8 percent for white men.[7] These disparities are more stark among men between the ages of twenty and thirty-four with less than a high school education. Between 1980 and 2008, the incarceration rate for black men with less than a high school education had increased from 10.6 percent to 37.2 percent, a 272 percent increase over the twenty-eight-year period. Among white men with less than a high school education, the incarceration rate had increased from 2.4 percent to 12 percent, a 400 percent increase over the same time period.[8] So while the increase in the incarceration rate was actually greater for whites, the percentage of incarcerated individuals was markedly greater for blacks. Indeed, more than one in three young black men with less than a high school education was in prison in 2008, suggesting that a greater share of young black men with less than a high school education were in prison than employed.[9] These are just a few sobering statistics regarding the magnitude of racial disparities in imprisonment in the United States.

These facts have implications for understanding the findings in this book. All of the analyses conducted in this study, and nearly all other studies on racial disparities in the United States, are based on samples of the non-institutionalized population of the United States. That is, imprisoned individuals are excluded from the analysis. The sociologist Becky Pettit has shown that failing to account for the more than 3 million individuals residing in prison, most of them black, could create biased estimates of racial disparities and the changes in social and economic outcomes among blacks. According to Pettit, the social and economic outcomes of black Americans would look considerably worse if appropriate adjustments were made for the incarcerated population. The percentage of blacks, particularly black men, who did not complete high school, who are unemployed or in the labor force, who are married, or who own homes would be considerably lower than the estimates produced in this book and in prior studies. For example, including inmates in estimates of the percentage of blacks with less than a high school education would increase the percentage of blacks who did not complete high school by 40 percent.[10]

Moreover, the mass incarceration of black Americans does not reflect differences in rates of offending. As Pettit notes:

> There is general agreement that the massive buildup in the size of the penal population has not been due to large-scale changes in crime and criminality. Instead, a host of changes at the local, state, and federal levels with respect to law enforcement and penal policy are implicated in the expansion of the prison system. Law enforcement agencies have stepped up policing, prosecutors have more actively pursued convictions, and there have been myriad changes in sentencing policy that now mandate jail or person time.[11]

Consequently, the findings contained in this book pertain exclusively to individuals who were not institutionalized at the time of the survey. More research is needed to better understand the implications of mass incarceration on within-race variation in social and economic outcomes.

REPORTING DOMINICAN RACIAL IDENTITY

Second, across the outcomes studied, black immigrants from the Dominican Republic tend to have worse outcomes than other black immigrant subgroups. Although these findings reflect the group's negative reception context (being both black and Hispanic), they are also likely to be driven by the complexities of reporting racial identity among group members. For example, most Latino immigrants migrate from countries where the system of racial identification does not center on the two-tiered black-white racial classification model dominant in the U.S. mainland. Thus, some findings in this book might result from measurement issues in racial reporting as Dominican immigrants attempt to identify themselves in an unfamiliar categorization scheme.

The findings might also reflect resistance to identifying as black in light of the complex histories and contexts in which Dominican national identity and racial identity developed in the presence of Spanish, French, and Haitian colonization.[12] Moreover, racial identification in the Dominican Republic follows a three-tiered racial classification system in which dominant categories include black, white, and mulatto or *indio* (Indian) and racial identity is based on phenotype or skin color and physical attributes such as hair texture.[13] Thus, resistance to co-opting a black racial identity might confound estimates of race-based disparities. Future research should examine Latino subgroup variation in the relationship between phenotype or skin color and various social and economic outcomes.[14]

Final Thoughts

In the 1980s, scholars and policy makers argued that black immigrants from the English-speaking Caribbean were a "model minority" because they achieved labor market success despite experiencing the same degree of racism and discrimination as black Americans. These arguments led many to conclude that cultural deficiencies in attitudes toward work among black Americans, rather than racism and discrimination, were responsible for their poor labor market outcomes.[15]

Much of this early debate resulted from a failure of researchers to clearly understand the empirical facts. In chapter 3, I argued that a key component of any culture-of-work framework must take into account disparities in the willingness of groups to work, most succinctly captured by labor force participation. I analyzed disparities in labor force participation between black Americans and black immigrants from the English-speaking Caribbean, the two groups examined in most of the literature on labor market disparities among blacks. I found that after controlling for a basic set of social and demographic characteristics, black immigrants from the English-speaking Caribbean are indeed more likely to participate in the labor force than black Americans. I also found, however, that black immigrants from the English-speaking Caribbean are more likely to participate in the labor market than white Americans as well. Moreover, after residing in the United States for more than twenty years, black immigrant women from the English-speaking Caribbean earn more than both black and white American women.

If researchers had started with these two facts in the 1980s, the discourse concerning the impact of black immigrants on American society would have surely gone in a different direction. The nuanced earnings and labor force participation profiles of black and white women challenge notions that black Americans have a cultural deficit in work attitudes. Indeed, the findings imply that if a cultural deficit exists among black Americans, white Americans suffer from a similar deficit. Obviously, such conclusions are shortsighted. Note that these data patterns existed in the 1980s, when scholars first began to blame the poor outcomes of black Americans on cultural inferiority. I contend that such narratives result from a poor understanding of the basic facts.

Far too often researchers move to the development and testing of theoretical frameworks before clearly understanding the data regularities needed to generate good theories. After reading several decades of research on disparities among blacks in the United States, I became increasingly discontented with theoretical and conceptual contentions that were incongruent with the basic facts, which led me to write this book. Although I hope this book provides theoretical insights that advance our understanding of the sources of racial disparities in the United States, I began this project with the unabashed goal of outlining the facts, nuances, and patterns needed to inform a substantive debate and lead to the creation of sound theories. I hope that the details contained in this book provide a map for researchers seeking to understand the ways in which black immigrants are changing the landscape of black America in the twenty-first century.

METHODOLOGICAL APPENDIX

Chapter 4

DEPENDENT VARIABLES

To evaluate labor market disparities, I construct three dependent variables. First, to evaluate disparities in labor force participation, I generate a dichotomous variable that equals 1 for all individuals who report being in the labor force and 0 for all other individuals. Second, the employed variable equals 1 if a person who reports being in the labor force also reports being employed, and 0 for individuals who are in the labor force but are not employed.

Last, I examine weekly earnings. My preferred earnings variable is the sum of wage or salary income and business income. However, the 2000 U.S. census and the 2010 to 2014 American Community Survey combine business income with farm income.[1] Consequently, total earnings is the sum of the respondent's wage or salary income and any positive business or farm income reported by the respondent divided by the reported number of weeks worked in the previous year.

INDEPENDENT VARIABLES

Each dependent variable in the chapter is regressed on a standard set of social and demographic characteristics. Because education and work experience are standard predictors of each outcome, regression models include years of education (or literacy) and predicted work experience (age-education-6) (not available from 1910 to 1930).[2] To capture the nonlinear effect of work experience on labor market outcomes, work experience squared is also included in each model. Research suggests that labor market outcomes vary by marital status.[3] To account for this effect, regression models include a variable that identifies whether an individual is married. In addition, because some immigrants do not speak English or speak English poorly, regressions include an indicator variable that equals 1 if an individual reports not speaking English or not speaking English well and 0 otherwise.[4] (English proficiency is not available from 1910 to 1940.) Because a high percentage of black immigrants tend to cluster in particular states (such as New York), models using data from 1980 to 2014 also include indicators for state of current residence. And because a slightly higher percentage of black immigrants reside in urban and metropolitan areas than do native blacks, the regression models using data from 1980 to 2014 control for metropolitan area status.

Research suggests that immigrants have less favorable labor market outcomes than native blacks when they first arrive in the United States because they are unfamiliar with the U.S. labor market. As they adapt to the host labor market, however, their labor market outcomes improve.[5] To further explore this possibility, I estimate models stratified by country of birth for each outcome and examine labor market differences between native black movers and immigrants at different tenures of U.S. residence.

EMPIRICAL MODEL

$$Y_i^* = \beta_0 + \beta_1 white\ American_i + \beta_2 black\ American\ mover_i + Birthplace_i \eta$$

$$+ X_i\theta + T_i\chi + \mu_i \qquad\qquad\qquad \text{(equation 1)}$$

Equation 1 represents the fully specified regression model. Y_i^* represents the labor market outcome of interest (log(weekly earnings), labor force participation, employment, and occupational prestige, [historical analysis (1910–1940) only]. Equation 1 is estimated using ordinary least squares (OLS) regression. Because employment and labor force participation are dichotomous variables, OLS regression estimates produce linear probability models (LPMs) of employment and labor force participation.

An LPM measures the conditional probability of achieving a particular outcome. For example, in this chapter, LPM measures $P(Y_i^* = 1|X)$, where Y_i^* is equal to being either employed or in the labor force. Therefore, the coefficients in the LPM measures the change in the probability of achieving $Y_i^* = 1$ when a particular independent variable changes, ceteris paribus. Robustness checks show that LPM provides approximately the same marginal effects as logistic and probit regression models. Additionally, the signs and significance levels are the same in each type of model, but because LPM is *linear,* interpreting changes in the underlying probability of experiencing the event of interest is more straightforward.[6]

In equation 1, X is a vector of social and demographic characteristics that includes experience (not available from 1910 to 1930), experience squared (not available from 1910 to 1930), education (literacy in 1910, 1920, and 1930), and indicator variables for whether the respondent is married, speaks English poorly (not available for historical (1910–1940) results), or resides in a metropolitan area as well as his or her current state of residence. T is a vector that identifies the survey year. *Birthplace* is a vector for each immigrant birth-country category.

LABOR MARKET TRAJECTORIES

$$Y_i = \beta_0 + \beta_1 white\ American_i + \beta_2 black\ American\ mover_i + X_i\theta + A_i\gamma + T_i\chi + \mu_i$$

(equation 2)

Equation 2 contains all the variables in equation 1 except the birthplace controls, plus a vector (A) of variables that captures immigrants' arrival cohort. This model is estimated separately for each immigrant subgroup and natives in the following periods: 1910, 1920, and 1930 and then for 1980, 1990, 2000, and the 2010–2014 period. The results from these models are used to create figures of labor market trajectories.

Chapter 5

OUTCOMES

To examine nativity differences in homeownership among blacks in the United States, I use the U.S. census question on homeownership. This variable indicates whether a housing unit was rented or owned by its inhabitants. Using this measure, I generate a dichotomous variable that equals 1 for all household heads who reported owning a home and equals 0 for all other household heads.

INDEPENDENT VARIABLES

Research on the determinants of homeownership identifies several characteristics of the household head that are strongly correlated with the likelihood of owning a home, including age and sex, citizenship, veteran status, level of education (replaced with literacy for analysis using data from 1910 to 1940), marital status, English-language proficiency (not available for historical [1910–1940] results), household income (not available prior to 1940), residence in a metropolitan area, and U.S. region of residence. In addition to these factors, characteristics associated with the composition of the household impact the likelihood of owning a home, including household size, whether the spouse is present for married individuals, number of household members, number of household members younger than eighteen, and number of household members older than sixty-four.

EMPIRICAL MODEL

Taking these variables into consideration, I estimate linear probability regression models examining differences in the probability of owning a home among blacks and whites in the United States. Equation 3 describes this empirical model.

$$Y_i = \beta_0 + \beta_1 white\ American_i + \beta_2 black\ American\ mover_i + Birthplace_i \eta$$
$$+ X_i \theta + T_i \chi + \mu_i \qquad \text{(equation 3)}$$

In equation 3, Y_i represents the outcome variable of interest: whether the household head reports owning the home in which they reside. X represents a vector of social and demographic characteristics. T is a vector that identifies the survey year. *Birthplace* is a vector for each immigrant birth-country category, where the reference category for all nativity groups is black American movers.

This analysis is followed by analysis based on equation 4, which examines how the probability of owning a home varies among black immigrants by arrival cohort and tenure of U.S. residence.

$$Y_i = \beta_0 + \beta_1 white\ American_i + \beta_2 black\ American\ mover_i + X_i\theta + A_i\gamma + T_i\chi + \mu_i$$

(equation 4)

This equation contains all the variables in equation 3 except the birthplace controls, plus a vector of variables that identify immigrant arrival cohorts. This model is estimated for each immigrant subgroup and natives in the following time periods: 1910, 1920, and 1930 and for 1980, 1990, 2000, and the 2010–2014 period. Household weights are used in all analyses. Robust standard errors are used to determine significance.

Chapter 6

OUTCOME

The March CPS is most centrally designed to measure unemployment. However, in 1996 the data were augmented to include a self-rated health variable. This variable is a subjective measure of health that asks respondents to rate their current health on a five-point scale as "excellent," "very good," "good," "fair," or "poor." We dichotomize this variable to 1 if a respondent reports their health as fair or poor and 0 if otherwise.

INDEPENDENT VARIABLES

Demographic, social, and economic factors related to health are included as control variables in the analysis of self-rated health. I also include controls for age and age-squared and a dummy indicator for gender. Moreover, since access to health care and exposure to environmental factors that impact health vary by U.S. region of residence and urban or rural status, I control for U.S. region of current residence and whether or not an individual lives in a metropolitan area.

To account for the impact of socioeconomic status on health, the regression models control for a respondent's level of education and marital status. Income is also highly correlated with health. However, there is a bidirectional association between current income and health.[7] In an effort to avoid the problems associated with the potential endogeneity of income, I control for measures of permanent income, including whether an individual owns or rents their current residence, the type of housing structure an individual resides in, and whether or not an individual receives investment income.

EMPIRICAL MODELS

$Y_i = \beta_0 + \beta_1 white\ American_i + \beta_2 black\ American\ mover_i + Birthplace_i \eta$

$\quad + X_i \theta + T_i \chi + \mu_i$ (equation 5)

In equation 5, X is a vector of social and demographic characteristics that includes age, age-squared, gender, U.S. region of residence, urban or rural status, whether or not the respondent lives in a metropolitan area, the respondent's level of education, marital status, whether the respondent owns or rents their current residence, the type of housing structure the respondent resides in, and whether or not the respondent receives investment income. T is a vector that identifies the survey year. *Birthplace* is a vector for each immigrant birth-country category.

As shown by Borjas, Antecol and Bedard, and McDonald and Kennedy, when multiple cross-sections of data are available, it is possible to separately identify the impact of duration of U.S. residence and the cohort of entry among immigrants.[8] Following Antecol and Bedard, the estimation equation used in this chapter is as follows:[9]

$Y_i = \beta_0 + \beta_1 white\ American_i + \beta_2 black\ American\ mover_i + X_i \theta + C \omega + D_i \gamma + T_i \chi + \mu_i$

(equation 6)

In this model, Y_i is the health outcome of interest. X is a vector of variables that control for demographic, social, and economic correlates of health, including age, age squared, gender, educational attainment, marital status, region of residence, metropolitan area status, and a set of proxies for permanent income. D is a vector of dummy variables indicating how long an immigrant has lived in the United States; this variable is set to 0 for U.S.-born adults. C is a vector of dummy variables identifying immigrant arrival cohorts. T is a vector of dummy variables indicating the survey year.

To identify both cohort of arrival and duration of U.S. residence effects, equation 6 imposes the restriction that the period effect on health is the same for both immigrants and natives. Therefore, the period effect is estimated for black natives, and this information is used to identify cohort and assimilation effects for immigrants.[10] Equation 6 will be used to estimate linear probability regression models of fair or poor health. The models are used to estimate regression health assimilation models that account for both duration of U.S. residence and arrival cohort for black immigrants from Africa and the Caribbean. Estimates from the models are used to create figures 6.2.

Chapter 7

MARRIAGE

Chapter 7 presents an analysis of marriage and intermarriage patterns among blacks and whites in the United States. Three variables are generated for the analysis. First, to study marriage I construct a variable that equals 1 if a respondent is married (with a spouse present or absent) and 0 otherwise.

Empirical Model

Chapter 7 also contains regression analysis examining disparities in marriage patterns between blacks and whites in the United States. Equation 7 describes the empirical model used in the chapter.

$$Y_i = \beta_0 + \beta_1 white\ American_i + \beta_2 black\ American\ mover_i + Birthplace_i \eta$$

$$+ X_i \theta + T_i \chi + \mu_i \qquad \text{(equation 7)}$$

In equation 7, Y_i represents the outcome variable of interest: whether an individual is married at the time of the survey. X represents a vector of social and demographic characteristics, including age, education, region of current residence, and whether the respondent resides in a metropolitan area. T is a vector that identifies the survey year. *Birthplace* is a vector for each immigrant birth-country category. To evaluate marriage differences between black immigrants, black American movers, black American nonmovers, and white Americans, equation 7 includes a dummy variable that indicates whether a respondent is a black American nonmover, a white American, or a member of one of the fourteen focal black immigrant categories. The reference category for each of these variables is black

American movers. Equation 7 is estimated using linear probability regression models.

INTERMARRIAGE

Outcomes

To study intermarriage, intramarriage, and endogamy among blacks in the United States, three variables are generated. "Intermarried" is strictly defined as marriages between blacks (of any ethnicity) with white Americans. Among married individuals, the intermarried variable equals 1 if a black respondent is married to a white American and is equal to 0 otherwise. To identify cross-ethnic unions among married blacks, I create an "intramarried" variable that equals 1 if a black immigrant is married to a black American or a black American is married to a black immigrant and is equal to 0 otherwise. Third, "endogamy" measures marriages among individuals of the same race and the same nationality. Among married individuals, endogamy equals 1 if the members of the union share the same race and birth country (for example, two black Americans, two white Americans, or two black Nigerian immigrants) and is equal to 0 otherwise.

Empirical Models

$$Y_i = \beta_0 + \beta_1 white\ American_i + \beta_2 black\ American\ mover_i + Birthplace_i \eta$$

$$+ X_i \theta + T_i \chi + \mu_i \qquad \text{(equation 8)}$$

In equation 8, X is a vector of social and demographic characteristics that includes age, age-squared, state of residence, urban or rural status, whether or not the respondent lives in a metropolitan area, the respondent's level of education, annual earnings, and whether the respondent speak poor English. T is a vector that identifies the survey year. *Birthplace* is a vector for each immigrant birth-country category.

NOTES

Chapter 1: Introduction

1. Anderson 2015, 1.
2. Alba and Nee 1997; Lee and Bean 2010, 17.
3. Lee and Bean 2010, 31.
4. Lee and Bean 2010, 19.
5. Author's calculation.
6. Flynn et al. 2017. In this book, I use the terms "black Americans," "native-born blacks," and "U.S.-born blacks" interchangeably to refer to black Americans born in the United States. I use the term "black population" to refer to all those living in the United States, both immigrants and native-born residents, who self-identify as black.
7. Sowell 1978.
8. Sowell 1978.
9. Sowell 1981, 187.
10. Throughout the book, I use "English-speaking Caribbean" and "West Indies" interchangeably.
11. Beer 1986.
12. Patterson 2006.
13. Domingo 1925; Ottley 1943; Reid 1939/1969.
14. Johnson 1930; Ottley 1943; Reid 1939/1969.
15. Beer 1986; Glazer and Moynihan 1970; Obama 2010.
16. Johnson 1930; Reid 1939/1969.
17. Model 2008.
18. Waters, Kasinitz, and Asad 2014.
19. Flynn et al. 2017.
20. Flynn et al. 2017.
21. Waters 1999.
22. Feliciano 2005; Model 2008.
23. Imoagene 2017.

24. Imoagene 2017.
25. Jasso et al. 2004.
26. In 2015, the minimum wage was $10.50 per hour in Washington, D.C.
27. Black immigrants are defined as individuals who were born outside of the United States and who self-identify their race as black. I exclude individuals who report multiple races.
28. The small sample sizes of the immigrant flows from the remaining African countries do not provide sufficient statistical power to generate reliable estimates across the range of outcomes studied in the book.
29. Black Americans are defined as individuals who were born in the United States who also self-identify their race as black (excluding individuals who reported multiple races). I also restrict the black American sample to individuals who do not report Hispanic ethnicity.
30. Borch and Corra 2010b; Dodoo 1999; Dodoo and Takyi 2002.
31. Butcher 1994.
32. Some individuals reside in their birth states but resided in a different state at some point between birth and the time of the survey.
33. Kochhar and Fry 2014.
34. Oliver and Shapiro 2006.
35. Tesfai 2015.
36. Livingston and Brown 2017; Kalmijn 1998; Lee and Bean 2010; Qian and Lichter 2001, 2007.
37. Lee and Bean 2010.

Chapter 2: A Demographic Portrait of Black America

1. Model 2008.
2. Palmer 1974, 6.
3. Model 2008; Palmer 1974.
4. Palmer 1974.
5. Model 2008, 13–14.
6. Model 2008.
7. Model 2008.
8. Palmer 1974, 7.
9. Daniels 2004; Model 2008.
10. Daniels 2004, 53.
11. Reid 1939/1969.
12. Kasinitz 1992.
13. Palmer 1974.
14. Model 2008.
15. Abrahámová 2008.
16. Model 2008.
17. "Africa" and "African" refers to sub-Saharan Africa throughout this book.
18. Model 2008.
19. Model 2008; Palmer 1974.

20. Kasinitz 1992, 28.
21. Model 2008, 23.
22. Palmer 1974.
23. Kent 2007.
24. Kent 2007.
25. Thomas 2016.
26. Anderson 2015; Kent 2007.
27. Kent 2007.
28. Anderson 2015; Kent 2007; Thomas 2012.
29. Lobo 2001; Thomas 2011a.
30. Anderson 2015.
31. Thomas 2014.
32. Because the U.S. Department of Homeland Security's *Yearbook of Immigration Statistics* does not contain data on immigrants by race, figure 2.2 shows trends for all permanent residents from these regions regardless of race-ethnicity.
33. For detailed explanations of each visa category, see U.S. Department of State, Bureau of Consular Affairs, "Diversity Visa Program—Entry," https://travel.state. gov/content/travel/en/us-visas/immigrate/diversity-visa-program-entry.html, accessed December 13, 2018.
34. Anderson 2015.
35. Anderson 2015.
36. The maps in figures 2.9 and 2.10 are for immigrants from the Caribbean and Africa, regardless of race. However, the estimates in table 2.2 indicate the maps are representative of the spatial distribution of black immigrants.
37. Model 2008; Palmer 1974.
38. Kent 2007.

Chapter 3: Theoretical Considerations

1. Altonji and Blank 1999; Glazer and Moynihan 1970; Hamilton, Austin, and Darity 2011.
2. Conley 2010; Kijakazi et al. 2016; Oliver and Shapiro 2013.
3. Shapiro 2004.
4. Shapiro 2004, 49.
5. Kochhar and Fry 2014.
6. Harris 2011; Hummer 1996; Massey and Denton 1993.
7. Bryce-Laporte 1972. Ogbu 1991; Sowell 1975.
8. Glazer and Moynihan 1970; Light and Gold 2000; Sowell 1983.
9. Ifatunji 2016.
10. Sowell 1978, 42.
11. Reid 1939/1969.
12. Johnson 1930; Reid 1939/1969.
13. Johnson 1930, 130.
14. Sowell 1978, 1981, 1983.

15. Obama 2004.
16. Ogbu 1991.
17. Patterson 1997.
18. Harris 2011, 40.
19. Harris 2011, 34.
20. Harris 2011.
21. Sowell 1975, 1978, 1981.
22. Sowell 1975, 1978, 1981, 1983.
23. Vickerman 1998.
24. Waters 1999.
25. Waters 1999, 140.
26. On perceptions of different treatment by whites, see Waters 1999.
27. Waters 1999.
28. Foner 1985.
29. Foner 1985.
30. Grosfoguel 2003.
31. Imoagene 2017.
32. Foner 2018.
33. Goldsmith, Hamilton, and Darity 2007; Monk 2014.
34. Frank, Akresh, and Lu 2010; Hersch 2002, 2011.
35. Rosenblum et al. 2016.
36. Chiswick 1978.
37. Chiswick 1978.
38. Chiswick 1978.
39. Borjas 1994.
40. Borjas 1994.
41. Feliciano 2005; Feliciano and Lanuza 2017.
42. Imoagene 2017.
43. Borch and Corra 2010a; Butcher 1994; Corra and Borch 2014; Corra and Kimuna 2009; Dodoo 1991, 1997, 1999; Dodoo and Takyi 2002; Ifatunji 2016, 2017; Kalmijn 1996; Model 2018.
44. Model 2008.
45. Model 2008.
46. Model 2008, 111.
47. Butcher 1994.
48. Boustan 2016; Wilkerson 2011.
49. Tolnay 2003.
50. Collins and Wanamaker 2014.
51. Boustan 2016.
52. Eichenlaub, Tolnay, and Alexander 2010.
53. Black et al. 2015.
54. Adelman, Morett, and Tolnay 2000; Crowder, Tolnay, and Adelman 2001; Tolnay and Eichenlaub 2006.
55. Borjas 1986, 1987, 1999.

56. Borjas 2014.
57. Antecol and Bedard 2006.
58. Borjas 1994, 1995; Hamilton 2014; Hamilton and Hummer 2011; Model 2008.
59. Model 2008.
60. Hamilton 2014.
61. Waters 1999; Arnold 1984; Grosfoguel 2003; Foner 1985.
62. Model 2008, 142.
63. See, for example, Sowell 1978.
64. Thomas 2011b, 2016.
65. Thomas 2014.
66. Alba and Foner 2015; Foner 2018; Waters, Kasinitz, and Asad 2014.
67. Harris 2011; Massey and Denton 1993; Western 2006.
68. Katznelson 2005.
69. Flynn et al. 2017.
70. Dodoo 1991, 1997; Hamilton 2014; Mason 2010. See the methodological appendix for more detailed definitions of employment and labor force participation.
71. Ifatunji 2016.
72. I define labor force participation as the proportion of the population between the ages of twenty-five and sixty-four who are working or actively looking for work.
73. Model 2008.
74. Hamilton 2014; Ifatunji 2016; Model 2008.
75. Portes and Rumbaut 2014.
76. All country-level data in this chapter come from the United Nations Development Program's *Human Development Reports* (hdr.undp.org/en/data).
77. Portes and Rumbaut 2014.
78. Borjas 2014.
79. Massey, Durand, and Malone 2002.
80. Massey, Durand, and Malone 2002.
81. Massey, Durand, and Malone 2002, 11.
82. Stark and Bloom 1985.
83. Massey, Durand, and Malone 2002.
84. Massey, Durand, and Malone 2002, 11–12.
85. Massey, Durand, and Malone 2002, 12.
86. Stark and Bloom 1985.
87. Castells 1989; Portes and Walton 1981; Wallerstein 1976, 2017.
88. Portes and Rumbaut 2014.
89. Anderson 2015.
90. Anderson 2015.
91. Piore 1979.
92. Massey, Durand, and Malone 2002, 16.
93. Portes and Rumbaut 2014, 139.
94. Anderson 2015.
95. Anderson 2015.

96. Portes and Rumbaut 2014.

97. Farley 1996; Model 2008.

98. Kirschenman and Neckerman 1991.

99. Foner 1995, 2009; Hamilton, Easley, and Dixon 2018. Research also suggests, however, that the similarity in labor market outcomes between black and white women may result from differential patterns of selection into the labor market. Because of the relatively poor labor market outcomes of black American men, during the childbearing years, black American women are more likely to maintain full-time employment and to work jobs at their skill level. Because white women with young children are more likely to have a husband in the labor market, they can more easily switch to a more flexible job for lower wages, which might also explain the lower disparities between white and black American women.

100. Portes and Rumbaut 2014.

101. Model 2008; Foner 1995; Hamilton, Easley, and Dixon 2018; Kasinitz 1992; Vickerman 1998.

102. Waldinger 1999.

103. Portes and Rumbaut 2014.

104. Portes and Rumbaut 2014, 141.

105. Kasinitz 1992, 93.

106. Kasinitz 1992.

107. Kasinitz 1992.

108. Kasinitz 1992, 95–96.

109. Foner 1985.

110. Foner 1985.

111. Flynn et al. 2017.

112. Palmer 1974.

113. Model 2008.

114. Model 2008; Palmer 1974.

115. Kasinitz 1992.

116. Kasinitz 1992.

117. Kasinitz 1992.

118. Kasinitz 1992, 44.

119. Kasinitz 1992, 50.

120. Kasinitz 1992.

121. Bowen and Bok 1998; Massey et al. 2007; Murrell and Jones 1996.

122. Hamilton 2014; Model 2008.

123. Model 2008.

124. Smith and Welch 1979.

125. Margo 1990.

126. Margo 1990, 8.

127. Margo 1990.

128. Margo 1990.

129. Margo 1990.

130. Massey and Denton 1993.

131. Massey and Denton 1993; Wilson 1987.

132. Flynn et al. 2017.

133. Hamilton and Darity 2010.

134. Flynn et al. 2017.

135. Darity, Dietrich, and Guilkey 2001.

136. The data in table 3.1 refers to the years 2010 to 2014 or 2015. Many immigrants, however, left their home countries in the more distant past. As a result, this snapshot is a somewhat crude picture of the relative characteristics of origin and destination.

137. Feliciano and Lanuza 2017.

138. Model 2008; Hamilton 2014.

139. Darity 2003, 81.

140. Model 2008.

141. Sowell 1978, 1981, 1983.

142. Fernández-Kelly, forthcoming, 5.

143. Foner 1985; Waters 1999.

144. Model 2008.

145. Massey and Denton 1993; Wilson 1978.

146. Thompson-Miller, Feagin, and Picca 2014.

147. Margo 1990.

Chapter 4: Historical and Contemporary Labor Market Disparities

1. Flynn et al. 2017.

2. Flynn et al. 2017.

3. Flynn et al. 2017.

4. Domingo 1925; Osofsky 1966/1996; Ottley 1943; Reid 1939/1969.

5. Domingo 1925; Osofsky 1966/1996; Ottley 1943; Reid 1939/1969.

6. Author's calculations.

7. Domingo 1925; Haynes 1912; McKay 1940; Ottley and Weatherby 1967; Reid 1939/1969.

8. Domingo 1925, 345.

9. Domingo 1925; Reid 1939/1969.

10. Johnson 1930, 130.

11. For one such prior study, see Reid 1939/1969.

12. Model 2008.

13. A major component of my theoretical argument relates to the importance of selective migration, a framework that pertains to adult primary movers. As a result, I exclude immigrants who migrated before age eighteen from all analysis. Unfortunately, however, the 1940 U.S. census does not contain data on year of immigration, which is needed to make this restriction. As discussed in chapter 2, there was a significant reduction in immigration from the Caribbean during the

1930s. Because I am not able to restrict the 1940 sample to individuals who migrated to the United States as adults, the 1940 Caribbean population in this study is artificially larger than the Caribbean population in 1930.

14. Boustan 2016; Tolnay 1998.

15. Boustan 2016, 54. For studies arguing that black American migrants were positively selected, see Lieberson 1978; Long and Heltman 1975; Masters 1972.

16. Margo 1990.

17. Model 2008, 16.

18. Roberts 1957; Reid 1939/1969.

19. Model 2008.

20. Again, these estimates are for the entire population between the ages of twenty-five and sixty-four in the respective years.

21. See, for example, Eichenlaub et al. 2010.

22. Borjas 1985, 1995, 1999.

23. Domingo 1925; Reid 1939/1969.

24. Portes and Rumbaut 2014.

25. All estimates in the chapter pertain to individuals between the ages of twenty-five and sixty-four. The immigrant sample is restricted to individuals who migrated after age eighteen.

26. Portes and Rumbaut 2014, 117.

27. Portes and Rumbaut 2014, 117.

28. Portes and Rumbaut 2014, 118–19.

29. The online appendix is available at https://www.russellsage.org/publications/immigration-and-remaking-black-america.

30. Reid 1939/1969; Domingo 1925; Haynes 1912.

31. Model 2008.

32. On patterns of labor market discrimination against native and immigrant populations, see Foner (1985, 2001).

33. Bean and Bell-Rose 2003; Waldinger 1999; Wilson 2003.

34. Foner 2009.

Chapter 5: Achieving the American Dream:
Past and Present Homeownership Disparities

1. Conley 2010.

2. Shapiro 2004.

3. Shapiro 2004.

4. Kochhar and Fry 2014.

5. Kochhar and Fry 2014.

6. Oliver and Shapiro 2006.

7. Flynn et al. 2017.

8. Oliver and Shapiro 2013.

9. Dymski 1995; Munnell et al. 1996; Murrell and Jones 1996; Squires, Velez, and Taeuber 1991.

10. Kim and Squires 1995.
11. Kim and Squires 1995.
12. Tesfai 2015.
13. Anderson 2015.
14. Tesfai 2015; Dustmann and Mestres 2010; Owusu 1998.
15. Haan 2007.
16. Tesfai 2015.
17. Borjas 2002; Haan 2007.
18. Borjas 2002.
19. Borjas 2002; Haan 2007.
20. Anderson 2015; Haan 2007.
21. Tesfai 2015.
22. Collins and Margo 2011.
23. Collins and Margo 2001, 2011.
24. Collins and Margo 2011.
25. Collins and Margo 2011.
26. Collins and Margo 2001, 2011.
27. Collins and Margo 2001, 2011.
28. Margo 1990.
29. Collins and Margo 2011.
30. Frey 2009.
31. Eichenlaub, Tolnay, and Alexander 2010.
32. Collins and Margo 2011.
33. Rothstein 2017.
34. Collins and Margo 2011.
35. Rothstein 2017.
36. Rothstein 2017, 64.
37. Rothstein 2017, 64.
38. Rothstein 2017, 65.
39. Rothstein 2017, 65.
40. Rothstein 2017, 70.
41. Katznelson 2005.
42. Katznelson 2005, 123–40.
43. Flynn et al. 2017; Katznelson 2005; Portes and Rumbaut 2006.
44. Flynn et al. 2017.
45. Flynn et al. 2017.
46. Pager and Shepherd 2008.
47. Farley and Frey 1994.
48. Rothstein 2017.
49. Borjas 1985.
50. Model 2008.
51. Johnson 1930; Reid 1939/1969.
52. Rothstein 2017.
53. Collins and Margo 2001.

54. Massey and Denton 1993.
55. De La Cruz-Viesca et al. 2016; Kijakazi et al. 2016; Muñoz et al. 2015.
56. Portes and Rumbaut 2006.
57. Foner 1979; Handa and Kirton 1999; Mequanent 1996.
58. Tesfai 2015, 8.
59. Ratner 1997; Tesfai 2015.
60. Flippen 2004; Galster and Godfrey 2005; Ross and Turner 2005; Turner and Ross 2005.

Chapter 6: Health Disparities

1. Hummer 1993, 1996.
2. Morris et al. 2010; Williams and Mohammed 2009; Williams et al. 1997.
3. Bickell et al. 2006; Gross et al. 2008; Ward et al. 2004.
4. Hummer 1993; Rice et al. 2017.
5. Green and Hamilton 2018.
6. Arias 2016; Hummer 1993; Levine et al. 2016.
7. On black immigrants' self-reported health profiles, see Acevedo-Garcia et al. (2010b), Hamilton and Hummer (2011), and Jackson and Antonucci (2005); on immigrants' infant and child health outcomes, see Collins, Wu, and David (2002), Elo, Vang, and Culhane (2014), and Hendi, Mehta, and Elo (2015). See Elo, Mehta, and Huang (2011) for immigrants' lower disability rates; Antecol and Bedard (2006) and Mehta et al. (2015) for their lower rates of obesity; and Singh and Siahpush (2002a) for their lower rates of adult mortality.
8. Acevedo-Garcia et al. 2010a; Antecol and Bedard 2006; Newbold 2005; Cho et al. 2004; Jasso et al. 2004; McDonald and Kennedy 2004, 2005.
9. Abraido-Lanza, Chao, and Flórez 2005; Abraido-Lanza, Chao, and Gates 2005; Akresh 2007; Amaro et al. 1990; Angel, Buckley, and Sakamoto 2001; Cho et al. 2004; Finch et al. 2001; Hummer et al. 1999b; Lopez-Gonzalez, Aravena, and Hummer 2005.
10. On the factors associated with the healthy immigrant effect, see Marmot, Adelstein, and Bulusu (1984), Palloni and Ewbank (2004), Sharma, Michalowski, and Verma (1990), and Turra and Elo (2008) for the influence of age; Jasso et al. (2004) for differences in the value of skills across countries; and Feliciano (2005) for the influence of education.
11. Feliciano 2005.
12. Palloni and Arias 2004.
13. Palloni and Arias 2004.
14. Abraido-Lanza et al. 1999; Hummer et al. 2007; Markides and Eschbach 2005; Turra and Elo 2008.
15. Hummer 1996; Levine et al. 2014; Soto, Dawson-Andoh and BeLue 2011; Williams 1999.
16. Skloot 2017; Washington 2006.
17. LaVeist, Sellers, and Neighbors 2001.

18. LaVeist, Sellers, and Neighbors 2001.
19. Collins, Wu, and David 2002.
20. Skloot 2017; Washington 2006.
21. Carlisle 2012; Erving 2011; Hamilton and Hummer 2011; Jackson and Antonucci 2005.
22. Collins, Wu, and David 2002; David and Collins 1997; Finch et al. 2009; Hummer et al. 1999a; Hummer et al. 1999b; Singh and Siahpush 2002b.
23. Antecol and Bedard 2006.
24. Hamilton and Hummer 2011.
25. Elo, Mehta, and Huang 2008; Read and Emerson 2005.
26. Lacey et al. 2015.
27. Warner and Hayward 2006; Zhang, Gu, and Hayward 2008.
28. Read and Emerson 2005.
29. Elo, Mehta, and Huang 2008.
30. Elo, Mehta, and Huang 2011; Feliciano 2005; Kennedy et al. 2014; Lacey et al. 2015; Landale, Gorman, and Oropesa 2006; Landale, Oropesa, and Gorman 2000.
31. Kristin Butcher (1994) first used this analytic approach to study nativity differences in earnings among blacks. These health models are usually estimated using data on immigrants and natives of the same race or ethnicity (see Antecol and Bedard 2006; Hamilton and Hummer 2011).
32. DeSalvo et al. 2006; Idler, Russell, and Davis 2000.
33. Finch, Kolody, and Vega 2000.
34. Dowd and Zajacova 2007, 2010.
35. Dowd and Todd 2011.
36. Dowd and Todd 2011.
37. Dowd and Todd 2011.
38. Angel and Guarnaccia 1989.
39. Viruell-Fuentes et al. 2011.
40. Hamilton 2015.
41. Head and Seaborn Thompson 2017; Kiecolt, Momplaisir, and Hughes 2016; Levine et al. 2014; Marshall and Rue 2012; Molina and James 2016; Soto, Dawson-Andoh, and BeLue 2011; Washington 2006; Woodward 2011.

Chapter 7: Forming Unions and Crossing Racial-Ethnic Boundaries

1. Bean and Stevens 2003.
2. Alba and Nee 2003.
3. Bean and Stevens 2003.
4. Bean and Stevens 2003; Drachsler 1920; Pagnini and Morgan 1990.
5. Bean and Stevens 2003.
6. Bean and Stevens 2003, 173.
7. Bean and Stevens 2003, 173.

8. Bean and Stevens 2003.

9. Bean and Stevens 2003.

10. Livingston and Brown 2017.

11. Bean and Stevens 2003.

12. Lee and Bean 2010.

13. Lee and Bean 2010, 93.

14. Lee and Bean 2010, 97.

15. Qian 1997.

16. Qian and Lichter 2001.

17. Model and Fisher 2001.

18. Batson, Qian, and Lichter 2006, 670.

19. Ruggles 1994.

20. Ruggles 1994.

21. Ruggles 1994, 141.

22. Raley and Sweeney 2009.

23. Lichter et al. 1992.

24. Raley, Sweeney, and Wondra 2015.

25. Raley and Sweeney 2009.

26. Raley, Sweeney, and Wondra 2015, 94.

27. Wilson and Neckerman 1987.

28. Raley, Sweeney, and Wondra 2015.

29. Raley, Sweeney, and Wondra 2015, 96.

30. Raley, Sweeney, and Wondra 2015.

31. Raley, Sweeney, and Wondra 2015.

32. Western 2006, 13.

33. Pettit 2012.

34. Pettit 2012.

35. Charles and Luoh 2010.

36. Charles and Luoh 2010.

37. All mortality estimates are taken from the Centers for Disease Control and Prevention (CDC) (https://www.cdc.gov/nchs/, accessed December 13, 2018).

38. Some studies restrict married couples to those with both spouses present in the household. Because members of some married immigrant couples move to the United States at different times, I use a marriage variable that captures this dynamic.

39. Bean and Stevens 2003.

40. See the methodological appendix for a complete description of the regression models.

41. Up to this point, I have focused on fourteen immigrant-sending countries. Because the best data sources do not produce reliable estimates in the earlier time periods for relatively recent immigrant flows (for example, immigrants from the Sudan and Somalia), for the trend analysis I focus on the eight countries with immigrant samples large enough to produce reliable estimates.

42. Kalmijn 1998; Mare 1991; Schwartz 2013.

43. Choi and Tienda 2017.
44. Balistreri, Joyner, and Kao 2015; Bany, Robnett, and Feliciano 2014; Choi and Tienda 2017.
45. Choi and Tienda 2017; Kalmijn 1998.
46. Choi and Tienda 2017.
47. Choi and Tienda 2017; Kalmijn and van Tubergen 2010; Qian and Lichter 2007.
48. Choi and Tienda 2017; Jiménez 2010.
49. Choi and Tienda 2017.
50. Bean and Stevens 2003.

Chapter 8: Conclusion

1. Margo 1990; Patterson 2006; Patterson with Fosse 2015; Sowell 1978.
2. Reid 1939/1969.
3. Thompson-Miller, Feagin, and Picca 2014.
4. Darity, Dietrich, and Guilkey 2001; Darity 2003; Harris 2011; Massey and Denton 1993; Pager 2003.
5. Darity, Dietrich, and Guilkey 2001.
6. On the incarceration of the black men, see Western 2006.
7. Pettit 2012.
8. Pettit 2012.
9. Pettit 2012, 8.
10. Pettit 2012.
11. Pettit 2012, 11–12.
12. Candelario 2001; Howard 2007; Torres-Saillant 1998.
13. Candelario 2001; Duany 1996.
14. Duany 1996.
15. Patterson 2006; Sowell 1978, 1981.

Methodological Appendix

1. Ruggles et al. 2018.
2. Borjas 1986, 1987; Model 2008.
3. Correll, Benard, and Paik 2007; Korenman and Neumark 1991.
4. Chiswick 1991; Chiswick and Miller 1995.
5. Borjas 1985.
6. Wooldridge 2015.
7. Ettner 1996.
8. Borjas 1985, 1987; Antecol and Bedard 2006; McDonald and Kennedy 2004, 2005.
9. Antecol and Bedard 2006.
10. Antecol and Bedard 2006; Borjas 1987.

REFERENCES

Abrahámová, Natalie. 2008. *Immigration Policy in Britain since 1962* (PhD diss., Masarykova Univerzita, Filozofická Fakulta).

Abraido-Lanza, Ana F., Maria T. Chao, and Karen R. Flórez. 2005. "Do Healthy Behaviors Decline with Greater Acculturation? Implications for the Latino Mortality Paradox." *Social Science and Medicine* 61(6): 1243–55.

Abraido-Lanza, Ana F., Maria T. Chao, and Charisse Y. Gates. 2005. "Acculturation and Cancer Screening among Latinas: Results from the National Health Interview Survey." *Annals of Behavioral Medicine* 29(1): 22–28.

Abraido-Lanza, Ana F., Bruce P. Dohrenwend, Daisy S. Ng-Mak, and Blake Turner. 1999. "The Latino Mortality Paradox: A Test of the 'Salmon Bias' and Healthy Migrant Hypotheses." *American Journal of Public Health* 89(10): 1543–48.

Acevedo-Garcia, Dolores, Lisa M. Bates, Theresa L. Osypuk, and Nancy McArdle. 2010a. "The Effect of Immigrant Generation and Duration on Self-Rated Health among U.S. Adults 2003–2007." *Social Science and Medicine* 71(6): 1161–72.

———. 2010b. "The Effect of Immigrant Generation and Duration on Self-Rated Health among U.S. Adults 2003–2007." *Social Science and Medicine* 71(6): 1161–72.

Adelman, Robert M., Chris Morett, and Stewart E. Tolnay. 2000. "Homeward Bound: The Return Migration of Southern-Born Black Women, 1940 to 1990." *Sociological Spectrum* 20(4): 433–63.

Akresh, Ilana Redstone. 2007. "Dietary Assimilation and Health among Hispanic Immigrants to the United States." *Journal of Health and Social Behavior* 48(4): 404–17.

Alba, Richard, and Nancy Foner. 2015. *Strangers No More: Immigration and the Challenges of Integration in North America and Western Europe*. Princeton, N.J.: Princeton University Press.

Alba, Richard, and Victor Nee. 1997. "Rethinking Assimilation Theory for a New Era of Immigration." *International Migration Review* 31(4): 826–74.

———. 2003. *Remaking the American Mainstream: Assimilation and Contemporary Immigration.* Cambridge, Mass.: Harvard University Press.

Altonji, Joseph G., and Rebecca M. Blank. 1999. "Race and Gender in the Labor Market." In *Handbook of Labor Economics,* vol. 3, edited by Orley Ashenfelter and David Card. Amsterdam: Elsevier.

Amaro, Hortensia, Rupert Whitaker, Gerald Coffman, and Timothy Heeren. 1990. "Acculturation and Marijuana and Cocaine Use: Findings from HHANES 1982–84." *American Journal of Public Health* 80(suppl): 54–60.

Anderson, Monica. 2015. "A Rising Share of the U.S. Black Population Is Foreign Born." Washington, D.C.: Pew Research Center (April).

Angel, Jacqueline L., Cynthia J. Buckley, and Art Sakamoto. 2001. "Duration or Disadvantage? Exploring Nativity, Ethnicity, and Health in Midlife." *Journals of Gerontology, Series B: Psychological Sciences and Social Sciences* 56(5): S275–84.

Angel, Ronald J., and Peter J. Guarnaccia. 1989. "Mind, Body, and Culture: Somatization among Hispanics." *Social Science and Medicine* 28(12): 1229–38.

Antecol, Heather, and Kelly Bedard. 2006. "Unhealthy Assimilation: Why Do Immigrants Converge to American Health Status Levels?" *Demography* 43(2): 337–60.

Arias, Elizabeth. 2016. "Changes in Life Expectancy by Race and Hispanic Origin in the United States, 2013–2014." Data Brief 244. U.S. Department of Health and Human Services, Centers for Disease Control and Prevention, National Center for Health Statistics.

Arnold, F. W. 1984. "West Indians and London's Hierarchy of Discrimination." *Ethnic Groups* 6: 47–64.

Balistreri, Kelly Stamper, Kara Joyner, and Grace Kao. 2015. "Relationship Involvement among Young Adults: Are Asian American Men an Exceptional Case?" *Population Research and Policy Review* 34(5): 709–32.

Bany, James A., Belinda Robnett, and Cynthia Feliciano. 2014. "Gendered Black Exclusion: The Persistence of Racial Stereotypes among Daters." *Race and Social Problems* 6(3): 201–13.

Batson, Christie D., Zhenchao Qian, and Daniel T. Lichter. 2006. "Interracial and Intraracial Patterns of Mate Selection among America's Diverse Black Populations." *Journal of Marriage and Family* 68(3): 658–72.

Bean, Frank D., and Stephanie Bell-Rose. 2003. *Immigration and Opportunity: Race, Ethnicity, and Employment in the United States.* New York: Russell Sage Foundation.

Bean, Frank D., and Gillian Stevens. 2003. *America's Newcomers and the Dynamics of Diversity.* New York: Russell Sage Foundation.

Beer, William R. 1986. "Real-Life Cost of Affirmative Action." *Wall Street Journal,* August 7.

Bickell, Nina A., Jason J. Wang, Soji Oluwole, Deborah Schrag, Henry Godfrey, Karen Hiotis, Jane Mendez, and Amber A. Guth. 2006. "Missed Opportunities:

Racial Disparities in Adjuvant Breast Cancer Treatment." *Journal of Clinical Oncology* 24(9): 1357–62.

Black, Dan A., Seth G. Sanders, Evan J. Taylor, and Lowell J. Taylor. 2015. "The Impact of the Great Migration on Mortality of African Americans: Evidence from the Deep South." *American Economic Review* 105(2): 477–503.

Borch, Casey, and Mamadi K. Corra. 2010a. "Differences in Earnings among Black and White African Immigrants in the United States, 1980–2000: A Cross-sectional and Temporal Analysis." *Sociological Perspectives* 53(4): 573–92.

———. 2010b. "Differences in Earnings among Black and White African Immigrants in the United States, 1980–2000: A Cross-sectional and Temporal Analysis." *Sociological Perspectives* 53(4): 573–92.

Borjas, George J. 1985. "Assimilation, Changes in Cohort Quality, and the Earnings of Immigrants." *Journal of Labor Economics* 3(4): 463–89.

———. 1986. "The Self-Employment Experience of Immigrants." *Journal of Human Resources* 21(4): 485–506.

———. 1987. "Self-Selection and the Earnings of Immigrants." *American Economic Review* 77(4): 531–53.

———. 1994. "The Economics of Immigration." *Journal of Economic Literature* 32(4): 1667–1717.

———. 1995. "Assimilation and Changes in Cohort Quality Revisited: What Happened to Immigrant Earnings in the 1980s." *Journal of Labor Economics* 13(2): 201–45.

———. 1999. "The Economic Analysis of Immigration." In *Handbook of Labor Economics,* vol. 3, edited by Orley Ashenfelter and David Card. Amsterdam: Elsevier.

———. 2002. "Homeownership in the Immigrant Population." *Journal of Urban Economics* 52(3): 448–76.

———. 2014. *Immigration Economics.* Cambridge, Mass.: Harvard University Press.

Boustan, Leah Platt. 2016. *Competition in the Promised Land: Black Migrants in Northern Cities and Labor Markets.* Princeton, N.J.: Princeton University Press.

Bowen, William G., and Derek Bok. 1998. *The Shape of the River: Long-Term Consequences of Considering Race in College and University Admissions.* Princeton, N.J.: Princeton University Press.

Bryce-Laporte, Roy Simon. 1972 "Black Immigrants: The Experience of Invisibility and Inequality." *Journal of Black Studies* 3(1): 29–56.

Butcher, Kristin F. 1994. "Black Immigrants in the United States: A Comparison with Native Blacks and Other Immigrants." *Industrial and Labor Relations Review* 47(2): 265–84.

Candelario, Ginetta E. B. 2001. "'Black Behind the Ears'—and Up Front Too? Dominicans in the Black Mosaic." *Public Historian* 23(4): 55–72.

Carlisle, Shauna K. 2012. "Nativity Differences in Chronic Health Conditions between Nationally Representative Samples of Asian American, Latino

American, and Afro-Caribbean American Respondents." *Journal of Immigrant and Minority Health* 14(6): 903–11.

Castells, Manuel. 1989. *The Informational City: Information Technology, Economic Restructuring, and the Urban-Regional Process.* Oxford: Blackwell Oxford.

Charles, Kerwin Kofi, and Ming Ching Luoh. 2010. "Male Incarceration, the Marriage Market, and Female Outcomes." *The Review of Economics and Statistics* 92(3): 614–27.

Chiswick, Barry R. 1978. "The Effect of Americanization on the Earnings of Foreign-Born Men." *Journal of Political Economy* 86(5): 897–921.

———. 1991. "Speaking, Reading, and Earnings among Low-Skilled Immigrants." *Journal of Labor Economics* 9(2): 149–70.

Chiswick, Barry R., and Paul W. Miller. 1995. "The Endogeneity between Language and Earnings: International Analyses." *Journal of Labor Economics* 13(2): 246–88.

Cho, Youngtae, W. Parker Frisbie, Robert A. Hummer, and Richard G. Rogers. 2004. "Nativity, Duration of Residence, and the Health of Hispanic Adults in the United States." *International Migration Review* 38(1): 184–211.

Choi, Kate H., and Marta Tienda. 2017. "Marriage-Market Constraints and Mate-Selection Behavior: Racial, Ethnic, and Gender Differences in Intermarriage." *Journal of Marriage and Family* 79(2): 301–17.

Collins, James W., Jr., Shou-Yien Wu, and Richard J. David. 2002. "Differing Intergenerational Birth Weights among the Descendants of U.S.-Born and Foreign-Born Whites and African Americans in Illinois." *American Journal of Epidemiology* 155(3): 210–16.

Collins, William J., and Robert A. Margo. 2001. "Race and Home Ownership: A Century-Long View." *Explorations in Economic History* 38(1): 68–92.

———. 2011. "Race and Home Ownership from the End of the Civil War to the Present." *American Economic Review* 101(3): 355–59.

Collins, William J., and Marianne H. Wanamaker. 2014. "Selection and Economic Gains in the Great Migration of African Americans: New Evidence from Linked Census Data." *American Economic Journal: Applied Economics* 6(1): 220–52.

Conley, Dalton. 2010. *Being Black, Living in the Red: Race, Wealth, and Social Policy in America.* Berkeley: University of California Press.

Corra, Mamadi K., and Casey Borch. 2014. "Socioeconomic Differences among Blacks in America: Over Time Trends." *Race and Social Problems* 6(2): 103–19.

Corra, Mamadi K., and Sitawa R. Kimuna. 2009. "Double Jeopardy? Female African and Caribbean Immigrants in the United States." *Journal of Ethnic and Migration Studies* 35(6): 1015–35.

Correll, Shelley J., Stephan Benard, and In Paik. 2007. "Getting a Job: Is There a Motherhood Penalty?" *American Journal of Sociology* 112(5): 1297–1339.

Crowder, Kyle D., Stewart E. Tolnay, and Robert M. Adelman. 2001. "Intermetropolitan Migration and Locational Improvement for African American Males, 1970–1990." *Social Science Research* 30(3): 449–72.

Daniels, Roger. 2004. *Guarding the Golden Door: American Immigration Policy and Immigrants since 1882.* New York: Hill and Wang.

Darity, William, Jr. 2003. "Employment Discrimination, Segregation, and Health." *American Journal of Public Health* 93(2): 226–31.

Darity, William, Jr., Jason Dietrich, and David K. Guilkey. 2001. "Persistent Advantage or Disadvantage? Evidence in Support of the Intergenerational Drag Hypothesis." *American Journal of Economics and Sociology* 60(2): 435–70.

David, Richard J., and James W. Collins. 1997. "Differing Birth Weight among Infants of U.S.-Born Blacks, African-Born Blacks, and U.S.-Born Whites." *New England Journal of Medicine* 337(17): 1209–14.

De La Cruz-Viesca, Melany, Zhenxiang Chen, Paul M. Ong, Darrick Hamilton, and William A. Darity Jr. 2016. "The Color of Wealth in Los Angeles." Report produced by Duke University, the New School, and the University of California, Los Angeles.

DeSalvo, Karen B., Nicole Bloser, Kristi Reynolds, Jiang He, and Paul Muntner. 2006. "Mortality Prediction with a Single General Self-Rated Health Question." *Journal of General Internal Medicine* 21(3): 267–75.

Dodoo, Francis Nii-Amoo. 1991. "Earnings Differences among Blacks in America." *Social Science Research* 20(2): 93–108.

———. 1997. "Assimilation Differences among Africans in America." *Social Forces* 76(2): 527–46.

———. 1999. "Black and Immigrant Labor Force Participation in America." *Race and Society* 2(1): 69–82.

Dodoo, Francis Nii-Amoo, and Baffour K. Takyi. 2002. "Africans in the Diaspora: Black-White Earnings Differences among America's Africans." *Ethnic and Racial Studies* 25(6): 913–41.

Domingo, Wilfred Adolphus. 1925. "Gift of the Black Tropics." In *The New Negro: An Interpretation*, edited by Alain Locke. New York: Albert and Charles Boni.

Dowd, Jennifer Beam, and Megan Todd. 2011. "Does Self-Reported Health Bias the Measurement of Health Inequalities in U.S. Adults? Evidence Using Anchoring Vignettes from the Health and Retirement Study." *Journals of Gerontology, Series B: Psychological Sciences and Social Sciences* 66(4): 478–89.

Dowd, Jennifer Beam, and Anna Zajacova. 2007. "Does the Predictive Power of Self-Rated Health for Subsequent Mortality Risk Vary by Socioeconomic Status in the U.S.?" *International Journal of Epidemiology* 36(6): 1214–21.

———. 2010. "Does Self-Rated Health Mean the Same Thing across Socio-economic Groups? Evidence from Biomarker Data." *Annals of Epidemiology* 20(10): 743–49.

Drachsler, Julius. 1920. *Democracy and Assimilation: The Blending of Immigrant Heritages in America.* New York: Macmillan.

Duany, Jorge. 1996. "Transnational Migration from the Dominican Republic: The Cultural Redefinition of Racial Identity." *Caribbean Studies* 29(2): 253–82.

Dustmann, Christian, and Josep Mestres. 2010. "Savings, Asset Holdings, and Temporary Migration." *Annals of Economics and Statistics/Annales d'Économie et de Statistique* 97/98(1): 289–306.

Dymski, Gary Arthur. 1995. "The Theory of Bank Redlining and Discrimination: An Exploration." *Review of Black Political Economy* 23(3): 37–74.

Eichenlaub, Suzanne C., Stewart E. Tolnay, and J. Trent Alexander. 2010. "Moving Out but Not Up: Economic Outcomes in the Great Migration." *American Sociological Review* 75(1): 101–25.

Elo, Irma, Neil Mehta, and Cheng Huang. 2008. "Health of Native-Born and Foreign-Born Black Residents in the United States: Evidence from the 2000 Census of Population and the National Health Interview Survey." PARC Working Paper Series 08-04. Philadelphia: University of Pennsylvania (July 3).

———. 2011. "Disability among Native-Born and Foreign-Born Blacks in the United States." *Demography* 48(1): 241–65.

Elo, Irma T., Zoua Vang, and Jennifer F. Culhane. 2014. "Variation in Birth Outcomes by Mother's Country of Birth among Non-Hispanic Black Women in the United States." *Maternal and Child Health Journal* 18(10): 2371–81.

Erving, Christy L. 2011. "Gender and Physical Health: A Study of African American and Caribbean Black Adults." *Journal of Health and Social Behavior* 52(3): 383–99.

Ettner, Susan L. 1996. "New Evidence on the Relationship between Income and Health." *Journal of Health Economics* 15(1): 67–85.

Farley, Reynolds. 1996. *The New American Reality: Who We Are, How We Got Here, Where We Are Going*. New York: Russell Sage Foundation.

Farley, Reynolds, and William H. Frey. 1994. "Changes in the Segregation of Whites from Blacks during the 1980s: Small Steps toward a More Integrated Society." *American Sociological Review* 59(1): 23–45.

Feliciano, Cynthia. 2005. "Educational Selectivity in U.S. Immigration: How Do Immigrants Compare to Those Left Behind?" *Demography* 42(1): 131–52.

Feliciano, Cynthia, and Yader R. Lanuza. 2017. "An Immigrant Paradox? Contextual Attainment and Intergenerational Educational Mobility." *American Sociological Review* 82(1): 211–41.

Fernández-Kelly, Patricia. Forthcoming. "Reclaiming the Black and Asian Journeys: A Comparative Perspective on Culture, Class, and Immigration." In *Routledge Handbook of Migration Studies*, 2nd edition, edited by Steven J. Gold and Stephanie J. Nawyn. New York: Routledge.

Finch, Brian Karl, D. Phuong Do, Reanne Frank, and Teresa Seeman. 2009. "Could 'Acculturation' Effects Be Explained by Latent Health Disadvantages among Mexican Immigrants?" *International Migration Review* 43(3): 471–95.

Finch, Brian Karl, Robert A. Hummer, Bohdan Kolody, and William Armando Vega. 2001. "The Role of Discrimination and Acculturative Stress in the Physical Health of Mexican-Origin Adults." *Hispanic Journal of Behavioral Sciences* 23(4): 399.

Finch, Brian Karl, Bohdan Kolody, and William Armando Vega. 2000. "Perceived Discrimination and Depression among Mexican-Origin Adults in California." *Journal of Health and Social Behavior* 41(3): 295–313.

Flippen, Chenoa. 2004. "Unequal Returns to Housing Investments? A Study of Real Housing Appreciation among Black, White, and Hispanic Households." *Social Forces* 82(4): 1523–51.

Flynn, Andrea, Susan R. Holmberg, Dorian T. Warren, and Felicia J. Wong. 2017. *The Hidden Rules of Race: Barriers to an Inclusive Economy*. New York: Cambridge University Press.

Foner, Nancy. 1979. "West Indians in New York City and London: A Comparative Analysis." *International Migration Review* 13(2): 284–97.

———. 1985. "Race and Color: Jamaican Migrants in London and New York City." *International Migration Review* 19(4): 708–27.

———. 1995. *The Caregiving Dilemma: Work in an American Nursing Home*. Berkeley: University of California Press.

———. 2001. *Islands in the City: West Indian Migration to New York*. Berkeley: University of California Press.

———. 2009. "Gender and Migration: West Indians in Comparative Perspective." *International Migration* 47(1): 3–29.

———. 2018. "Race in an Era of Mass Migration: Black Migrants in Europe and the United States." *Ethnic and Racial Studies* 41(6): 1113–30.

Frank, Reanne, Ilana Redstone Akresh, and Bo Lu. 2010. "Latino Immigrants and the U.S. Racial Order: How and Where Do They Fit In?" *American Sociological Review* 75(3): 378–401.

Frey, William H. 2009. "The Great American Migration Slowdown." Washington, D.C.: Brookings Institution.

Galster, George, and Erin Godfrey. 2005. "By Words and Deeds: Racial Steering by Real Estate Agents in the United States in 2000." *Journal of the American Planning Association* 71(3): 251–68.

Glazer, Nathan, and Daniel Patrick Moynihan. 1970. *Beyond the Melting Pot: The Negroes, Puerto Ricans, Jews, Italians, and Irish of New York City*. Cambridge, Mass.: MIT Press.

Goldsmith, Arthur H., Darrick Hamilton, and William Darity Jr. 2007. "From Dark to Light: Skin Color and Wages among African-Americans." *Journal of Human Resources* 42(4): 701–38.

Green, Tiffany, and Tod Hamilton. 2018. "Maternal Educational Attainment and Infant Mortality in the United States: Does the Gradient Vary by Race and Nativity?" *Demographic Research* (unpublished).

Grosfoguel, Ramán. 2003. "Race and Ethnicity or Racialized Ethnicities?" *Ethnicities* 4(3): 315–36.

Gross, Cary P., Benjamin D. Smith, Elizabeth Wolf, and Martin Andersen. 2008. "Racial Disparities in Cancer Therapy: Did the Gap Narrow between 1992 and 2002?" *Cancer* 112(4): 900–908.

Haan, Michael. 2007. "The Homeownership Hierarchies of Canada and the United States: The Housing Patterns of White and Non-White Immigrants of the Past Thirty Years." *International Migration Review* 41(2): 433–65.

Hamilton, Darrick, Algernon Austin, and William Darity Jr. 2011. "Whiter Jobs, Higher Wages: Occupational Segregation and the Lower Wages of Black Men." Washington, D.C.: Economic Policy Institute (February 25).

Hamilton, Darrick, and William Darity Jr. 2010. "Can 'Baby Bonds' Eliminate the Racial Wealth Gap in Putative Post-racial America?" *Review of Black Political Economy* 37(3–4) : 207–16.

Hamilton, Tod G. 2014. "Selection, Language Heritage, and the Earnings Trajectories of Black Immigrants in the United States." *Demography* 51(3): 975–1002.

———. 2015. "The Healthy Immigrant (Migrant) Effect: In Search of a Better Native-Born Comparison Group." *Social Science Research* 54: 353–65.

Hamilton, Tod G., Janeria A. Easley, and Angela R. Dixon. 2018. "Black Immigration, Occupational Niches, and Earnings Disparities between U.S.-Born and Foreign-Born Blacks in the United States." *Russell Sage Foundation Journal of the Social Sciences* 4(1): 60–77.

Hamilton, Tod G., and Robert A. Hummer. 2011. "Immigration and the Health of U.S. Black Adults: Does Country of Origin Matter?" *Social Science and Medicine* 73(10): 1551–60.

Handa, Sudhanshu, and Claremont Kirton. 1999. "The Economics of Rotating Savings and Credit Associations: Evidence from the Jamaican Partner." *Journal of Development Economics* 60(1): 173–94.

Harris, Angel L. 2011. *Kids Don't Want to Fail: Oppositional Culture and the Black-White Achievement Gap.* Cambridge, Mass.: Harvard University Press.

Haynes, George Edmund. 1912. *The Negro at Work in New York City: A Study in Economic Progress.* London: P. S. King and Son, for Columbia University.

Head, Rachel N., and Maxine Seaborn Thompson. 2017. "Discrimination-Related Anger, Religion, and Distress: Differences between African Americans and Caribbean Black Americans." *Society and Mental Health* 7(3): 159–74.

Hendi, Arun S., Neil K. Mehta, and Irma T. Elo. 2015. "Health among Black Children by Maternal and Child Nativity." *American Journal of Public Health* 105(4): 703–10.

Hersch, Joni. 2002. "Skin Color, Immigrant Wages, and Discrimination." In *Racism in the 21st Century,* edited by Ronald E. Hall. New York: Springer New York.

———. 2011. "The Persistence of Skin Color Discrimination for Immigrants." *Social Science Research* 40(5): 1337–49.

Howard, David. 2007. "Development, Racism, and Discrimination in the Dominican Republic." *Development in Practice* 17(6): 725–38.

Hummer, Robert A. 1993. "Racial Differentials in Infant Mortality in the U.S.: An Examination of Social and Health Determinants." *Social Forces* 72(2): 529–54.

———. 1996. "Black-White Differences in Health and Mortality: A Review and Conceptual Model." *Sociological Quarterly* 37(1): 105–25.

Hummer, Robert A., Monique Biegler, Peter B. De Turk, Douglas Forbes, W. Parker Frisbie, Ying Hong, and Starling G. Pullum. 1999a. "Race/Ethnicity, Nativity, and Infant Mortality in the United States." *Social Forces* 77(3): 1083–1117.

Hummer, Robert A., Daniel A. Powers, Starling G. Pullum, Ginger L. Gossman, and W. Parker Frisbie. 2007. "Paradox Found (Again): Infant Mortality among the Mexican-Origin Population in the United States." *Demography* 44(3): 441–57.

Hummer, Robert A., Richard G. Rogers, Charles B. Nam, and F. B. LeClere. 1999b. "Race/Ethnicity, Nativity, and U.S. Adult Mortality." *Social Science Quarterly* (University of Texas Press) 80(1): 136–53.

Idler, Ellen L., Louise B. Russell, and Diane Davis. 2000. "Survival, Functional Limitations, and Self-Rated Health in the NHANES I Epidemiologic Follow-up Study, 1992." *American Journal of Epidemiology* 152(9): 874–83.

Ifatunji, Mosi Adesina. 2016. "A Test of the Afro Caribbean Model Minority Hypothesis: Exploring the Role of Cultural Attributes in Labor Market Disparities between African Americans and Afro Caribbeans." *Du Bois Review: Social Science Research on Race* 13(01): 109–38.

———. 2017. "Labor Market Disparities between African Americans and Afro Caribbeans: Reexamining the Role of Immigrant Selectivity." *Sociological Forum* 32(3): 522–43.

Imoagene, Onoso. 2017. *Beyond Expectations: Second-Generation Nigerians in the United States and Britain*. Berkeley: University of California Press.

Jackson, James S., and Toni C. Antonucci. 2005. "Physical and Mental Health Consequences of Aging in Place and Aging out of Place among Black Caribbean Immigrants." *Research in Human Development* 2(4): 229–44.

Jasso, Guillermina, Douglas S. Massey, Mark R. Rosenzweig, and James P. Smith. 2004. "Immigrant Health: Selectivity and Acculturation." In *Critical Perspectives on Racial and Ethnic Differences in Health in Late Life*, edited by Norman B. Anderson, Rodolfo A. Bulatao, and Barney Cohen. Washington, D.C.: National Academies Press.

Jiménez, Tomás R. 2010. *Replenished Ethnicity: Mexican Americans, Immigration, and Identity*. Berkeley: University of California Press.

Johnson, James Weldon. 1930. *Black Manhattan*. New York: Alfred A. Knopf.

Kalmijn, Matthijs. 1996. "The Socioeconomic Assimilation of Caribbean American Blacks." *Social Forces* 74(3): 911–30.

———. 1998. "Intermarriage and Homogamy: Causes, Patterns, Trends." *Annual Review of Sociology* 24(1): 395–421.

Kalmijn, Matthijs, and Frank van Tubergen. 2010. "A Comparative Perspective on Intermarriage: Explaining Differences among National-Origin Groups in the United States." *Demography* 47(2): 459–79.

Kasinitz, Philip. 1992. *Caribbean New York: Black Immigrants and the Politics of Race*. Ithaca, N.Y.: Cornell University Press.

Katznelson, Ira. 2005. *When Affirmative Action Was White: An Untold History of Racial Inequality in Twentieth-Century America*. New York: W. W. Norton & Co.

Kennedy, Steven, Michael P. Kidd, James Ted McDonald, and Nicholas Biddle. 2014. "The Healthy Immigrant Effect: Patterns and Evidence from Four Countries." *Journal of International Migration and Integration* 16(2): 317–32.

Kent, Mary Mederios. 2007. "Immigration and America's Black Population." *Population Bulletin* 62(4): 1–16.

Kiecolt, K. Jill, Hans Momplaisir, and Michael Hughes. 2016. "Racial Identity, Racial Discrimination, and Depressive Symptoms among African Americans and Afro-Caribbeans." In *New Directions in Identity Theory and Research,* edited by Jan E. Stets and Richard T. Serpe. New York: Oxford University Press.

Kijakazi, Kilolo, Rachel Marie Brooks Atkins, Mark Paul, Anne E. Price, Darrick Hamilton, and William A. Darity Jr. 2016. "The Color of Wealth in the Nation's Capital." Washington, D.C.: Urban Institute (November).

Kim, Sunwoong, and Gregory D. Squires. 1995. "Lender Characteristics and Racial Disparities in Mortgage Lending." *Journal of Housing Research* 6(1): 99–113.

Kirschenman, Joleen, and Kathryn M. Neckerman. 1991. "'We'd Love to Hire Them, But . . .': The Meaning of Race for Employers." *Urban Underclass* 203(1991): 203–32.

Kochhar, Rakesh, and Richard Fry. 2014. "Wealth Inequality Has Widened along Racial, Ethnic Lines since End of Great Recession." Washington, D.C.: Pew Research Center (December 12), 1–15.

Korenman, Sanders, and David Neumark. 1991. "Does Marriage Really Make Men More Productive?" *Journal of Human Resources* 26(2): 282–307.

Lacey, Krim K., Karen Powell Sears, Ishtar O. Govia, Ivy Forsythe-Brown, Niki Matusko, and James S. Jackson. 2015. "Substance Use, Mental Disorders, and Physical Health of Caribbeans At-Home Compared to Those Residing in the United States." *International Journal of Environmental Research and Public Health* 12(1): 710–34.

Landale, Nancy S., Bridget K. Gorman, and R. S. Oropesa. 2006. "Selective Migration and Infant Mortality among Puerto Ricans." *Maternal and Child Health Journal* 10(4): 351–60.

Landale, Nancy S., R. S. Oropesa, and Bridget K. Gorman. 2000. "Migration and Infant Death: Assimilation or Selective Migration among Puerto Ricans?" *American Sociological Review* 65(6): 888–909.

LaVeist, Thomas A., Robert Sellers, and Harold W. Neighbors. 2001. "Perceived Racism and Self and System Blame Attribution: Consequences for Longevity." *Ethnicity and Disease* 11(4): 711–21.

Lee, Jennifer, and Frank D. Bean. 2010. *The Diversity Paradox: Immigration and the Color Line in Twenty-First Century America.* New York: Russell Sage Foundation.

Levine, Debra Siegel, Joseph A. Himle, Jamie M. Abelson, Niki Matusko, Nikhil Dhawan, and Robert Joseph Taylor. 2014. "Discrimination and Social Anxiety Disorder among African-Americans, Caribbean Blacks, and Non-Hispanic Whites." *Journal of Nervous and Mental Disease* 202(3): 224–30.

Levine, Robert S., James E. Foster, Robert E. Fullilove, Mindy T. Fullilove, Nathaniel C. Briggs, Pamela C. Hull, Baqar A. Husaini, and Charles H. Hennekens. 2016. "Black-White Inequalities in Mortality and Life Expectancy, 1933–1999: Implications for Healthy People 2010." *Public Health Reports* 116(5): 474–83.

Lichter, Daniel T., Diane K. McLaughlin, George Kephart, and David J. Landry. 1992. "Race and the Retreat from Marriage: A Shortage of Marriageable Men?" *American Sociological Review* 57(6): 781–99.

Lieberson, Stanley. 1978. "A Reconsideration of the Income Differences Found between Migrants and Northern-Born Blacks." *American Journal of Sociology* 83(4): 940–66.

Light, Ivan H., and Steven J. Gold. 2000. *Ethnic Economies*. Bingley, U.K.: Emerald Group Publishing.

Livingston, Gretchen, and Anna Brown. 2017. "Intermarriage in the U.S. 50 Years after *Loving v. Virginia.*" Washington, D.C.: Pew Research Center, Social & Demographic Trends (May 18).

Lobo, Arun Peter. 2001. "U.S. Diversity Visas Are Attracting Africa's Best and Brightest." *Population Today* 29(5):1–2.

Long, Larry H., and Lynne R. Heltman. 1975. "Migration and Income Differences between Black and White Men in the North." *American Journal of Sociology* 80(6):1391–1409.

Lopez-Gonzalez, Lorena, Veronica C. Aravena, and Robert A. Hummer. 2005. "Immigrant Acculturation, Gender, and Health Behavior: A Research Note." *Social Forces* 84(1): 577–89.

Mare, Robert D. 1991. "Five Decades of Educational Assortative Mating." *American Sociological Review* 56(1): 15–32.

Margo, Robert A. 1990. *Race and Schooling in the South, 1880–1950: An Economic History*. Chicago: University of Chicago Press.

Markides, Kyriakos S., and Karl Eschbach. 2005. "Aging, Migration, and Mortality: Current Status of Research on the Hispanic Paradox." *Journals of Gerontology, Series B: Psychological Sciences and Social Sciences* 60(special issue 2): S68–75.

Marmot, M. G., A. M. Adelstein, and L. Bulusu. 1984. "Lessons from the Study of Immigrant Mortality." *Lancet* 323(8392): 1455–57.

Marshall, Gillian L., and Tessa C. Rue. 2012. "Perceived Discrimination and Social Networks among Older African Americans and Caribbean Blacks." *Family and Community Health* 35(4): 300–311.

Mason, Patrick L. 2010. "Culture and Intraracial Wage Inequality among America's African Diaspora." *American Economic Review* 100(2): 309–15.

Massey, Douglas S., and Nancy A. Denton. 1993. *American Apartheid: Segregation and the Making of the Inderclass*. Cambridge, Mass.: Harvard University Press.

Massey, Douglas S., Jorge Durand, and Nolan J. Malone. 2002. *Beyond Smoke and Mirrors: Mexican Immigration in an Era of Economic Integration*. New York: Russell Sage Foundation.

Massey, Douglas S., Margarita Mooney, Kimberly C. Torres, and Camille Z. Charles. 2007. "Black Immigrants and Black Natives Attending Selective Colleges and Universities in the United States." *American Journal of Education* 113(2): 243–71.

Masters, Stanley H. 1972. "Are Black Migrants from the South to the Northern Cities Worse Off Than Blacks Already There?" *Journal of Human Resources* 7(4): 411–23.

McDonald, James Ted, and Steven Kennedy. 2004. "Insights into the 'Healthy Immigrant Effect': Health Status and Health Service Use of Immigrants to Canada." *Social Science and Medicine* 59(8): 1613–27.

———. 2005. "Is Migration to Canada Associated with Unhealthy Weight Gain? Overweight and Obesity among Canada's Immigrants." *Social Science and Medicine* 61(12): 2469–81.

McKay, Claude. 1940. *Harlem: Negro Metropolis.* New York: E. P. Dutton & Co.

Mehta, Neil K., Irma T. Elo, Nicole D. Ford, and Karen R. Siegel. 2015. "Obesity among U.S.- and Foreign-Born Blacks by Region of Birth." *American Journal of Preventive Medicine* 49(2): 269–73.

Mequanent, Getachew. 1996. "The Role of Informal Organizations in Resettlement Adjustment Process: A Case Study of Iqubs, Idirs, and Mahabers in the Ethiopian Community in Toronto." *Refuge: Canada's Journal on Refugees* 15(3): 30–40.

Model, Suzanne. 2008. *West Indian Immigrants: A Black Success Story?* New York: Russell Sage Foundation.

———. 2018. "Selectivity Is Still in the Running: A Comment on Ifatunji's 'Labor Market Disparities.'" *Sociological Forum* 33(2): 539–46.

Model, Suzanne, and Gene Fisher. 2001. "Black-White Unions: West Indians and African Americans Compared." *Demography* 38(2): 177–85.

Molina, Kristine M., and Drexler James. 2016. "Discrimination, Internalized Racism, and Depression: A Comparative Study of African American and Afro-Caribbean Adults in the U.S." *Group Processes and Intergroup Relations* 19(4): 439–61.

Monk, Ellis P., Jr. 2014. "Skin Tone Stratification among Black Americans, 2001–2003." *Social Forces* 92(4): 1313–37.

Morris, Arden M., Kim F. Rhoads, Steven C. Stain, and John D. Birkmeyer. 2010. "Understanding Racial Disparities in Cancer Treatment and Outcomes." *Journal of the American College of Surgeons* 211(1): 105–13.

Munnell, Alicia H., Geoffrey M. B. Tootell, Lynn E. Browne, and James McEneaney. 1996. "Mortgage Lending in Boston: Interpreting HMDA Data." *American Economic Review* 86(1): 25–53.

Muñoz, Ana Patricia, Marlene Kim, Mariko Chang, Regine Jackson, Darrick Hamilton, and William A. Darity. 2015. "The Color of Wealth in Boston." March 26.

Murrell, Audrey J., and Ray Jones. 1996. "Assessing Affirmative Action: Past, Present, and Future." *Journal of Social Issues* 52(4): 77–92.

Newbold, K. Bruce. 2005. "Self-Rated Health within the Canadian Immigrant Population: Risk and the Healthy Immigrant Effect." *Social Science and Medicine* 60(6): 1359–70.

Obama, Barack. 2004. "2004 Democratic National Convention Keynote Address." Speech delivered July 27, 2004, Fleet Center, Boston. Available at: https://www.americanrhetoric.com/speeches/PDFFiles/Barack%20Obama %20-%202004%20DNC%20Address.pdf (accessed December 13, 2018).

———. 2010. "State of the Union Address." Delivered January 27, 2010, Washington. Available at: https://www.americanrhetoric.com/speeches/PDFFiles/ Barack%20Obama%20-%20State%20of%20the%20Union%202010.pdf (accessed December 13, 2018).

Ogbu, John U. 1991. "Immigrant and Involuntary Minorities in Comparative Perspective." In *Minority Status and Schooling: A Comparative Study of Immigrant and Involuntary Minorities,* edited by Margaret A. Gibson and John U. Ogbu. New York: Garland.

Oliver, Melvin L., and Thomas M. Shapiro. 2006. *Black Wealth, White Wealth: A New Perspective on Racial Inequality,* 2nd ed. New York: Taylor & Francis.

———. 2013. *Black Wealth/White Wealth: A New Perspective on Racial Inequality,* ebook edition. New York: Taylor & Francis.

Osofsky, Gilbert. [1966] 1996. *Harlem: The Making of a Ghetto: Negro New York, 1890–1930.* New York: Harper & Row; Reprint, Chicago: Ivan R. Dee.

Ottley, Roi. 1943. *"New World a-Coming": Inside Black America.* Boston: Houghton Mifflin.

Ottley, Roi, and William J. Weatherby, eds. 1967. *The Negro in New York: An Informal Social History.* New York: Praeger.

Owusu, Thomas Y. 1998. "To Buy or Not to Buy: Determinants of Home Ownership among Ghanaian Immigrants in Toronto." *Canadian Geographer/Le Géographe canadien* 42(1): 40–52.

Pager, Devah. 2003. "The Mark of a Criminal Record." *American Journal of Sociology* 108(5): 937–75.

Pager, Devah, and Hana Shepherd. 2008. "The Sociology of Discrimination: Racial Discrimination in Employment, Housing, Credit, and Consumer Markets." *Annual Review of Sociology* 34(1): 181–209.

Pagnini, Deanna L., and S. Philip Morgan. 1990. "Intermarriage and Social Distance among U.S. Immigrants at the Turn of the Century." *American Journal of Sociology* 96(2): 405–32.

Palloni, Alberto, and Elizabeth Arias. 2004. "Paradox Lost: Explaining the Hispanic Adult Mortality Advantage." *Demography* 41(3): 385–415.

Palloni, Alberto, and Douglas C. Ewbank. 2004. "Selection Processes in the Study of Racial and Ethnic Differentials in Adult Health and Mortality." In *Critical Perspectives in Racial and Ethnic Differences in Health in Late Life,* edited by Norman B. Anderson, Rodolfo A. Bulatao, and Barney Cohen. Washington, D.C.: National Academies Press.

Palmer, Ransford W. 1974. "A Decade of West Indian Migration to the United States, 1962–1972: An Economic Analysis." *Social and Economic Studies* 23(4): 571–87.

Patterson, Orlando. 1997. "The Ordeal of Integration: Progress and Resentment in America's 'Racial' Crisis." Washington, D.C.: Civitas Counterpoint.

———. 2006. "A Poverty of the Mind." *New York Times,* March 26.

Patterson, Orlando, ed., with Ethan Fosse. 2015. *The Cultural Matrix: Understanding Black Youth*. Cambridge, Mass.: Harvard University Press.

Pettit, Becky. 2012. *Invisible Men: Mass Incarceration and the Myth of Black Progress*. New York: Russell Sage Foundation.

Piore, Michael J. 1979. *Birds of Passage: Migrant Labor and Industrial Societies*. New York: Cambridge University Press.

Portes, Alejandro, and Rubén G. Rumbaut. 2006. *Immigrant America: A Portrait*. Berkeley: University of California Press.

———. 2014. *Immigrant America: A Portrait*, revised, updated, and expanded edition. Berkeley: University of California Press.

Portes, Alejandro, and John Walton. 1981. "Unequal Exchange and the Urban Informal Sector." In *Labor, Class, and the International System*, edited by Charles Tilly and Edward Shorter. Amsterdam: Elsevier.

Qian, Zhenchao. 1997. "Breaking the Racial Barriers: Variations in Interracial Marriage between 1980 and 1990." *Demography* 34(2): 263–76.

Qian, Zhenchao, and Daniel T. Lichter. 2001. "Measuring Marital Assimilation: Intermarriage among Natives and Immigrants." *Social Science Research* 30(2): 289–312.

———. 2007. "Social Boundaries and Marital Assimilation: Interpreting Trends in Racial and Ethnic Intermarriage." *American Sociological Review* 72(1): 68–94.

Raley, R. Kelly, and Megan M. Sweeney. 2009. "Explaining Race and Ethnic Variation in Marriage: Directions for Future Research." *Race and Social Problems* 1(3): 132–42.

Raley, R. Kelly, Megan M. Sweeney, and Danielle Wondra. 2015. "The Growing Racial and Ethnic Divide in U.S. Marriage Patterns." *Future of Children* 25(2): 89–109.

Ratner, Carl. 1997. *Cultural Psychology and Qualitative Methodology: Theoretical and Empirical Considerations*. New York: Springer Science & Business Media.

Read, Jen'nan Ghazal, and Michael O. Emerson. 2005. "Racial Context, Black Immigration, and the U.S. Black/White Health Disparity." *Social Forces* 84(1): 181–99.

Reid, Ira De Augustine. [1939] 1969. *The Negro Immigrant, His Background, Characteristics, and Social Adjustment, 1899–1937*. New York and London: Columbia University Press and P. S. King & Son; reprint, New York: Arno Press.

Rice, Whitney S., Samantha S. Goldfarb, Anne E. Brisendine, Stevie Burrows, and Martha S. Wingate. 2017. "Disparities in Infant Mortality by Race among Hispanic and Non-Hispanic Infants." *Maternal and Child Health Journal* 21(7): 1581–88.

Roberts, George W. 1957. *The Population of Jamaica*. Cambridge: Cambridge University Press.

Rosenblum, Alexis, William Darity Jr., Angel L. Harris, and Tod G. Hamilton. 2016. "Looking through the Shades: The Effect of Skin Color on Earnings by Region of Birth and Race for Immigrants to the United States." *Sociology of Race and Ethnicity* 2(1): 87–105.

Ross, Stephen L., and Margery Austin Turner. 2005. "Housing Discrimination in Metropolitan America: Explaining Changes between 1989 and 2000." *Social Problems* 52(2): 152–80.

Rothstein, Richard. 2017. *The Color of Law: A Forgotten History of How Our Government Segregated America.* New York: Liveright Publishing.

Ruggles, Steve. 1994. "The Origins of African-American Family Structure." *American Sociological Review* 59(1): 136–51.

Ruggles, Steven, Sarah Flood, Ronald Goeken, Josiah Grover, Erin Meyer, Jose Pacas, and Matthew Sobek. 2018. *IPUMS USA: Version 8.0* [dataset]. Minneapolis, Minn.: IPUMS. DOI: 10.18128/D010.V8.0.

Schwartz, Christine R. 2013. "Trends and Variation in Assortative Mating: Causes and Consequences." *Annual Review of Sociology* 39(1): 451–70.

Shapiro, Thomas M. 2004. *The Hidden Cost of Being African American: How Wealth Perpetuates Inequality.* New York: Oxford University Press.

Sharma, R. D., M. Michalowski, and R. B. P. Verma. 1990. "Mortality Differentials among Immigrant Populations in Canada." *International Migration* 28(4): 443–50.

Singh, Gopal K., and Mohammad Siahpush. 2002a. "Ethnic-Immigrant Differentials in Health Behaviors, Morbidity, and Cause-Specific Mortality in the United States: An Analysis of Two National Data Bases." *Human Biology* 74(1): 83–109.

———. 2002b. "Ethnic-Immigrant Differentials in Health, Behaviors, Morbidity, and Cause-Specific Mortality in the United State: An Analysis of Two National Data Bases." *Human Biology* 74(1): 83–109.

Skloot, Rebecca. 2017. *The Immortal Life of Henrietta Lacks.* New York: Broadway Books.

Smith, James P., and Finis Welch. 1979. "Inequality: Race Differences in the Distribution of Earnings." *International Economic Review* 20(2): 515–26.

Soto, José A., Nana A. Dawson-Andoh, and Rhonda BeLue. 2011. "The Relationship between Perceived Discrimination and Generalized Anxiety Disorder among African Americans, Afro Caribbeans, and Non-Hispanic Whites." *Journal of Anxiety Disorders* 25(2): 258–65.

Sowell, Thomas. 1975. *Race and Economics.* New York: D. McKay Co.

———. 1978. "Three Black Histories." In *Essays and Data on American Ethnic Groups,* edited by Thomas Sowell and Lynn D. Collins. Washington, D.C.: Urban Institute.

———. 1981. *Ethnic America: A History.* New York: Basic Books.

———. 1983. *The Economics and Politics of Race: An International Perspective.* New York: William Morrow.

Squires, Gregory D., William Velez, and Karl E. Taeuber. 1991. "Insurance Redlining, Agency Location, and the Process of Urban Disinvestment." *Urban Affairs Quarterly* 26(4): 567–88.

Stark, Oded, and David E. Bloom. 1985. "The New Economics of Labor Migration." *American Economic Review* 75(2): 173–78.

Tesfai, Rebbeca. 2015. "The Interaction between Race and Nativity on the Housing Market: Homeownership and House Value of Black Immigrants in the United States." *International Migration Review* 50(4): 1005–45.

Thomas, Kevin J. A. 2011a. "What Explains the Increasing Trend in African Emigration to the US?" *International Migration Review* 45(1): 3–28.

———. 2011b. "What Explains the Increasing Trend in African Emigration to the U.S.?" *International Migration Review* 45(1): 3–28.

———. 2012. "A Demographic Profile of Black Caribbean Immigrants in the United States." Washington, D.C.: Migration Policy Institute (April).

———. 2014. *Diverse Pathways: Race and the Incorporation of Black, White, and Arab-Origin Africans in the United States.* East Lansing: Michigan State University Press.

———. 2016. "Highly Skilled Migration from Africa to the U.S.: Exit Mechanisms, Demographic Determinants, and the Role of Socioeconomic Trends." *Population Research and Policy Review* 35(6): 825–49.

Thompson-Miller, Ruth, Joe R. Feagin, and Leslie H. Picca. 2014. *Jim Crow's Legacy: The Lasting Impact of Segregation.* Lanham, Md.: Rowman & Littlefield.

Tolnay, Stewart E. 1998. "Educational Selection in the Migration of Southern Blacks, 1880–1990." *Social Forces* 77(2): 487–514.

———. 2003. "The African American 'Great Migration' and Beyond." *Annual Review of Sociology* 29(1): 209–32.

Tolnay, Stewart E., and Suzanne C. Eichenlaub. 2006. "Southerners in the West: The Relative Well-being of Direct and Onward Migrants." *Social Forces* 84(3): 1639–63.

Torres-Saillant, Silvio. 1998. "The Tribulations of Blackness: Stages in Dominican Racial Identity." *Latin American Perspectives* 25(3): 126–46.

Turner, Margery Austin, and Stephen L. Ross. 2005. "How Racial Discrimination Affects the Search for Housing." In *The Geography of Opportunity: Race and Housing Choice in Metropolitan America*, edited by Xavier de Souza Briggs and William Julius Wilson. Washington, D.C.: Brookings Institution Press.

Turra, Cassio M., and Irma Elo. 2008. "The Impact of Salmon Bias on the Hispanic Mortality Advantage: New Evidence from Social Security Data." *Population Research and Policy Review* 27(5): 515–30.

United Nations Development Program (UNDP). 2014. *Human Development Report: Sustaining Human Progress: Reducing Vulnerabilities and Building Resistance.* New York: UN.

U.S. Department of Homeland Security (DHS). 2014. *Yearbook of Immigration Statistics.* Washington: DHS.

Vickerman, Milton. 1998. *West Indian Immigrants and Race.* New York: Oxford University Press.

Viruell-Fuentes, Edna A., Jeffrey D. Morenoff, David R. Williams, and James S. House. 2011. "Language of Interview, Self-Rated Health, and the Other Latino Health Puzzle." *American Journal of Public Health* 101(7): 1306.

Waldinger, Roger D. 1999. *Still the Promised City? African-Americans and New Immigrants in Postindustrial New York.* Cambridge, Mass.: Harvard University Press.

Wallerstein, Immanuel. 1976. *The Modern World-System: Capitalist Agriculture and the European World Economy in the Sixteenth Century.* New York: Academic Press.

———. 2017. "The Modern World-System." In *Social Theory: The Multicultural, Global, and Classic Readings,* edited by Charles Lemert. Boulder, Colo.: Westview Press.

Ward, Elizabeth, Ahmedin Jemal, Vilma Cokkinides, Gopal K. Singh, Cheryll Cardinez, Asma Ghafoor, and Michael Thun. 2004. "Cancer Disparities by Race/Ethnicity and Socioeconomic Status." *CA: A Cancer Journal for Clinicians* 54(2): 78–93.

Warner, David F., and Mark D. Hayward. 2006. "Early-Life Origins of the Race Gap in Men's Mortality." *Journal of Health and Social Behavior* 47(3): 209–26.

Washington, Harriet A. 2006. *Medical Apartheid: The Dark History of Medical Experimentation on Black Americans from Colonial Times to the Present.* New York: Doubleday Books.

Waters, Mary C. 1999. *Black Identities: West Indian Immigrant Dreams and American Realities.* New York and Cambridge, Mass.: Russell Sage Foundation and Harvard University Press.

Waters, Mary C., Philip Kasinitz, and Asad L. Asad. 2014. "Immigrants and African Americans." *Annual Review of Sociology* 40(1): 369–90.

Western, Bruce. 2006. *Punishment and Inequality in America.* New York: Russell Sage Foundation.

Wilkerson, Isabel. 2011. *The Warmth of Other Suns: The Epic Story of America's Great Migration.* New York: Vintage.

Williams, David R. 1999. "The Monitoring of Racial/Ethnic Status in the USA: Data Quality Issues." *Ethnicity and Health* 4(3): 121–37.

Williams, David R., and Selina A. Mohammed. 2009. "Discrimination and Racial Disparities in Health: Evidence and Needed Research." *Journal of Behavioral Medicine* 32(1): 20.

Williams, David R., Yan Yu, James S. Jackson, and Norman B. Anderson. 1997. "Racial Differences in Physical and Mental Health Socio-economic Status, Stress, and Discrimination." *Journal of Health Psychology* 2(3): 335–51.

Wilson, Franklin D. 2003. "Ethnic Niching and Metropolitan Labor Markets." *Social Science Research* 32(3): 429–66.

Wilson, William Julius. 1978. *The Declining Significance of Race: Blacks and Changing American Institutions.* Chicago: University of Chicago Press.

———. 1987. *The Truly Disadvantaged: The Inner City, the Underclass, and Public Policy.* Chicago: University of Chicago Press.

Wilson, William Julius, and Kathryn M. Neckerman. 1987. "Poverty and Family Structure: The Widening Gap between Evidence and Public Policy Issues." In *Fighting Poverty: What Works and What Doesn't,* edited by Sheldon Danziger and Daniel Weinberg. Cambridge, Mass.: Harvard University Press.

Woodward, Amanda Toler. 2011. "Discrimination and Help-Seeking: Use of Professional Services and Informal Support among African Americans, Black Caribbeans, and Non-Hispanic Whites with a Mental Disorder." *Race and Social Problems* 3(3): 146–59.

Wooldridge, Jeffrey M. 2015. *Introductory Econometrics: A Modern Approach.* Boston, Mass.: Cengage Learning.

Zhang, Zhenmei, Danan Gu, and Mark D. Hayward. 2008. "Early Life Influences on Cognitive Impairment among Oldest Old Chinese." *Journal of Gerontology, Series B: Psychological Sciences and Social Sciences* 63(1): S25–33.

INDEX

Boldface numbers refer to figures and tables.